Clare Jenkins's BBC Radio 4 program— ~~~~~~~~ at
Peggy's, was broadcast on 1 ̄ ̄   e
included:

'Vividly evocative... Clare Jer
samosas with Peggy as she ren.   picnics, pet
mongooses, Mulligatawny soup,   ̄ung on Anglo-Indian
life today'

Gillian Reynolds, *Sunday Telegraph*

'Captures a vanishing way of life... In their unique culture, Tower
of London fridge magnets and toad in the hole are compatible
with samosas and exotic tales of pet mongooses'

Stephanie Billen, *The Observer*

'Catches something of the special atmosphere of a culture and
way of life that are fast disappearing'

Susan Jeffrey, *Daily Mail*

'[Captain Abbott is] Born and bred in India "but as British as you
come". You could almost hear his handlebar moustache in his big,
booming voice flecked with the up-and-down lilt of Hindi'

Kate Chisholm, *The Spectator*

'The programme made me want to take tea with Peggy'

David McGillivray, *Radio Times*

'I think Peggy has to be one of my favourite non-fiction
characters ever'

Ross Dickinson, author and copy editor

DEDICATION

For Peggy (1923–2016) and Roy (1926–2017)

'An Anglo-Indian means a person whose father or any of whose other male progenitors in the male line is or was of European descent…'
The Constitution of India, Article 366 (2)

'In the old days, Anglo-Indians identified themselves with their British past – they always felt England was their home. But not any more. Now, this is our home.'
Harry MacLure, editor of *Anglos in the Wind* magazine

'We're happy in India, where we are in our own little sphere.'
Peggy Cantem

'It means a lot to be Anglo-Indian. I'm proud to be so. I wouldn't want to be anything else.'
Gwendoline Khan

STEPHEN MCCLARENCE
& CLARE JENKINS

TEATIME
AT PEGGY'S

A GLIMPSE OF ANGLO-INDIA

First published in the UK in June 2024 by
Journey Books, an imprint of Bradt Guides Ltd
31a High Street, Chesham, Buckinghamshire, HP5 1BW, England

www.bradtguides.com

Text copyright © 2024 Stephen McClarence & Clare Jenkins
Edited by Ross Dickinson
Cover illustration/cover design by Jasmine Hortop
Layout and typesetting by Ian Spick
All photographs by Stephen McClarence

Production managed by Sue Cooper, Bradt Guides & Page Bros

ISBN: 9781804692424
British Library Cataloguing in Publication Data
A catalogue record for this book is available from the British Library
Digital conversion by www.dataworks.co.in
Printed in the UK by Page Bros

To find out more about our Journey Books imprint, visit www.
bradtguides.com/journeybooks

ABOUT THE AUTHORS

Stephen McClarence is an award-winning travel writer whose work has appeared in *The Times*, *Sunday Times*, *Daily* and *Sunday Telegraph*, *Daily* and *Sunday Express*, *Yorkshire Post*, *National* *Geographic Traveler* and *DestinAsian* magazine. A finalist in (and winner of) numerous travel writing awards, he won the major National Daily Travel Writer of the Year award for a *Times* article about Ramji, a rickshaw driver he met in Varanasi. He has also reviewed books for *The Times* and been an exhibiting photographer.

Clare Jenkins has been a regular contributor to Radio 4's *Woman's Hour*, including reporting on women's lives in India. She has also made hundreds of features and documentaries for  BBC Radio, including some from India, latterly via her production company, Pennine Productions. Among these: *Teatime at Peggy's* bbc.co.uk/programmes/b05tpwc7.

She has previously published books about women's relationships with Roman Catholic priests, and people's experiences of bereavement, and is a member of the Oral History Society.

Teatime at Peggy's is a joint project, although the narrative is written in Stephen's voice. The couple, who have visited India regularly for over twenty years, are now working on a sequel, about their encounters with other people in India who have British connections.

ACKNOWLEDGEMENTS

We have many people to thank for enabling us to visit India so many times over the course of twenty-odd years. Chief among these, in terms of getting us there and then getting us around, has to be Katie Cosstick, formerly of Cox & Kings. Not only did she organise so many of our trips east, she showed endless patience and flexibility when asked if we could incorporate a trip to Jhansi within many of our itineraries.

Then there are the various newspaper travel editors and commissioning editors – among them Tom Chesshyre, Duncan Craig, Michael Hickling, Steve Keenan, Michael Kerr, Jane Knight, Cath Urquhart – who commissioned so many of Stephen's articles about India. Tom and Michael Kerr have continued to give very helpful advice about the publishing industry, as has India expert Hugh Rayner, founder of Indiabooks.

On the radio side, Matthew Dodd, Lindsay Leonard and Alistair Wilson were among those who commissioned India-based features and documentaries from Clare for BBC Radio 3 and 4. At Pennine Productions, Janet Graves has been a hugely skilful and astute executive producer, while Mike Thornton is a superb studio manager.

Our friends Virgil Miedema and Barbara Spaid (and their daughters Stephanie and Allison) opened their house in Delhi to us for twelve years of visits, enabling us to go off wandering, recording, making notes. We have Virgil to thank, too, for endless trips around old British cemeteries all over India, and for introducing us to BACSA, the British Association for Cemeteries in South Asia.

James Verona has been very helpful in explaining the intricacies of his cousin Captain Roy Abbott's family tree, while Harry MacLure of the Chennai-based magazine *Anglos in the Wind* has provided extremely useful background information about the Anglo-Indian community worldwide.

The team at Bradt Journey Books, including editorial director Anna Moores for her seemingly endless patience, help and advice, and editor Ross Dickinson for his superb editing skills. Also many thanks to Jasmine Hortop for her wonderfully evocative cover art.

Last but not least, we thank all the friends we made in Jhansi over the course of fifteen years. Thanks to you, we really did – as Peggy said – have a ball.

CONTENTS

CHAPTER 1

THE HOLY MAN AND PEGGY

January 2004

Outside our hotel, two dozen people were standing around a sadhu, an elderly, grey-bearded holy man, who was sprawled on the busy road.

'Can you believe it?' said an American tourist about to board a coach for Khajuraho's erotic sculptures. 'He was knocked down by a motorcyclist. Went right over the handlebars and cartwheeled ten feet into the air.'

The American climbed into the coach, and it pulled away, its passengers straining to see what they were leaving behind.

The holy man, his stick and cloth bundle of belongings beside him, was looking dazed and trying to sit up. A few feet away, a young female motorcyclist was sitting on a kerbstone rubbing her head. With so many people around them, things seemed to be in hand, so Clare and I went into the hotel, stepping carefully over the open drain in front of it, collected our key in the dim, chilly reception – 'No electricity,' sighed a fellow guest – and went up to our room.

Ten minutes later, as we were unpacking, we glanced out of the window, which faced the road. The crowd and the motorcyclist had gone, but the holy man was still there, stretched out in the road, with the traffic dodging around him. Clare picked up the room phone and dialled nine. A leaden voice answered: 'Reception.'

'There's an elderly man lying in the road outside,' said Clare. 'He's been knocked over. Would someone be able to go out and see if he's all right, please?'

There was a pause. 'Yes, ma'am.' And he put the phone down.

Ten minutes later, the holy man was still there. We went downstairs and asked to see the manager. A harassed-looking, henna-haired man emerged from a back room brushing food from his scuffed black jacket. Clare explained about the holy man.

'He's just lying down,' the manager said.

'In the middle of a busy road?'

He shrugged. 'I will see to it, ma'am,' he said.

Back in the room, we looked out of the window. The holy man had struggled on to his side and was vomiting on to the road. Clare rang reception again. 'This man needs to be taken to hospital. He's obviously ill – he's being sick in the road.'

The manager finally registered our concern. 'Ma'am, I tell you what I do. I will move you to another room.'

'We don't want another room! We want this man looked after!'

'Ma'am, I will come to your room.'

He came to our room.

'Sir, ma'am,' he said, shifting awkwardly. 'I will arrange for the man to be moved. He can be taken to the basement.'

'But he's hurt. He needs to go to hospital.'

He stared at the silent TV set in embarrassment. 'See, we cannot get involved. Once a man fell over and hit his head on a stone outside the hotel. I had him taken to hospital but he died the next day. A policeman came to see us. He said: "Unless you give me ten thousand rupees, I will charge you with assault." I had to pay up. So you see, it is not in our interests to get involved. Here in India you cannot afford to be a Good Samaritan.'

He left, and we reflected. An hour after he had been knocked over, the holy man staggered to his feet and limped away. All that was left was a small pool of vomit. Soon afterwards, a cow ambled past and licked it up.

The Hotel Sita was a utilitarian-looking 1970s building. Though far from plush, it was clean, and away from the chaos and relentless noise of Jhansi, a large, if unremarkable, railway town in the north Indian state of Uttar Pradesh. In 2004, it was probably Jhansi's most modern hotel, though it was still undeniably shabby. Clapped-out air-conditioning units were stacked on its echoey landings between small piles of abandoned masonry. Old mattresses leaned against the walls. Our room's drab brown curtains drooped from their rods and the shower splashed water into every corner of the bathroom floor.

There was, though, a good restaurant, its door guarded by a life-sized dark green stone turtle, and many rungs up the catering ladder from the restaurant across town that offered 'Milk-Fed Baby Lamb Leg Steak'. Even so, our first breakfast was a basic affair. According to the menu, we had ordered Milk with Cornflakes, Toast-Butter-Jam and Tea in Pot ('Separate tea', with tea, milk and sugar all separate, rather than India's staple chai, where everything was boiled up together). Were eggs available, I asked.

'No Bolied Eggs,' the waiter said, reading from the menu. No Tit-bits Veg, no Tit-bits Non-veg. No Omelette with Finger Chips.

The rooms at the rear of the hotel overlooked an alley. A young man was wheeling along it a trolley covered by a mountainous pile of green chillies. Another man strolled around brushing his teeth. A small child played with a tiny dog. On the flat roof of the house across the alley a woman rolled chapatis, another hung out long lines of washing, and a third spread out rice to dry on large mats. The roof space of another house, hemmed in by higher buildings, had been converted into a luxuriant garden, with potted shrubs and hanging baskets. Neighbours gossiped, a man hurried along selling pink candyfloss, ringing a bell to alert potential customers. Two other men brought out a dining chair and cut each other's hair. It was the quintessence of local neighbourhood India.

Later that afternoon, we met Peggy Cantem, the eighty-two-year-old known throughout the town as 'Aunty Peggy' (or, just as often, 'Peggy Aunty'). We'd heard a great deal about her in the four years we had been visiting Jhansi, but somehow our paths hadn't yet crossed. Now, alerted to our presence by the Anglo-Indian grapevine, she came to meet us at our hotel.

Small, sallow, slightly hunched, with shrewdly darting eyes and short white hair, she was wearing dark blue slacks, a red, green and white checked shirt and a blue fleece. A widow, she had no children but an immense network of friends and contacts. As president of Jhansi's Anglo-Indian Association, she was also, we gradually discovered, an inveterate marriage maker, English teacher, charity organiser, friend of the great and the good, the rich and the poor – and the doughty custodian of the European cemetery, with its rich social history of the town's British and Anglo-Indian inhabitants.

She herself was the granddaughter of a British soldier and his Indian wife. Usually Christian and regarding English as their mother tongue, there were around half a million Anglo-Indians (also then known as Eurasians) in India at Partition in 1947. Many subsequently emigrated to Britain, the USA, Canada or Australia. There were now fewer than 150,000 throughout India (the exact number remains unknown), concentrated mainly in Delhi, Bangalore, Chennai, Hyderabad and Kolkata. In Jhansi, numbers had dwindled over the years to around thirty families.

Peggy arrived on the arm of Billy, a young man in tight jeans, tight white shirt and back-to-front baseball cap. He described himself as a doctor but, when asked what kind of doctor, clarified that he was, in fact, a trainee cosmetologist.

A what?

'A cosmetologist – see, I am working on reversing the wrinkling process,' he told Clare, peering at her face. 'I can rid you of all those wrinkles round your eyes and…'

'Those wrinkles,' Clare interrupted firmly, 'are the songlines of my existence. I'm not having them touched.'

'I can also see that you have dry skin…'

Clare laughed at his cheek, but it was clear that the four of us together was not the best combination, so Billy disappeared to check his emails.

'Now, my dears,' said Peggy, smoothing over this awkwardness, 'you must come to my house for tea and ginger cake.'

She called Anish Khan, her 'taxi fellow' or 'two-seater fellow' as she variously referred to him. The three of us squeezed on to the back seat of his rickety-rackety autorickshaw and juddered our way to Peggy's house, round curving lanes and narrow alleys, past gutters full of rubbish and past the old, rather dilapidated-looking British St Martin's Church.

'We used to have the Armistice service in that church,' Peggy said sadly. 'In the old days, there were fields all around it. But now the fields are all built over.'

Her home was in the Civil Lines area, on the edge of the army cantonment. She had lived there for forty years and paid rent of 150 rupees (about £1.50) a month. Her flat occupied the ground floor of a cramped house at the end of a long, narrow, blank-ended alley lined by more upmarket homes. Built in the 1930s for railway workers, the house – like the church – had originally been in open country but had gradually been hemmed in by piecemeal development.

'Welcome to my little abode, darlings,' she said, her accent somehow simultaneously clipped and lilting, as, with some effort, she climbed the three front steps. The house used to have a garden, she said, but someone had built another house directly in front. So now her front door faced a concrete wall. 'Jackals were here when I first came. This area used to be known as Jackal Square; it was like a jungle at the back. I used to have a jackal running through the house, and three or four dogs chasing it.'

She pulled aside the curtain across the entrance.

'Sheela!' she called. 'Chai!'

We stepped into a cluttered kitchen-cum-dining room. Over to the right, Sheela Chauhan, Peggy's smiling, seemingly unflappable cook, started boiling up milk on a two-ring gas hob, Peggy's only cooker. Wearing a lemon and turquoise sari, she hummed quietly as she stirred the tea, milk, sugar and spices together in a battered pan. Pages from old newspapers were taped to the wall behind the 'cooker' to catch any splashes.

'Here, darlings,' said Peggy. 'Sit!'

We sat on plastic chairs around a large table with a 1960s floral tablecloth. Letters were piled on it, along with a glass vase of plastic roses, salt and pepper pots, a collection of sauce bottles and a jar jammed full of pens and pencils. Religious posters, including a Sacred Heart, were hung on the walls, together with an out-of-date calendar from the nearby Shrine of St Jude. Statuettes, including a couple of St Jude himself, gazed at each other across shelves stacked with a jumble of aluminium plates, unmatching crockery and screw-top pickle jars that looked like specimens from a medical museum. A two-foot-high plastic model of the Eiffel Tower dominated the top shelf.

Tea cloths, displayed on the walls like posters, were decorated with Ladybird-style pictures of British wildlife – robins, hedgehogs, foxes. An oil lamp stood ready and waiting for the regular power cuts (daily 8am to noon; 5pm to 7pm).

The outsized fridge – a Godrej Pentacool – was covered with magnets including a kangaroo, a chilli, a banana, a picture of Lourdes, the Sydney Harbour Bridge, Jesus with one hand on his bleeding heart, a kitsch angel and an even kitscher koala. A fading print of *The Last Supper* was propped up on the electricity generator.

In a corner was a slightly foxed framed photograph of Peggy in her forties. She had immaculately permed dark hair and lipsticked lips, and wore small pearl earrings and a trim blouse.

As we waited for the tea to boil, she disappeared behind another curtain. 'I am fetching the ginger cake,' she called from what turned out to be her storeroom.

Reeking of mothballs, the room was piled high with dusty documents, family photos and more ornaments. Old suitcases, trunks and shoeboxes crammed with papers were stacked up alongside an almirah, a large grey iron locker in which plastic-wrapped tablecloths, linen and spare towels could be protected from monsoon damp. The room was cluttered with more religious paraphernalia, gifts to hand out to guests (expected and unexpected), more tablecloths and a cache of cakes and biscuits. A statuette of Christ stood next to an old cardboard box that had once contained a pop-up toaster.

Peggy returned with a packet of Good Day biscuits – 'I don't know what I've done with that ginger cake.' As Sheela brought the chai, a cow nosed through the doorway and she shooed it away.

This dining room, we soon discovered, was an unofficial community centre for Anglo-Indian Jhansi, an audience hall with Peggy at its centre; there was – in a favourite phrase of hers – much *aana aur jaana* (coming and going). It was always open house and at times it resembled a salon, with Peggy holding court and half a dozen others pitching in to the discussion.

Several different conversations might be going on at once, everyone talking over everyone else in English, Hindi or a mixture of both, and often shrieking with laughter. It was like vaudeville, a riotous Restoration comedy, a conversational free-for-all. The phone, in its hand-knitted holder, would constantly ring, from underneath newspapers, documents and towels, or in Peggy's handbag. When she had a moment to herself, she would leaf through her battered contacts book and dial someone. As everything got curiouser and curiouser, we often felt we had fallen down the rabbit hole and joined the Mad Hatter's tea party.

Her speech was full of charmingly anachronistic phrases. 'Everything is kept higgledy-piggledy,' she would say, shaking her head over the state of her storage room. Sentences would come out of nowhere. 'My mongoose hasn't come this morning,' she would suddenly announce, apropos of nothing. Or: 'Rodney Titus – you can give him all the dope on the Anglo-Indians.' Or: 'My English is not even colloquial.'

She suddenly dropped the name Mark Tully into the conversation. The BBC's celebrated India correspondent had once sat at the table. 'And have you heard of William Dalrymple? They both write to me because of the Anglo-Indian community.'

According to an article I later read in an Anglo-Indian newsletter, other visitors had included the maharajah of a former princely state and the leader of India's transgender *hijra* community. 'Her home became a landmark,' the article declared, 'and she, a legend.'

High commissioners and consuls would call, 'and I have friends in Alaska also, they send help for the cemetery. And in Nova Scotia – Thelma Bliss and all.'

In the 1950s, she had shown John Masters around Jhansi when the film of *Bhowani Junction* – his classic study of racial tensions in post-Partition India – was being planned, with stars including Ava Gardner and Stewart Granger.

'I showed him the old style of the Anglo-Indians. He liked our houses – they were in the railway quarters. When I was married, we had a C-type house, thirteen rooms, for two people. He said: "These houses would suit beautifully".'

In the event, the film was shot in Pakistan.

Sheela brought more chai and the conversation broadened out. 'We kept the houses well because of our servants. We still want to live in the good old British days when we had servants at our beck and call,' said Peggy. 'That is one fault in us Anglo-Indians.'

She still employed two: Sheela and May Coutinho, her small, thin, elderly-looking domestic help whose large, round glasses emphasised her pleading look. Both women were widows and to some extent dependent on Peggy. While we talked, a quiet, rather hurt-looking young woman moved slowly around in the shadows of the bedroom, cleaning.

'This is my friend's servant,' said Peggy. 'She's a sleepy-head, I think!'

Suddenly the lights went out.

'Oh, what a nuisance! Power cut... Sheela! Torches!' Sheela took two torches from the top of the fridge, where they were kept alongside a large, rather grubby-looking plastic water filter.

Clare mentioned the incident with the holy man.

'The average Indian is tired of this country with all its corruption,' sighed Peggy. 'The country is going to the dogs. One man I know tried to free three hundred thousand rupees – about three thousand pounds in your money, I think? – from a trust and the judge wanted one hundred thousand rupees to give him permission. In court the clerk openly said: "How much will you pay me to deal with this case quickly?"

'See,' she added sadly, 'here the lawyers are liars, but you have to pay them.'

An autorickshaw spluttered down the alley and shuddered to a halt outside. A frail old man with a plaid scarf wound tightly round his head and neck staggered down from the passenger seat, carrying a net shopping bag.

'Ah! Here is Pastor Rao!' cried Peggy. 'Pastor Rao – come in, come in! You have arrived just in time for tea and biscuits! Here, sit!'

He did so, unwinding his scarf to reveal thin white hair and a grizzly beard.

'Meet my good friends, Stephen and Clare, journalists from the BBC in England.'

The word 'England' hit the Pastor like a thunderbolt. 'Ah, you are from London!' he cried. 'I had the honour to shake hands with Dr Robert Runcie, the 102nd Archbishop of Canterbury.' He struggled back to his feet, his eyes lighting up behind thick, black-framed government glasses. 'I remember hearing your great leader Churchill's speeches,' he said with stentorian pride. He cleared his throat, gripped the back of the chair and launched into the politician's 'We shall fight on the beaches' speech, declaiming in a quavery voice: 'There has never been a period in all these long centuries of which we boast when an absolute guarantee against invasion, still less against serious raids, could have been given to our people…'

We all listened, even Anish, who spoke little English but understood much more. He stood in the doorway, tilted his head to one side and smiled.

'We,' the Pastor concluded with a rhetorical pause and raising his voice to a full Churchillian shout, '*shall never surrender!*' He smiled broadly as we applauded, cleared his throat and, almost trembling, sat down. 'This really was their finest hour,' he said and reached for his cup of chai.

As we were to discover over the next few years, the Anglo-Indians' own finest hour lasted through two centuries of British rule. They would not have existed had it not been first for the East India Company and then the British Raj.

The community began on the subcontinent in the 1630s, with the founding of a British settlement in Madras, since renamed Chennai. Many of the early settlers – British, French, Portuguese, Dutch – married Indian women or took them as mistresses. Their offspring became known as Eurasians or Anglo-Indians (though the term originally simply meant Brits who returned home from India). Calcutta's founder, Job Charnock, married an Indian. William Pitt's grandmother was Anglo-Indian. More recently, so were Cliff Richard and the Hollywood actress Merle Oberon.

Closer to home, one of Clare's great-uncles, a tea planter in Assam, had married an Indian woman working on his estate and had two children with her. At some point, though, she simply disappeared from the picture. While her son found work with the Indian Civil Service, her husband returned to Britain, followed eventually by their daughter, who never mentioned her mother, not even to her own children and grandchildren. And so the family's Indian connection has remained shrouded in mystery – despite attempts by Clare and her cousins to find out more, both in Britain and here in India.

CHAPTER 2

CAPTAIN ABBOTT – BRITISH INDIA PRESERVED IN ASPIC

Our *Alice in Wonderland* journey into Anglo-Indian life had started four years earlier, in the first month of the millennium, during a busy three-week press trip across Uttar Pradesh. Together with twenty or so other journalists, I was visiting some of the area's major tourist highlights: Haridwar, Rishikesh, Corbett National Park, Lucknow, Varanasi and, inevitably, Agra, for the Taj Mahal.

By comparison, Jhansi – where our group was scheduled to spend three nights – was very small beer: a dusty town of half a million people, some three hundred miles or so south of Delhi and a main junction for trains from the capital to Mumbai and Chennai. Few foreign visitors lingered very long there. Most simply used it as a lunch stop on their way to the intricately carved temples of Khajuraho, or to Orchha, the atmospherically abandoned medieval town a half-hour drive away.

Those who did linger usually learned about the Rani of Jhansi, Lakshmibai. During the First Indian War of Independence (aka the 1857 Mutiny), 'India's Joan of Arc', as she was subsequently known, became a symbol of the country's freedom struggle. Disguising herself as a man, she had gripped her horse's reins between her teeth and, wielding her sword in both hands, reputedly leapt from the ramparts of the town's hilltop fort and died fighting the British. By doing so, she gave Jhansi its one moment of fame.

Statues of her on her rearing horse, baby son strapped to her back, towered over the station taxi rank. Otherwise this garrison town had been infamous, in the days of the Raj, as a 'hardship' or 'punishment' posting, with summer temperatures often reaching 50°C at midday.

'I don't think there were many stations in India worse than Jhansi,' Stephen Bentley, a regimental 'band boy' who served in India from 1927 to 1933, told Charles Allen for his classic book *Plain Tales from the Raj*. 'The barracks were miles away from the town and what town there was was really only a small railway settlement.'

It had 'a very poor bazaar of about ten or twenty shops' and a corrugated-iron cinema, but no cafés. 'The population,' Bentley added, was 'principally Anglo-Indian or half-caste'. It was, Allen wrote, 'a twilight community'.

After an ill-advised curry the night before, I'd spent a bilious morning in bed and now needed some fresh air – or at any rate air as fresh as a traffic-choked Indian town could offer. I was making my careful way along a frantically busy, cow-dung-spattered, bus-honking road near the town's army cantonment area when, beyond a couple of wild boars snuffling through a pile of rubbish, I spotted a sign: 'Turn right to the luxurious Jhansi Hotel'. I turned right and, set back from the road, a long, low, whitewashed building stretched out.

The rambling single-storey hotel had, I later gathered, opened in 1910 and looked little changed since. It may once have been the focus of British social life, the place where the *burra-sahibs*, the colonial big cheeses, hung up their pith helmets and downed their

G & Ts, but, half a century after Indian Independence, it was frayed and faded, with broken chairs outside many of its rooms. Luxurious rather overstated it.

Mid-afternoon the hotel was quiet, so the longest-serving of its seventeen staff – Mr Singh, a waiter with a frayed towel draped over his shoulder – offered me a guided tour. The high, dim rooms opened off a wide veranda lined with antlers, lilac-painted planters' chairs and air-conditioning units as big as wardrobes. Faded old master prints hung in the smaller of the two dining rooms. In one corner was a vast dinner gong; in another, the grandest of grandfather clocks ticked steadfastly away.

Ceiling fans whirred in the cavernous main dining room, with its solid pillars, Louis XV-style chairs and weathered Victorian portraits of British worthies. The cream-painted walls were grubby, the ceiling nicotine-brown, the whole room terminally neglected. At one end was a small stage once used by dance bands.

'This used to be the ballroom when the British Raj was here,' said Mr Singh, handing me a menu. It included a dish called 'Cheese Gatwick'. None of the staff were quite sure what this was, as no guest in living memory had ordered it.

How many bedrooms were there? This prompted a keen debate between Mr Singh and his fellow waiters. After several minutes and many disagreements, they settled on twenty.

Understandably, it wasn't 'costly' – a word we often heard – to stay here. Yogesh Mehrotra, the hotel's personable chief executive, wrote the room rate (from £6 a night) on a card and handed it to me. 'The prices are negotiable,' he said.

Could I have a look around?

'Of course.'

He led me along the back veranda to what he called a 'special' room at the far end, No 14. With a discreet flourish, he pushed open the door.

'In this room lived Dr Righton,' he said reverently. 'He was a single gentleman and he stayed here for fifty years.'

Dr Major J. A. (Joe) Righton had, I later learned, been a member of the Indian Army Medical Corps. During World War II, he had served under General Montgomery, Lord Wavell and Viscount Slim in Burma. He had 'stayed on' after Independence, to work as a doctor for Indian Railways, and lived in this one room-plus-bathroom. After retirement, his health declined, and he was almost totally deaf and blind when he died in 1988, aged eighty-five.

At the end he was still paying the same room rate he had paid when he first moved in – ten annas (around ten pence) a day. 'And it was including two meals and one breakfast per day,' said Mr Mehrotra. 'It was our hospitality, as he was our old customer. He got a pension from the railways and his family back in England used to send a little money for him, a five-pound postal order. He was typically British but he was used to Indian culture.'

We edged around the high, dim room, with its stately bed, baronial fireplace and empty shelves.

'When Dr Righton was here, books were there, and clothes and all,' said Mr Mehrotra. 'In his old days, he just spent his time walking round the hotel.'

So he must have been the very last Brit living in Jhansi after Independence?

'No, no, sir, there is still Captain Abbott in Lalitpur Road. Shall I ring?'

A servant answered the call. I said I was British and wondered if I could come to see the Captain. I could hear rapid consultation in the background and the servant came back on the phone: 'Can you come at 5pm?'

Mr Mehrotra checked his watch. It was 3.30pm. 'Captain-Sahib will be at lunch,' he explained.

At 5pm I was hunched in an autorickshaw as it turned through a gate with the name 'Captain N. R. Abbott' stencilled on one of its posts. The initials, I later discovered, stood for Niel Royston, though everyone knew him as Roy. The boundary wall was painted mustard yellow with diamond shapes etched out in ochre. The rickshaw spluttered up a long gravel drive lined by terracotta pots of marigolds, regimentally manicured lawns and immaculately kept beds of snapdragons, pompom dahlias, roses, pansies and nasturtiums. With asters, sweet peas, white alyssum, daisies and phlox, it could have been a suburban English garden, except for the tamarind trees and coconut palms, the guavas and papayas. All told, the estate covered four and a half acres.

In the centre of the lawn, a white marble statue of a doleful angel with clipped wings cast her eyes to the ground. A vegetable plot was planted with cabbages, tomatoes and lettuce; beyond that were an orange orchard and a tennis court. A *mali*, or gardener, squatted by a small fire, spooning food from a chrome tin. Nearby were two dogs' graves, one 'erected in memory of our Poochie – a small dog with a big heart. Died 25.1.1965 RIP', the other to 'Prince, born 7/3/71, died 23/8/71'.

At the top of the drive was a grand cream-painted bungalow – four-square, flat-roofed, colonnaded and colonial. Wicker planters' chairs were ranged along its pillared veranda, whose walls – like those at the hotel – bristled with antlers. I asked the rickshaw driver to wait and rang the bell on the side door.

'Is sahib at home?' I asked the rather distracted-looking man who answered. He ushered me through a door curtain into a small office lined with framed sepia photographs of Victorian and Edwardian Brits and disappeared behind another curtain. Seconds later an English voice – firm, fruity, ringing with military authority – boomed, 'Come in! Come in!'

I parted the curtain and discovered British India preserved in aspic.

Sitting at a large desk stacked high with official-looking files and folders was Captain Royston Abbott, a widower and, I was later told, the last British landowner, or zamindar, in India. In his mid-seventies and with the air of a Surrey bank manager from the 1940s, he seemed imposingly, impeccably English. With his dark blue blazer and cravat, a silk handkerchief perfectly folded in his top pocket, he could have been dressed for a Rotary meeting or an evening at a Home Counties golf club. On the wall behind him a tiger's head mounted on a shield snarled silently. In front of him, a sign on the desk instructed – ironically, as I was later to discover – 'Observe Silence'.

He gestured me to a sofa. 'Tea? I'll just tell the fellow.'

He strode stiffly down a long corridor and I took in the high-ceilinged room. With French windows opening on to the veranda, it could have been a stage set for a play based on Charles Allen's book. A leopard skin was splayed out on one wall, the stuffed head of a crocodile and the head of a flying fox were hung on another. There were fading 1920s wedding photographs and displays of sabres, machetes, pistols and tennis racquets.

The bookshelves housed Nevil Shute novels, ten-year-old *Reader's Digest*s, *Gone With the Wind* and *Bhowani Junction*. The Captain's edition was dated 1955, the year after it was first published – he later told me he hadn't reread it since. Next to a Coronation picture of the Queen and Prince Philip were calendars advertising farm machinery manufacturers and medals, shields, cups and certificates from flower show competitions. A room full of trophies: floral and animal.

Alongside a gently humming tank of exotic fish was a hand-tinted copy of a photograph of the Captain as a young officer, khaki bush hat rakishly tilted. Generations of Abbotts stared out from the walls. In pride of place were retouched colour photographs of the Captain, his late wife Lillian (a beautiful woman with a hint of Ava Gardner about her, despite severe horn-rimmed glasses and hair tied back in a bun), and their daughter Penny. A month after Christmas, the frames were still garlanded with tinsel.

Directly opposite the desk was a grand portrait in oils of a stocky man with a handlebar moustache and bowler hat, plus fours and a riding crop. 'My great-grandfather,' said the Captain as he strode back in. 'William Lumsden Abbott.' Born in Scotland in 1828, William, he said, had been the first of the four generations of Abbotts to settle in India, enlisting in the army and sailing East in 1850.

The Captain himself had been born in Jhansi and joined the army as an eleven-year-old cadet.

'I went through the Indian Military Academy in Dehra Dun – "the Indian Sandhurst" as it was called. Left in 1943 and got a regular commission in the Indian Army, the Royal Garhwal Rifles. It was a lovely little regiment. I had a great time there, absolutely wonderful. In those days, there was no better army in the world. Not one. I was in Java and Sumatra against the Japanese – that was fun for a couple of years.'

He left the army in 1951, retaining his military title, joined the family farming business and took over the running of the Jhansi Hotel, which his grandfather had built.

'In those days it was…'

He got no further. The door curtain parted and a ghostly vision materialised. It was 'the fellow' – the bearer, an old man in a white uniform with white Nehru cap, white shoes and white gloves. He shuffled towards us carrying a tray. Without a word, he bowed and gravely lowered the tray in front of me. I poured tea from a silver-plated teapot into a rose-flowered china cup and took a slice of chocolate cake.

'That's Chuman,' said the Captain. 'He's very old. His father worked for my father. I look after the fellow, look after his medical bills. They appreciate that kind of thing. Been with me forty years.'

The bungalow, he said, had been built around 1900 for an army brigadier, and subsequently bought by his own parents. It was one of over a dozen Jhansi bungalows once owned by the Abbotts.

'There was one near the Jhansi Hotel. It had an aviary – a huge place with hundreds of lovely birds. At the front there were four large frogs made from cement, with waterspouts for mouths.'

The Captain now divided his time between Jhansi and 'the farms' – six hundred acres of land near the small town of Khurai, one hundred miles south.

'There's a bungalow with mango orchards. It's very, very peaceful… I'm very much involved in social work there, you know. I tell the villagers: "Look, we need a road here. You provide the labour and I'll meet the costs." Otherwise you wait for the government to do things and that never happens. I've built two schools, wells, a little community centre, a Hindu temple, whatever comes up. I find them very willing to participate in it all.'

As Chuman brought more tea, the Captain reflected on his decision to 'stay on' after Partition in 1947, something he didn't often get the chance to do, he admitted, with so few British visitors.

'When the British left India, I thought of going back, but I found it didn't affect us out here in the slightest way. Some Indians are so fed up with the conditions now that they say: "Sahib, why don't you let us vote for the British again?"' He threw back his head and laughed.

In the 1970s, he had bought a house near Eastbourne, where he had lived with Lillian and Penny for a couple of years.

'But I could never settle over there, y'know. I've been back a couple of times, but I don't stay long. The last time was eleven years ago.'

It was the difficulty so many India-based Brits faced when they went 'home' to Britain and found themselves in a world that was colder and duller than India, a world that flickered hesitantly in grainy black-and-white rather than shimmering in vibrant technicolour.

'I've no intention of leaving India now – no matter what happens,' he said. 'I'm too attached to this country and living in the villages has made me more pro-Indian. I always get together with the villagers, have a chat: we get on very well together. Everyone knows me. They always ask: "How are you?" I say: "I'm all right, how about you? Don't catch my diseases!" They don't always get my humour, don't always get what I'm talking about. But when I explain it to them, then they laugh.' He chuckled to himself. 'The climate is also a big factor in not leaving. And I've always been used to a very outdoor life – in the army, shooting, farming. Farming is probably the best thing an army officer can do. It's an open-air life; you're not sitting behind an office table.' He paused. 'And over here I get tremendous respect.'

So was it true, then, what many former expats said – that in India you could be 'somebody', but back in Britain you were 'nobody'?

'That's it!' he said, banging his hand on the desk. 'That's it!'

On his last trip to London, he had bumped into an old Anglo-Indian friend from Jhansi who had moved to the UK.

'He was delivering boxes for a Savile Row tailor – yet he had been an official here. He said: "What a mistake I made, Roy. I should never have left India. Look at what I'm doing now – carrying boxes around."'

The Captain showed me round the bungalow: three large bedrooms with bathrooms, a dim sitting room, and a windowless dining room in the centre of the house between the kitchens and his office – a refuge from scorching summer temperatures. On the wall was a framed plaque:

Christ is the head of this home,
The unseen guest at every meal,
The silent listener to every conversation.

At the end of the main corridor was a mournful bust of a veiled young woman. Another bust – of a ringletted Victorian girl – stood on a plinth at the far end of the sitting room, where three huge volumes were displayed in a glass case: *Masterpieces of Industrial Art & Sculpture at the International Exhibition, 1862.*

'We used to have some gay parties in here,' the Captain reflected.

The house now seemed silent, however, dim and sepulchrally still. It had once been considered, he said, as a location for the award-winning 1980s TV serialisation of Paul Scott's *The Jewel in the Crown.*

In the vestibule he pointed out a photograph of his father – also Roy – feeding pigeons in Trafalgar Square in 1932. Another showed an uncle with a 'catch', a newly shot tiger. Alongside was another of a dead tiger – with the half-eaten body of an Indian woman next to it, eyes bulging with fear.

'The tiger on the wall through there' – he pointed back towards the office – 'that was mine. It was ten miles from the farms. We beat the jungle out and the guns were all lined up at one end and this fellow came out straight in front of me. I was very fond of shooting, but now it's all so restricted.'

Two hours had passed, with the low hum of an electricity generator cutting in and out. Through the French windows, a full moon was rising over the orange orchard.

'There's no-one left out here in Jhansi now except me,' he said. 'I've got a few army friends, though, and I went to the Army Day celebrations the other day. Took me back to the way things used to be done. Very pukka.' He was still, he added, the official British representative in Jhansi – 'Though there's not much to represent now.'

Did he remember Dr Righton?

'Oh yes, he was one of my shooting partners. Particularly birds. We used to go out and do a lot of duck shooting together, before all the restrictions came in. A good fellow, Joe Righton.'

I said I must get back to the hotel where I was staying, the Hotel Sita. As I stood up to leave, I told the Captain I'd like to come back the following morning and photograph him.

'By all means,' he said, beaming.

Next day, I was due to catch a coach to Agra at 8.30am, so I arranged for another autorickshaw to pick me up from the Sita, a ten-minute drive away, at 7.30am.

'Sahib is dressing,' I was told when I arrived at the bungalow. I strolled anxiously around the garden, admiring the pompom dahlias. It was past 8am by the time the Captain emerged, immaculately turned out again, with his pocket handkerchief even more perfectly folded. I quickly photographed him on the veranda, the morning sun streaming dazzlingly across it, and the waiting rickshaw spluttered back to the Sita, where my journalist companions were already on the coach.

'Enjoy Agra,' the Captain said as I left (he pronounced it, '*Aaaargraahh*'). 'And call again, won't you, next time you're in Jhansi? You must come down to the farms. It's a different world down there. Bring your wife. And you could bring me some Cracker Barrel cheese, if you wanted. Just can't get the stuff over here.'

CHAPTER 3

'INCONVENIENCE CAUSED IS DEEPLY REGRETTED'

Almost exactly a year later, I was heading back to Jhansi with two packs of Cracker Barrel and my wife Clare. Early in January, halfway through our two-month trip to India, I had telephoned Captain Abbott from Lucknow and, as promised, he had invited us to visit him at 'the farms'.

He said his driver would pick us up in Jhansi, so we booked tickets from Lucknow on the Sabarmati Express – or the Varanasi-Ahmedabad Sabarmati Express as *Trains at a Glance*, the Indian equivalent of *Bradshaw's Guide*, more grandly called it. *Trains at a Glance* was an institution, a huge and detailed printed timetable still published years after the timetable system had been fully computerised. Its most intriguing feature was the Rail Travel Concessions chart which listed the arbitrary-seeming categories of passengers who could apply for discounts. They included 'Recipients of Indian Police Medal for Meritorious Service... Either of parents accompanying the child recipients of National Bravery Award... Girl students of govt. schools situated in rural areas... Students and non-students' and 'Artists – theatrical, musical concert, dancing, magician troupes'. Over hundreds of Indian train journeys, we never knowingly saw a magician troupe – unless, as a dazzling party piece, they had made themselves invisible.

❖ ❖ ❖ ❖

In Lucknow, we headed straight for the Residency, the gaunt, forlorn site of the infamous 1857 six-month siege, seven years after the Captain's great-grandfather had arrived in India. We bought our tickets at the official booth, the assistant handed them over the counter, we went through the turnstile, and he instantly emerged from the booth and demanded 'Tickets!' We handed them back and he tore them in half. The Residency compound had unexpectedly become a park, where families picnicked, children played shuttlecock and couples canoodled. A man was having a shower on the lawn, using a garden hose.

Afterwards, we took a taxi to La Martiniere, the celebrated boys' public school where Kipling's Kim was educated: a vast dinosaur of a building that looked as though the plans for half a dozen different stately homes had been accidentally jumbled together. It was built by Claude Martin, a one-time soldier who, as a display helpfully pointed out, 'experimented in hot-air ballooning and bladder surgery'. In the school library, I asked one of the pupils – about twelve years old – if he read Jane Austen.

'Sir,' he sighed, 'I am tired of the classics.'

The library's books looked as though they could have been bought at the city's Ram Advani bookshop, a sort of literary salon, a sophisticated Left Bank-ish place for cultural chit-chat accompanied by china cups of Darjeeling tea with milk in a silver jug. The most cultivated and courteous of men, Mr Advani had opened the shop shortly after Partition in 1948. Lucknow then, he told us during one of our visits, was 'a more gracious place. It had a charm, a grandeur and a sort of feudal society, like you have in England. Or used to have.'

We had booked into the Carlton Hotel, a former maharajah's palace – rambling and turreted – that had been a hotel for 120 years and had not worn well (it has since been renovated). The rooms were irredeemably dingy and cobwebbed, with moth-eaten carpets we hesitated to cross in bare feet and armchairs we hesitated to sit on in clean clothes. Every other door seemed to open into a storeroom piled high with rubbish. The staff – dozens of them hanging around – seemed bemused to have guests staying. The house rules included: 'Misuse of linen for the purpose other than it is meant is prohibited'.

We stayed one night, then moved on to another, slightly less moth-eaten, hotel. On our second morning there, the room phone rang.

'Sir,' said the man on reception. 'Would it be possible for you to shift rooms? We are insecticising rooms on your floor to get rid of the cockroaches.'

We shifted rooms. Near the hotel was an email and computer centre. I asked at the tourist office when it was generally open. 'Sir, it is open whenever the fellow is there.'

Alongside Lucknow's State Museum, a scruffy yard housed a dozen British imperial statues that had been plucked from their plinths after Independence and re-erected in a semicircle. They included four Queen Victorias, ranging in size from economy to semi-colossal. The Queen gazed across at her grandson, George V, and a group of sundry worthies replete with plumes, medals and imperial pride. Modern India had consigned them to a junkyard of the Raj.

We turned up at Lucknow's palatial crimson and white railway station in good time for the 9.50pm departure to Jhansi. A litter of puppies had bedded down on a heap of sand and two cows were ambling along the crowded platform, nosing through waste bins and pulling out choice bits of cardboard for supper. Swathed in a shawl, I dozed off on a bench, but woke a few minutes later as flute music wafted past me. A thin old man, white-haired and watery-eyed, was sitting cross-legged a few yards away playing a bright blue flute: haunting, plaintive music that seemed to blend ragas and Scottish reels. The high notes ricocheted off the station roof, drowning out the announcements about delays. Each began, as in every Indian station, with a patrician female voice intoning 'Your kind attention please...' and ended with 'Inconvenience caused is deeply regretted'. The old man seemed oblivious to them, staring penetratingly at me, occasionally waving his left hand in the air for money. Some of the two-dozen-strong audience gathered around this station-platform Krishna handed him a few rupees and he moved on.

The patrician lady announcer gave us regular updates and we offered her our kind attention. Our train was gradually delayed to 10.30, then 11.15, then 12.05, and finally 12.50am. It was an unremarkable delay by Indian standards. We were used to spending chilly nights on dark station platforms, strolling up and down, perhaps discovering an ambiguous sign over a doorway: 'Second Class Ladies Waiting Room'. We once turned up at a station at 11.25pm to catch a midnight 'Express'. At around 11.30 a train rolled in.

'This is amazing,' I said to the man standing next to me. 'Our train is half an hour early.'

'No, no,' he replied. 'This is yesterday's train. It is twenty-three and a half hours late.'

Over the years, we'd learned that delays could offer useful opportunities to take in platform life. First, though, you might have to clamber over people lying lengthwise on the steps of a passenger bridge and avoid passengers sleeping on luggage in the entrance hall or picnicking on the platforms. During the day, Indian railway stations can be manically bustling. At night, gloom descends. At Lucknow, under dim blue lighting, groups of tired-looking travellers were swathed in dun-coloured cardigans and shawls, camouflaged in the darkness. They wore hand-knitted woollen bonnets or wrapped thick scarves around their heads. We seemed to be drifting through a sludgy dream, surrounded by muffled, furtive-looking figures.

The station offered three hours of random snapshots. An elderly, skull-capped Muslim, wearing a finely embroidered coat, ate a banana with almost meditative concentration. A group of women sat silently on the ground in a circle. A child lay face down on sacking. An old woman picked her feet meticulously. An elderly Sikh woman in a peach-coloured sari strolled past with a dagger suspended from an orange rope swinging by her side. A magazine seller pushed his wooden trolley along the platform. Chanting 'Chai, chai chai', vendors poured steaming-hot tea from huge tin kettles into flimsy plastic cups that not only burned the fingers but also, eventually, would be thrown on to the railway line. A few years earlier, the cups had been biodegradable terracotta.

Police officers carrying lathis, their solid bamboo sticks, patrolled the platforms, ready to pounce on 'miscreants', as Indian newspapers often referred to criminals. Men hawked and blew their noses straight on to the platform.

'Usually the train is never late,' a fellow passenger told us. 'But today it is. Something must have happened.' We sprang on to a wooden bench the second it became vacant and waited and watched.

Just before 1am, the train finally pulled in with a deafening shriek of whistles, a screech of brakes, and a clatter of carriages ricocheting off each other as they shuddered to a halt. Passengers ran up and down the platforms, calling and shouting, pushing and shoving, rushing this way and that, dragging crying children behind them.

We had already hired a porter, who would generally – though not necessarily – know exactly where each carriage was likely to stop. If he had miscalculated, it could mean a frantic hundreds-of-yards dash from one end of the train to the other.

As our train stopped, our porter hoisted himself and our luggage up the carriage steps and continued pushing and shoving along the corridors until he found our seats, in a curtained-off compartment, with bunks overhead. He shoved our suitcases unceremoniously under the bottom bunks, took his fee (greatly enhanced for Westerners), then pushed and shoved his way back on to the platform.

We sorted out the luggage, locked it with padlocks and chained it to security loops, though we knew it might all need to be unlocked again if other passengers arrived with enough luggage for a four-year international expedition.

Each berth was designed for four passengers, but whole families were piling in. Initially, we'd worried about this, until we realised that most of them were a waving-off party, who would pile off again with shouts and tears and smiles as the train jolted into motion again. As we prepared for bed, an attendant came round dispensing impressively clean sheets, pillows and small rough towels. Around 1.30am, it was finally time to try to go to sleep.

Unlike our usual 'Second Class AC' compartments, this one – 'First Class Non-AC' – had no glass in its barred windows and was grubby, dark, dusty and, crucially, freezing cold. Passengers snored in the gloom. We huddled under our sheets and shawls as the train trundled on through the night. Drunken men in the next carriage bawled at each other, singing and hurling around what sounded like metal crates of bottles.

As dawn broke, the conductor checked tickets, negotiated seat changes and catnapped on a spare bunk, occasionally yawning loudly and scratching himself. Station stops always meant a great kerfuffle of comings and goings, with vendors selling pakoras, samosas and bananas from huge tin platters, vacuum-packed sweets, chocolate, peanuts and tubs of ice cream (best avoided).

As our 5.50am arrival in Jhansi stretched out to 9am, passengers got off at station stops to buy more food. A distinguished-looking Muslim carried a newspaper-covered tray of hot food in chilli sauce back to his carriage. A sadhu stared in wonder at the tray another passenger had just handed him. It was the sort of food we ate every lunchtime and evening when we were on trains – sloppy veg curry, even sloppier dahl, rice, chapatis, all served on compartmentalised chrome trays. Most of our fellow passengers had brought their own home-prepared food in steel tiffin boxes and would smile sympathetically at us.

Between talking, reading and writing up notes, we observed our fellow passengers and the scenes both inside and outside the carriage. A young man struggled to push his mobile phone charger into the charging point. An older man with hennaed hair took a pill bottle out of his pocket, sprinkled paan tobacco into his palm, ground it between his fingers and then cascaded it into his mouth. When a passenger across the aisle left the train, the attendant folded his crumpled blanket with almost obsessive precision and took his used sheets away.

Different landscapes passed – fields of sugarcane and gram, then wide, wide views peopled by stick-wielding cowherds wearing dhotis (loincloths), and labourers shielding themselves from the fierce sun with huge black umbrellas. Two men drove their water buffalo to the river. The animals waded in, until only their heads were visible above the water, like shiny jet-black stones. Chillies dried on low roofs, clothes dried on fencing. Because there was no glass in the windows we could see the landscape's colours in all their startling vibrancy. All too often in Second Class AC, the glass could be tinted yellow or orange, or was simply too filthy to see through, so that India trundled past as abstract blocks of grimy colour.

At one station, people sheltered from the heat under umbrellas and newspapers, while a goat wearing a blue pullover – its front legs down the sleeves – sunbathed on a wooden bench. Men urinated beside the train line at every turn. Ten feet from the line, a farmworker defecated in a field, hiding his head in his hands.

Our compartment became the unofficial railway office. The inspector – or 'Head Travelling Ticket Examiner' as his lapel badge proclaimed – compared charts ('data cards') with the conductor. Both wore impressively glinting signet rings, painstakingly transcribed information from a computerised list to a handwritten list, and carried clipboards with an air of consummate self-importance. But there were ink stains on their jacket chest pockets, where they each kept half a dozen pens. One eventually stapled his lists together, attached a scrap of paper, stapled it all again, spent a couple of minutes admiring his handiwork, got up, scratched his bottom and wandered off.

After a nine-hour journey, we arrived in Jhansi and took a taxi to the Jhansi Hotel.

'You are Australian?' asked the taxi driver.

'No, English.'

'From which country?' he asked.

'England.'

'You speak very nice English.'

Despite its smartly tended front gardens, the hotel seemed even more dilapidated than it had been the previous year (though not by the standards of Lucknow's Carlton). The television in our room had no plug, the air conditioning howled, the neglect was dispiriting. Outside the room, framed by plastic bucket chairs, the cooling system was a metal box stuffed with hay which would be drenched with water during the hot summer months. Tangled webs of electricity wires hung from the walls and an illuminated aquarium of goldfish added a little green gloom to the reception area.

In the dining room – dimmer than ever due to one of Jhansi's frequent power cuts – we ate stone-cold poached eggs with curled-up toast and frozen pats of butter. Men in long shawls occasionally loomed out of the shadows; one brought us a candle to add a little cosiness. Newspapers on a side table were full of the sort of burlesque headlines so loved by the Indian press. 'Mad Tusker Kills

Mahout', 'Dacoits Loot Go-Down near Jaipur', 'Synthetic Milk Centre Busted'.

As I was handing in our key at reception before exploring Jhansi, a well-dressed elderly man stepped out of the gloom.

'Ah, Mr McClarence!' He smiled. 'Would you like coffee? We can sit outside in the sunshine.'

It was the hotel manager, Omnath Mehrotra, Yogesh's father, a benign man who had been in charge since 1975. He spoke rapidly in Hindi to a waiter who hurriedly arranged a plastic table and chairs in the garden. With a soundtrack of car horns from the road about thirty feet away, Mr Mehrotra sketched the hotel's history from its founding ninety years before by the Captain's grandfather, 'the Honourable J. H. Abbott, OBE'.

Its heyday had been in the 1930s, when Jhansi had an international airport which became a stopover to Calcutta or Karachi for flights to and from Australia.

'At that time there were no hotels,' said Mr Mehrotra, 'and people were coming from outside – not Indians. So for a comfortable stay this was built – twenty rooms, nine cottages, a huge dining room, lounge. The hotel trade in India has become very popular in the last forty years: before then it was only for the very rich. There were very few tourists then, but Mr Abbott, he saw the necessity for having a hotel. The Jhansi Hotel was a travel agent also and made arrangements for people to travel abroad. They would hire or charter planes and take bookings.'

The image of fashionable colonial society dancing the night away here now seemed a little incongruous.

Mr Mehrotra took us down the corridor to Dr Righton's old room, seemingly untouched since my first visit. He became a shade melancholy. 'The morning that he died, when I passed by on this veranda, he wished me good morning and I wished him. There were Sisters of Charity here and so many times they asked him to shift to another hotel. But he said: "No, I am very happy here. Mr Mehrotra looks after me, the hotel staff look after me, I stay here." The Abbott family did a lot for him. They used to send him his evening meal. He lived here with just his books and his gun – an airgun he used for duck shooting – and his bicycle. After he got fractured in the hip, he stopped using it. I think he gave it to the postman as a gift.'

We took an autorickshaw to the Captain's house. He had already driven south to his village, but his bustlingly efficient housekeeper, Leela, a Keralan Christian in her forties, gave us a tour of the garden and the bungalow. Clare was impressed. It must, she said, be the best-kept house in Jhansi.

'I think so! You can find better houses, but well maintained – this is it. There are three, four – about five people just in the garden always.'

Leela, a nurse by training, had been part of the household since the Captain's wife Lillian had become ill. She had known the family for ten years before that, however – when she was lodging with 'an elderly Anglo-Indian lady who is a friend of this house'.

The elderly lady turned out to be Peggy Cantem, who had been at school with the Captain's sister and whom we would finally meet three years later. After which she would become, along with the Captain, the twin focus of our many visits to Jhansi.

'His wife was very fond of me,' said Leela, 'so they asked the doctor to keep me here, because I am all alone; I am not married. So I started staying here to look after her. Then I remained after her death also. And now I look after other things. Because most of the time, He…' She often seemed to capitalise the pronoun when talking of the Captain and never referred to him by name. It was always 'He' or 'Uncle'. '…He stays in the village, so somebody has to look after the house, otherwise the people would do everything as they like. You know, abroad you've got no servants so you've got no headaches, it's not a problem. But in India, once they've worked somewhere for a very long time, they think everything belongs to them. So to keep up a house like this, they will do it according to their own way. You need somebody about, to look after things…'

She broke off to shout sharply at a man riding a bicycle up the drive.

'See, that's one of the rules of the house. They cannot ride the cycle near the house – they have to get off down here, at the entrance. And there is another rule here. The children in the compound, they are not allowed to play around the house when he is here, not to make a noise, nothing. They are not allowed to go to the garden. Their relations, who are working here, they are also not allowed to go.' A picture was emerging of a small fiefdom regimented by rules and regulations.

The fifteen servants and their families, housed in modest one-, two- and three-room cottages to the side of the bungalow, were mostly from the Captain's village.

'Their parents worked for him or for his father, and he does everything for them – whitewash their houses, medical aid, everything he does. It's a community. This man here…' She indicated a man standing next to a four-wheel drive, who saluted as we approached. '...he is our driver, actually. His son had a little problem in his heart last year, so Uncle sent him to the hospital and they did checks and they found he only had six months left. Uncle spent about a lakh [roughly one thousand pounds] on him and the boy is now sitting here, hale and hearty. That's a lot of money and many people, even if they have it, they don't give it. He does a lot of social work like that. So all these servants and their children – when there are accidents, operations, they cannot afford them, so He is doing all that.'

A buffalo lolloped round the corner of the house.

'For our own milk purpose,' said Leela. She laughed. 'I tell Uncle, "It's better to be a buffalo in your farm because they are well looked after and have a cooler in their room for the summer! They are better protected than us!" Really, I tease him sometimes.'

She waved over to the servants' quarters.

'We have our own washing system for the clothes, our own dhobi, a sweeper, cook, bearer. Still according to those times when the British were here, Uncle is keeping it all up. I don't think anyone else is keeping things in such a way, because they don't think it is necessary. But his tradition is like this.' She broke off. 'You must come inside.'

We took off our shoes as we went into the outer office, where Mr Gopal, the manager, was photocopying papers.

'Half time Uncle stays here, half time in the village,' said Leela, sweeping past him.

Mr Gopal smiled. 'Salaams, sahib, memsahib.'

'Whenever they see you,' Leela explained, 'they have to say "Salaams". And there is another rule. You have to make an appointment to come and see Uncle. No appointment, you have to stay in here and some servant will go and inform him. If he says it is all right, then you can go in. His wife was also very particular with the rules. If it was afternoon time and they were resting, you were not allowed to come in. And suppose she was sitting there, the servants were not supposed to stand in front of her; they had to come and stand to her left. Come…'

We followed her through to the Captain's office, which seemed unnervingly silent without him. After the intense heat outside, it was welcomingly cool. Chuman Lal (to give him his full name), the elderly apparition who had served me tea the previous year, came slowly in, stooping over a tray with glasses of water on it. As before, he was all in white.

'He has been working here so many years, near about fifty years,' said Leela. 'He worked for Uncle's father also, as a kid. Uncle is very particular about his uniform. Even when he is not here, this man, he has to dress like that when serving me at table, otherwise I'll get hell from him!'

The room looked unchanged from before: possibly unchanged, indeed, since the Queen's Coronation.

'This is Uncle's daughter, Penny,' said Leela, pointing to a framed photograph of a young woman in a wheelchair, laughing, with her head lolling on one side. 'She is no more. She was absolutely handicapped. Could not walk, could not talk, her legs they were like this…' She shook her arms floppily. We later learned that Penny had been born with cerebral palsy, dying in 1991, aged thirty-five.

When I'd met the Captain the previous year, he hadn't mentioned that Lillian, his second wife, had died just three years earlier. She'd also been born in India, after her mother, who had married a railway engineer, emigrated from Britain to work as chief medical officer in a jungle area of the state of Orissa (now Odisha). Educated in Calcutta, Lillian had married an army officer and had a son who eventually emigrated to Australia. She married the Captain after both their marriages had broken down.

'His first wife is still alive: she is in England,' said Leela. 'Very brilliant woman she was, though I never met her. She couldn't cope with this Indian climate, Indian servants and all. So they divorced and she went back to England; their son was born there but is now in Australia.'

Leela's house tour was dizzyingly thorough. She swept us into the Captain's bedroom, telling us that all the ornaments were dusted every day. Staff were fined five or ten rupees for not replacing them in exactly the right place or for incorrectly folding his socks and handkerchiefs. Combs and nail files were arranged in drawers, shoes displayed on shelves with almost obsessive precision.

'Everything has to be…' said Leela, pausing momentarily, '…systematic.'

The staff, she continued, started sweeping and dusting before 7am, long before the Captain emerged for breakfast at 9.30. After dinner, they would often still be working at 11pm.

Clare wondered if he dressed for dinner.

'Perfectly!' Leela laughed. 'Dinner time he goes for his bath, spends one hour in the bathroom and when he finishes, he gives call from there. And he comes out perfectly dressed, his hanky and pen in his pocket, his watch, everything. Sometimes I ask: "And after all that, you are just going to watch TV or go to sleep?" When he was at school with his sister, the servants had to go to the school to give them dinner, breakfast or lunch. They served everything, with forks and knives – not like the other people who just took their tiffin and ate it where they were standing. No, they had to sit properly, lay the table in the school!'

The rules continued, thick and fast.

'Chuman Lal has to serve from the left, not in front of us. Every morning I have to check his nails for serving, his gloves, his clothes, his buttons, to make sure everything is clean. He's got a house here and when he retires he will stay here because he has no other place to go. He will get a pension and will be looked after well as long as Uncle is here.' She added that another member of staff had recently died: 'He is no more at the moment.

'In the evenings,' she continued, 'Uncle takes the report books and reads each and every one of them – what happened here, who came, who has gone, who had tea here, whose phone call came – all these things. He will ask you a hundred and ten questions! If someone is sick, "What is wrong with him? What doctor he sees? What medicines he is prescribed? Have you seen the doctor's report? How he came – by walking, by rickshaw, bicycle?" Everything he wants to know. If Uncle is not here, they take the report book to the village. We have a system here. Maybe I distribute something to them – vegetables. They have to say thanks. If they don't, you've got the right to fine them. He's keeping the house in such a way.'

Like a regiment?

'Yes,' she laughed, loudly. 'Like a regiment! In England you don't think of these things because you have no servants, because you have to do everything. But when you have servants, you are paying them, so you want some work from them. Or they are sitting around and gossiping. Servants are necessary evils, Mrs Abbott used to say. One hundred per cent I agree! Without servants you can't do anything.'

An elderly lady in a pale lemon sari sidled into the room.

'This is Lucy, she looked after Penny,' said Leela.

'Good morning,' the old lady smiled sweetly.

Leela explained that Lucy was Chuman Lal's wife and had joined the household in the 1960s, when the Captain's father was still alive. At first she had worked in the gardens but then she became the ayah, or nanny, to ten-year-old Penny and cared for her day and night for twenty-five years until she died. She still slept in 'Penny's Room', as the plaque on the door called it. It was preserved as a sort of shrine – Penny's large white cot still stood in one corner, together with the bed where she slept as she got older.

'We had to pull all the pillows around her – she was very heavy,' said Lucy. 'Very nice girl she was, very sweet, used to laugh all the time – "Hahaha!" – and kiss us. When she died, it was very sad, very sad.' She looked down and twisted the folds of her sari. 'Then her mother died, two years later, because she missed her daughter. She loved her very much, very much, all the time.'

A slight sadness descended. Despite all the people and activity the Captain had in his life, we wondered if he was ever lonely, given that he had no family nearby.

'Yes, he is lonely,' Lucy nodded. 'But we are here with him. Sometimes family comes – you saw their photos, no? Very nice people. And Mr Mehrotra, other friends he has, they come here. We all like to look after him. He is very nice, Captain-Sahib.'

Leela bustled us back to the servants' quarters at the side of the house. She pointed out the area where the dhobi-wallah boiled clothes and linen in a brass cauldron over a charcoal oven. 'Someone has to check that he is boiling properly. And then Uncle takes the clothes and smells them. Sheets, pillowcases, towels, all have to be boiled, washed, rinsed, dried, go for ironing. Then I have to see it is folded properly. If it is not, then I get it!'

I suggested that a man as busy as the Captain might have other things to worry about than how a sheet was folded.

Leela shrugged. Then, out of the blue: 'Have you been to the cemetery?' She meant the European cemetery, across the cantonment. 'You must go!'

Obeying orders, we took an autorickshaw further into the cantonment, a cleaner, greener, far more spacious area than the hectic, noisy streets of the main part of town. We veered off the road on to a scrubby path and bounced up and down to the entrance: a brick-built Victorian gatehouse resembling a miniature Gothic chapel. The gatekeeper's wife and children emerged from their modest home next door and watched as we spluttered to a halt. A dog barked and a small child slapped it away. The chowkidar himself, in shabby trousers and a loose shirt, emerged from the gatehouse, smiled a greeting and hovered in the background for the next hour as we explored the overgrown expanse of graves.

They reflected Jhansi's imperial history at its most tragic. All told, India's eight hundred European (mostly British) cemeteries housed the graves of perhaps a million Britishers. Jhansi's was one of the biggest, covering ten acres, with around four thousand graves dating back to 1840. Parts of it were well maintained, but at the far side the gravestones were swathed in creepers: a sea of gently undulating vegetation. Goats ambled around.

The gravestones, remembering Commissioners of Oaths and Quartermasters and their families, captured the reality of short European lives in a hot Eastern climate. The town's reputation as a 'hardship posting' was reflected by the gravestones of British soldiers who had died of heatstroke, cholera or plague.

Sergeant Major Arthur Horatio Barron of the East Surrey Regiment who died in 1898, aged thirty-three, was typical. 'He tried to do his duty' read his inscription. Ellen Moriarty (died in 1863, aged twenty-seven) shared a grave with her son Thomas ('aged four hours'). A much later memorial to 'Billy Boy', who died in 1946 aged five months, was inscribed 'This little bird so young'. Lieutenant Roger Louis Gerard Wathen of the Royal Norfolk Regiment died aged twenty-five in 1935 'through an accident at polo'.

The occupants of some of the graves could never have anticipated being buried in India. When an Air France plane flying from Calcutta to Jodhpur crashed and burst into flames near Datia, just north of Jhansi, in March 1938, all seven passengers and crew died and were buried here. Another grave was dedicated 'In Everloving Memory of…' There was no name but a wilting garland of marigolds had been left on it.

Cemented to the gatehouse's inner walls were memorials to the sixty-six Jhansi-based British and European victims of the 1857 Mutiny, when Indian troops turned on their rulers. A grey marble slab was carved with a list of them, including:

'Captain Alexander Skene, Mrs Skene & two children.

Mr Robert Andrews, Collector & Magistrate, Mrs Andrews & four children.

Mr DC Wilton, Patrol, Mrs Wilton, one child & two sisters of Mrs Wilton.

Mr DD Blyth, Assistant Revenue Surveyor, Mrs Blyth, her mother & four children…'

Another cobwebbed memorial remembered William Carshore (aged thirty-five), the Collector of Customs, his wife Mary (twenty-eight) and their children Arthur (four), Clara (three), Violet (two) and Herbert (eight months). They were all 'massacred on this spot by the rebels and mutinous native soldiers on the 14th June 1857'. The memorial had been placed there by Mary's 'sorrowing parents'.

Emerald-green parakeets squawked overhead as we wandered among memorials smothered by brambles, the scrubby ground scattered with debris. A blackened angel lurked in a thicket. It was a fascinating blend of death and life.

Down one of the main paths, we met the teenage son of an army colonel. The family driver, he told us, brought him here every evening after school for half an hour to soak himself in the peace and quiet. He said his grandfather remembered 'British days'. 'He used to say: "If you are properly educated an' all, the British are on your side".' He added that his family spoke English to each other at home.

On the far side of the cemetery, the flock of parakeets settled on a tamarind tree.

On the drive back to the Captain's bungalow, we noticed a roadside sign: Shrine of St Jude. As Clare's Catholic mother was a great believer in this patron saint of lost causes, we had to investigate. Down a quiet, semi-rural lane, this unexpectedly mosque-like 1960s building boasted a giant stone lotus-flower sculpture at its entrance. 'Open to Devotees', a sign said. The high-arched interior, echoing with chirping birds, was painted sky blue and apple green, with garlands strung between its pillars and a large mural of a haloed saint bearing the plea 'St Jude pray for us'. An altar dedicated to a garlanded Madonna holding the infant Jesus was framed by red, orange and pink light bulbs, like a theatre dressing-room mirror. Vases of pink paper flowers stood on it, adding to the colour. There was a slight hint of the fairground about it all.

Sister Raphael, a young nun, fetched a key and ushered us into a side room strung with drying vestments. She unlocked a metal cupboard and brought out a cross-shaped brass reliquary with a white linen cover draped over it. At the centre of the cross was a fragment of red cloth, reputedly from the coat of St Jude, a symbol of hope to Catholics in distress. Sister Raphael kissed it.

'Every year, during the annual Feast of St Jude, many thousands come here from all over the world,' she said. 'And every Saturday we have many miracles – cancer people getting healed, sick people getting well and getting jobs and good education. Broken families getting reunited. All the desperate cases, all they come to him. He is a miraculous friend to them.'

The gift shop had an impressive range of St Judeiana on sale: St Jude key rings and tiny statuettes, St Jude calendars and *The Voice of St Jude*, a bimonthly magazine then in its sixtieth year whose Editorial Board included Sister Raphael, Ms Mary Vaz and 'Uncle George'. And there was the name Peggy Cantem again, apparently one of the shrine's leading supporters.

Back at the Captain's bungalow, his driver loaded our luggage into a Sumo four-wheel drive for the five-hour journey south to the farms, 120 miles away. Their six hundred acres of gram, lentils and soya beans were at Behrol, a village near the pleasant little town of Khurai. Behrol appeared on only the most detailed maps, in very small print. While we sat at ease in the rear passenger seats, Mr Gopal and a guard with a loaded rifle squeezed beside the driver, and two other members of staff sat sideways in the back, surrounded by our luggage, a couple of tiffin carriers, a box full of food cooked in Jhansi and brightly coloured blankets.

The landscape became steadily more rural. There were wheat fields and haystacks, hedgerows and country lanes, but with tamarind and guava trees instead of the more familiar (to us) oaks, bullock carts instead of tractors, lolloping buffalo instead of grazing cows, and trim white temples instead of medieval churches. By the roadside, 'cow-dung cakes', used as fuel, were stacked on end, leaning on each other, like hands pressed together in a 'Namaste' salutation. Women, sitting on their haunches, washed clothes at wells. Roadside shrines housed small bronze idols wreathed in glittering cloth and tinsel.

We stopped in the small town of Lalitpur, where brass pots were piled up outside huts and STD telephone shops stood on every corner. In 2001, mobile phones had yet to find their way to village India. When they did, it was as though the whole subcontinent had been waiting impatiently for that moment, as everyone rushed out to buy one. We bought an intricately painted clay water pot from a female trader. She asked for ten rupees. Clare gave her twenty.

'Ten rupees only, madam,' said the woman in a reversal of the keen bargaining we often encountered.

Back on the road, canned music boomed from the cab of a lorry packed with people who, Mr Gopal told us, worked on the Captain's farm. We stopped to pick up an elderly man, a young woman and three children who lived in his village. They scrambled into the back, finding whatever space they could among the luggage and the tiffin carriers.

We bumped and jolted along increasingly rough roads, past a well the Captain had built and past villagers riding ancient bicycles. The driver pointed out a sati site – a large-trunked tree embedded with a rough stone memorial to a woman who had jumped, or been pushed, on to her late husband's funeral pyre. Although the practice had been outlawed during British times, it very occasionally, and controversially, survived in parts of rural India.

Finally, at dusk, minutes before it went suddenly and completely dark, we turned down a rutted dirt track, sending blackbuck leaping high across the fields. Swallows perched on the lone telegraph wire following the line of the road. Just past a mango orchard, we reached a gated compound, which was dominated by a huge banyan tree. The driver pressed hard on the horn: the signal for excited shouting. Children ran towards us, laughing and squabbling, and the chowkidar hurried out of his brick hut to open the wrought-iron gates, which had the letters A and F etched into them: Abbott's Farms. We could just about make out twinkly strings of Christmas lights ahead.

CHAPTER 4

A LIVING GOD AND A DANCING GIRL

We stopped in front of a bungalow with a corrugated-iron roof. A large satellite dish was screwed to the wall, a gold Christmas star was strapped to the chimney and a generator chugged loudly. A group of perhaps twenty villagers, mostly men in dhotis, surged towards us and greeted us with 'Salaams'. Some had walked eight miles across the fields to honour the friends of the 'Captain-Sahib'. They touched our feet and draped garlands of marigolds and rose petals around our necks, almost smothering us with fragrant flowers.

'Welcome, welcome!' boomed a deep bass voice from the bungalow and out strode the Captain. In his thick plaid dressing gown and slippers, his hair now lightly touched with henna, he looked less like a Home Counties golf-club Rotarian than he had the previous year. I handed him the Cracker Barrel and he laughed. 'How nice to see you! You must have thought that journey on the back road was never-ending!'

He took us into the house and Shyam Yadav, his wryly smiling bearer and right-hand man, brought us tea – 'Black tea, separate.' After asking if we wanted sugar - '*Chini?*' – he held out a plate of Good Day biscuits.

The bungalow, built by the Captain's grandfather in 1932, was a more modest affair than the one in Jhansi. It was vaguely hexagonal with a veranda, part of which served as a dining room (the 1960s-style mustard and beige curtains invariably closed), and a high-ceilinged living room, with solid 1940s furniture and

1950s-style décor. 'I suppose this has become "heritage" now,' said the Captain dryly. 'Like me.'

We sat in upright, cane-backed armchairs facing a brass coal scuttle and a television draped in a home-sewn cotton cloth. The walls were hung with watercolours of half-timbered English cottages, pictures of Christ (like illustrations from a children's book) and a black-and-white photograph of the Captain as a young man. Long-dead viceroys, including Lord Wavell, gazed out at us. Plaster ducks flew wonkily across one wall, two of them dive-bombing a bronze plaque of *The Last Supper*. Five silk butterflies fluttered diagonally across another wall, which they shared with a framed copy of Cecil Beaton's portrait of the Queen in her Coronation robes, the colours slightly faded, alongside a vase of equally faded silk flowers.

A cluster of knick-knacks included small plastic figures of a bride and groom, a wooden herd of black elephants and a statuette of an African warrior brandishing a spear. The bookcase was stacked with old paperbacks, *A King's Story* by the Duke of Windsor, *Our Friend the Alsatian* and a book for the conceited called *How to be Even More Successful*. A crackly radio in the background was tuned – badly – to the BBC World Service.

The room was a curious combination of suburban and subcontinental. Its wooden shutters (designed to keep it cool in summer) could make it cold and dim on even the sunniest days, but it became cosy when a fire was crackling in the grate. During rain showers, water dripped rhythmically, like gamelan music, on to the roof from overhanging tree branches.

The Captain's bedroom and bathroom led off one side and, through a chintzily curtained door, a small guest bedroom led off the other. Shyam ushered us inside. There were whitewashed walls, a barred window with wooden shutters, a small dark-wood wardrobe, a chest of drawers, a cane stool and twin beds covered with blankets so thick and heavy that we sometimes lay crushed under the weight. We draped our garlands around a picture of the Sacred Heart, next to a photograph of the Captain as a young soldier and a watercolour of flowers from an English cottage garden. The adjoining bathroom had an ancient claw-foot bath and a stack of neatly arranged cotton towels. Over the toilet was a small plaque with a cartoon of a 'cute' white child urinating, with the caption:

If you sprinkle when you tinkle
Please be sweet and wipe the seat.

Leading off the living room was another veranda, screened from prying eyes outside by latticework and thick curtains. Dominated by a desk piled with files and documents, it acted as the Captain's office. The kitchen and staff quarters were across a narrow yard.

The bungalow, like the one in Jhansi, had such a period atmosphere that you could be fooled into thinking you were still in Britain – albeit the Britain of the 1940s.

'Ha, yes!' said the Captain. 'A lot of people have said that. It's the atmosphere. My sister always used to say: "It's all very well you living out in India, but we're not in India when we come to your house. It's like being back in England – the atmosphere, the way you live." Which I think is very true.'

❖ ❖ ❖ ❖

The Abbott family had once owned a dozen villages; now there were just four – Behrol, Dhariya, Talapar and Khajuria. All told, the Captain oversaw the lives of around three thousand people, including fifty staff and servants. 'I don't know of any other foreigners doing the same thing today,' he said.

Interesting that, despite having been born and brought up in India, he sometimes referred to himself as a 'foreigner'.

'Any problems they have, they come to me and I try to help them as far as possible. Perhaps something to do with a wedding in the family. I arrange it for them, monetarily or with transport. Or a tractor may have broken down, so I send mine to get the fields cultivated or sown. I'm always willing to help as far as I can and they know that, so they don't hesitate to come and ask me.'

And so it proved. Before dinner, there was a constant trickle of villagers and, with the room lights dimming, brightening, and dimming again, the salaams and garlandings continued.

'They're very happy to have you here,' the Captain translated at one point. 'And they hope you will be back here some day. I told them that you make radio programmes and they all know BBC London. You can tell the smallest child – "Memsahib, BBC London!"'

The garlanding BBC enthusiasts were followed by villagers wanting to share their problems with the Captain, to thank him for gifts given and to express hopes of further gifts to come. Sitting in his office, on his grand swivel chair, he barked at them in the local dialect – genial, joshing, but firm – and signed chits, authorising payments for the most needy. They had a range of names for him: Rajah Sahib, Roy Rajah, Uncle Abbott, King Uncle. When the Captain – the last court of appeal in village disputes – went to fetch a ledger from his office, one villager declared: 'He is a living god!'

Back with his ledger, the living god continued to hold court. An asthmatic farmworker edged on to the veranda and pulled up his thin cotton shirt to show us many white scars. A 'holy man' had applied a red-hot iron seventy-five times to his chest, to try to cure him of asthma. It hadn't worked and the farmworker now needed money to pay for further treatment. He was pinning his hopes on the Captain.

'Many of these people suffer from asthma, but they don't want injections,' said the Captain. 'Instead they consult a holy man. They believe in it totally. That's why I give my staff regular check-ups, regular tablets for things like malaria.' It also improved efficiency, he said, and cut out one potential excuse for not working.

Queuing behind the farmworker were half a dozen other villagers with money, health and family problems. One by one they stepped forward and a sad litany of stories of poverty and hardship unfolded.

A distraught man wearing a dirt-stained dhoti and a headscarf wrapped turban-style around his head wept as he talked about his daughter who had killed herself two months earlier by jumping down the village well. She had been married for five years, had no children, and her husband and in-laws were constantly harassing her for her dowry. Such dowry deaths were 'a social evil', said the Captain. 'And what will happen now? The boy will probably find another wife.' He shrugged his disapproval.

A motorbike spluttered to a halt outside and a very old man, wearing only a dhoti and shawl, eased himself off the pillion. His grandson, a teacher, had driven him from his home six miles away.

'He's not been well,' said the Captain. 'He used to work for me but now he's retired and lives with his wife in a house he's built, with its own temple attached.'

The Captain had already bought him a walking frame, but now he needed medicine and could not afford the 250-rupee cost of a doctor's visit (around £2.50). Unfortunately, one of the motorbike's tyres had developed a puncture and they were hoping the Captain could help. After what seemed like hours of discussion, a deal was sealed and the old man was driven back home in the Sumo. The grandson, however, asked to be taken to another village to buy a new inner tube. After more discussion, he got his way. Everything here clearly involved much discussion.

Next, a woman whose hand had been mangled in a threshing machine begged for money. Then a man whose wife had burnt herself to death because he had been having an affair with another woman. He had tried to save her, failed, and set fire to himself, running screaming through the village; he was in hospital for two months.

Another man was lurking outside, speaking rapidly through the lattice screen, as though at a confessional, talking to the priest. He had sold two of his four acres of land to a moneylender for 100,000 rupees and remortgaged the rest to pay for his two daughters' weddings. Now he had injured his hand – it was heavily wrapped in bandages – and needed a job.

The Captain showed his exasperation. 'They often do this,' he sighed. 'They were given land by the government under their redistribution policy – the Land Ceiling Act of 1976 – but then they sell it and become landless again, having been landless to start with…'

The Land Ceiling Act, we were to discover over the next fifteen years, was a constant feature of the Captain's life, with court cases disputing his ownership of the villages dragging on and on like *Bleak House*'s Jarndyce vs Jarndyce.

It was 9.30pm and we were wondering if we'd ever be having dinner but thought it impolite to ask. Eventually, the Captain retreated to his bedroom to have his evening whisky and soda and his bath, its hot water brought from the kitchen by Lachoo Patel, his finely moustachioed deputy bearer. As we sat waiting, huddled in shawls, the World Service news crackled loudly from the bedroom ('Newcastle United offside'). The cultured BBC voices occasionally veered off into another channel screeching with Bollywood film music. Then Dolly Parton's 'Jolene' rang out followed by Jim Reeves's 'Green, Green Grass of Home'. The Captain, it turned out, was an unlikely country and western fan. 'I don't like this modern music,' he told us. 'Jazz an' all. Don't like it.'

Finally, at around 10.30pm, just as we were ready to crawl into bed, he emerged wearing a cravat and blazer, exactly as I had photographed him the previous year on his Jhansi veranda. Time for dinner, he said, and took us into the freezing dining area. It transpired that the meal was generally served at 10.15pm at the earliest – a range of light curries (aloo gobi, dahl, paneer) with rice and puris, followed by creme caramel, fruit salad and syrupy gulab jamun dumplings. Sometimes the Captain did not appear for dinner until midnight. After a few subsequent visits, Clare persuaded him to bring the meal forward to the ridiculously early hour of 9pm.

He told us he always changed for dinner, even if he was dining alone. 'I think it's just force of habit. I did it when my wife was alive… I'm just keeping up standards. New shirt, maybe new trousers, even if I'm on my own. My wife dressed up too and I've kept it up since. I'm a traditionalist and an incurable romantic. I love all the old things. I hate change of any kind because I think that old way of life was a lot better than it is today. It's much too casual today, the way people go round. I've seen people in their own homes, sitting at the dining table with their vest on. I just couldn't do that sort of thing.

'The traditions here are all handed down, I should say, from my grandfather's days. My mother and father also lived in this way, maintained all these standards. People are quite shocked to see the way I live. They feel it's not necessary any more, but I'm not prepared to give up. We've never lived in the Indian way at all.

'Having said that, I think I'm probably more Indian now than British. If anyone asks me "When are you going back to England?" or says "You're very British," I always say: "No, I'm not, I'm as much of an Indian as you are." And if the fellow is younger than me, I say: "I'm definitely more Indian than you are because I've lived here longer!" I've not adopted many Indian habits, though, except I do eat the betel nut. I love a paan after dinner,' he added, referring to the hugely popular Indian mouth freshener.

A smiling, comfortably built woman in a sari was hovering in the doorway.

'Ah! Lakshmi-Bai, my cook! Named after the warrior queen!' cried the Captain. She stepped back and Shyam stepped in, dressed, like Chuman in Jhansi, in white uniform, white gloves and Nehru cap. On the chilliest evenings, though, he would wear two or three pullovers, the Captain would put on his dressing gown and a scarf, and we would shiver under shawls.

The plates and cutlery were laid out on the table with geometrical precision, the knives sharpened so regularly over the decades that they were ground back to half their original width. In the centre of the table, a plastic condiments tray included a small jar of Colman's mustard, a large one of achaar (pickles) and pieces of jaggery (cane sugar).

Over dinner the Captain told us that during harvest or sowing time, when he could be here for up to two months, he might not speak a single word of English. Sometimes, he said, he found it difficult to remember the right English word or sentence construction.

'The standard of English here is rather poor. There are people who want to talk to you in English, maybe to brush up their own English, but I break into Hindi straight away because I don't quite know what they're trying to say. So I say: "Let's talk in Hindi and we'll understand each other better." Then I find it hard going back and speaking English again. You slip up on a few words here and there, maybe your grammar isn't so good.'

The farms, he said, represented 'real' India, very different from booming metropolitan India. Two-thirds of the nation's population, after all, lived in 700,000 villages, working on the land, and old attitudes lingered.

'The British were revenue collectors for the government, so we were virtually little kings or rajahs. I'm still known as Rajah Sahib. I say: "No, no, that's all finished." They say: "No, sahib, that will never be finished as far as we're concerned, because you were our owner, and you will always stay that way."

'I have a system here where everyone has to report to me. Every evening, they give me a report of all the work that's happened during the day. That can sometimes get a bit late if someone doesn't turn up on time – then dinner can be delayed. I try to stick to a time but it's not easy. Because here there's no such thing as someone asking for an interview in advance. They just turn up – as you've seen – and I don't like turning them away. They may have an important problem to discuss with me, if someone is very sick, so I just have a chat no matter what time it is. They come here maybe very late at night. I like to be available to them.'

The lights flickered from time to time as he elaborated on the family history he had sketched out the previous year. His great-grandfather, William Lumsden Abbott, whose portrait we had seen in Jhansi, had fought in the first Anglo-Afghan War and survived the Mutiny after being shot and injured by his own troops. His great-grandmother, aged just seventeen, survived the siege of Lucknow by hiding in an open grave with her small child. Reunited, the couple had subsequently sailed back to Scotland, before returning to India where, in 1880, William died of cholera at Morar near Gwalior.

That same year, the viceroy ordered the Maharajah of Gwalior to evacuate all the Europeans out of Morar and close down the cantonment. 'So they all had to move out. I suppose it was Hobson's choice to go north or go south and my grandfather, John Harold, opted for Jhansi. The whole family got in a bullock cart with their few belongings, penniless. John Harold, who was only eighteen at the time, was a pauper with no shoes on his feet.

'People thought every European would be a millionaire but there were lots of poor ones and he was one of them. They lived in a tin shed when they first arrived; it must have been dreadful in the summer, burning hot. One day he was sitting outside it and saw a whole lot of army mules and horses going down the road. And he thought: "I wonder what those animals live on; they must eat grass." So he went to see the brigadier to see if he could supply him with hay and got a contract and never looked back. From very small beginnings, he built himself up, became a very wealthy man and was known as the Hay King of Jhansi.'

As a leading figure in the Anglo-Indian community, John Harold also, we later learned, gathered together a force of six thousand Anglo-Indians to fight for Britain during World War I. One of the recruits was his son, the Captain's father.

There was a pause as Shyam cleared away the plates. 'He bought fifteen houses in the cantonment,' the Captain continued. 'And in 1932, he bought fifty villages. You took everything over, whatever was there. It was the old tenancy thing, you know. The government appointed you to look after the village and collect rent, on which it paid you a commission.'

Recapping on his early army life, he recalled Independence Day 1947, when he was doing security work near the town of Bareilly.

'It was very strange. The Hindus and Muslims were going after each other's throats, but you could walk straight through them as a Britisher. They weren't bothered about you. They were sorting out their own problems – as they're doing to this day.'

The Captain left the army four years later and took over the family farms when his father left India to run a small wheat farm in Saxmundham in Suffolk.

'It was windy, Suffolk. My goodness it was windy! And it was too cold. I visited but said: "I don't think I'll be coming back here again."'

In fact, as he had told me the previous year, he, Lillian and Penny did spend two years living in England in the late 1970s but they didn't stay.

'We were thinking that we might eventually be able to put Penny in a home there, but we decided that wouldn't be very suitable for her. We couldn't bear the thought of leaving her in England and us living out here. So we decided it would be better to have her out in India with us, where we could still get servants to look after her. Other than that, I've paid short visits to England, two to three months at a time, more on holiday than anything else. But I couldn't settle over there.'

He'd said the same thing the first time I'd met him. So – why couldn't he?

'It was the climate mainly. I found it too wet and too cold after getting used to the climate out here. And it was a totally different way of life to what I'd been used to out here. It would have meant changing my lifestyle completely and by that time I was too old to consider doing that. I wouldn't have been as independent as I've been out here, where I've been able to do a lot of things the way I've wanted to. If I'd gone to England, it would have meant getting a job, working somewhere to fixed timings, the old nine-to-five business, which wouldn't have suited me at all.

'Over here I can do things the way I want them to be done and I'll probably be here for the rest of my days. I'm sure I won't be short of company or of people looking after me. It's an open-air life, not sitting behind an office desk all day long. Even if I'm left with just a little plot of land, I love it here, so I'd probably stay in the village, cultivate my plot and be quite happy doing it.

'We've built schools here, at my cost – not only in this village but in Dhariya as well – wells, roads, bus shelters, an eye clinic. It's given me a great deal of satisfaction which I couldn't possibly have got in England. You know, I've more or less integrated with the villagers completely.'

So if his grandfather had been known as the Hay King of Jhansi, what was he known as?

He laughed loudly. 'I'm the Chota Rajah, the Little King, of this village! Though they may call me other things behind my back.

'I still try to impose a little army discipline among the workers here. I have a bell rung at all times of day. The first one rings at 5am – reveille. I have to be up early myself, at 6, to show the sahib's awake.'

At the end of the meal Shyam, shivering with cold, placed a large bedroom clock on the table in front of the Captain so he could check that the chowkidar was ringing the hourly bell on time. It seemed the bell had not been rung at 3am the previous night, which had led to a severe reprimand.

The Captain went back into his office to go through the day's accounts and report books. A group of admin staff were there, patiently waiting. As we went to bed, at midnight, teeth chattering, the petitioners were still turning up to consult this one-man welfare state. The beds were so cold during the night – despite hot-water bottles, swaddled in soft cotton covers – that we ended up sleeping in the same single bed, fully clothed, for warmth.

❖ ❖ ❖ ❖

The next morning, the village temple drums started at 5am, heralding predawn processions around the narrow alleys between the houses. We slept on as best as we could until Shyam brought us a tray of 'bed tea'. The sun was rising orange over the fields and the Captain was already in his office, booming orders. In the background, the crisp, quiet voices of the BBC World Service couldn't possibly compete.

'Did you hear the Indian great horned owl last night?' he asked as we went through for breakfast. '*Bubo* – that's its ornithological name, after its call. The villagers are very superstitious that it might be an ill omen, so I got the chowkidar to chase it away.'

The table was set as it had been every morning for decades – with turquoise place mats, crocheted food covers and water glasses protected from falling ants by plastic covers. We were served a half-grapefruit, porridge and poached eggs on toast – the Captain preferred 'rumble tumble' eggs (scrambled and spiced with tomato, onion and chillies). Then more toast, with marmalade, and chai. He was already well into his day, following the timetable of old British India: up at 5am in summer, 6am in winter.

'After I get up, I go and check on whether all the rest of the staff are out – what duties they've been allotted, have they started working yet? Then I come back here, have a wash, do my yoga, have my breakfast, then I get down to my books. I check up on what's going on outside, everything that goes on – the farm work, the machinery – make sure it's all kept in proper condition. There's work going on all the time, in the fields.' It was clearly a regime of near-military micromanagement.

He would have a late lunch, followed usually by an afternoon nap ('No more than half an hour – very refreshing, then I'm ready for the rest of the day'), more reports ('How much of the field was cut today?') and talk, seemingly endlessly, to staff, servants and villagers.

'If there's not much on, I'll be done by 6 or 7 and I can sit back here and catch up with a bit of reading, if there's nobody wanting to see me about some personal problem.'

And then the routine of bath, World Service, 'Jolene' and very late dinner that we had witnessed the night before. After dinner, he would read newspapers or magazines.

'You have to keep in touch with everything out here – keep in touch with what's going on in the world – or you can be quite cut off. I'm never in bed before midnight. Then up by 6am again.'

Routine and discipline were important to him in a way that sometimes bordered on the obsessive. 'I don't think anyone else would be as particular about these things as I am. Like the fellow serving at the table wearing gloves, Shyam. When my stepson was out here from Australia last year, I had to go to Jhansi for a few days and when I came back, the chap wasn't wearing his gloves. So I pulled him up straight away. "What's this?" "Well, sahib, the *baba*" – my stepson – "didn't insist on it." So I said: "Well, *you* should have insisted. Go off and put your gloves on. Now that I'm here, you will wear them."

'I'm a little more particular about these things than my father was. I feel it's good as it keeps them on their toes, instils a sense of discipline in them. I've had occasions here where I've found the fellow wearing dirty clothes or he hasn't had a shave, and I've sent him off: "Go off and I'll wait. I don't mind waiting, but I'm not prepared to have you serving me with my food when you're in that condition." If they're really naughty, or they do something they're not supposed to do, then they get fined. Not very much – ten rupees perhaps – depending on the crime. I say: "Now you will remember you were fined, so you won't do it again."

'And I won't have anyone walking through this place when I'm not here. I don't care who it is. This is my private residence and I want to keep it as such. Some of the government officials say to the staff, "May I see inside the house, how the sahib lives?" They're not allowed. Once Lakshmi-Bai and Lachoo did allow some people to snoop in here and go through the rooms. I heard about it and I fined them. Quite a heavy fine, about fifty rupees each.'

How much did the staff earn?

'It's not so much the earnings as the facilities,' he said, neatly sidestepping specifics. 'I give them lots of facilities. They may get sick, so I pay all the medical bills. I give them clothes, distribute the vegetables growing in the garden to them. If someone's getting married, I pay the wedding expenses, so it all mounts up to quite a bit. And they know this, they know where they're well off, where their bread is buttered.

'People often ask: "What do you do out there? I suppose you just sit back." They're very mistaken. There's plenty to do here! As you've seen yourselves, there's never a dull moment.'

After breakfast Clare and I sat in the garden to make the most of the warm sunshine. At the far end of the lawn was a small Hindu shrine, reputedly haunted. Beyond that, an idyllic view over wheat fields dotted with giant ferns, and tamarind and banana trees. As the Captain had promised the previous year, it was calm, quiet, peaceful – and clean. Meanwhile, he sat in his office telling the staff his plans for the day.

When he emerged, he took us on a tour of the village. It was a sort of royal progress, past a fenced-off area where a chital deer and a nilgai antelope were grazing: injured rescue animals that might otherwise be killed and eaten. He handed them something to eat. 'They love these little sugar tablets.'

He led us along narrow alleys clustered with whitewashed mud-walled houses and pointed out a small temple to Hanuman, the monkey god, which he had had built twenty-five years before.

'Do you see the screen over there? That's to prevent Hanuman-ji from looking on any female. He's very anti-female, that god. I don't go in, because you have to take your shoes off.'

He showed us a garage, where garlanded photographs of Lillian were displayed, and pointed out roads he had built, wells he had sunk, clinics he had funded. And he told us about the mass weddings he organised to save the villagers' money.

Goats bleated, tethered buffalo chewed the cud, children shouted 'Salaams, sahib!' then laughed and ran away. Women briskly tossed cowpats in their hands like pancakes before laying them out in the sun to dry. One woman, carrying a basket of these 'cow-dung cakes', hid her face from us with the loose end of her sari. The villagers could not afford gas stoves, said the Captain, and could not always find enough firewood, so they used the dung to cook food on. As we walked, he explained the different castes to which the village people belonged – the cattle-drover caste, the shoemaker caste, the basket weavers, the jewellers.

We stayed longest at the brick-built school, which had around a hundred pupils, aged six to eleven. Children sat in the yard, cross-legged in the sunshine on hessian sacking, small chalk slates on their laps, satchels, picture books and basic Hindi primers beside them. Some of the girls were wearing dresses they had outgrown, so the backs gaped open. They were chattering like the parakeets flying overhead but, as we approached, we were greeted with a chorus of 'Salaams, Uncle-ji! Salaams, sahib! Salaams, memsahib!' Some ran forward to touch his feet as a mark of respect.

A plaque read:

The school was constructed by Capt. N.R. Abbott for the children of Behrol and neighbouring villages. He thanks all the villagers who helped in the construction. Completed June 1964.

'I didn't realise it was that long ago,' he said with a laugh. 'They didn't have a school before that, so I decided one was badly needed. I still look after all the maintenance – all the whitewashing and all the repairs.'

The husband of the head teacher came out and spoke rapidly in Hindi.

'We had a little garden built in here to make it look a bit respectable,' the Captain said. 'But he is saying that goats came in and ate all the seedlings we had put down.' A cow ambled into the yard. 'We have a pound where you can take all these stray cattle – and then the owners have to pay to get them out again. That was started by the British, the impounding. It's one way of deterring them from letting their cattle loose.'

A plump woman carrying a toddler approached us, wiping her hands.

'This is the madam, the headmistress,' said the Captain. 'Happy New Year!'

She replied in Hindi and the Captain laughed.

'She says it will be a happy New Year when the new school is open.'

There had been plans to extend the school to create classes for older pupils but government officials had said that no land was allotted for the project, so the Captain would have to build on his own land.

The school consisted of just two large rooms with a bench for the teacher and two blackboards. The Hindi alphabet was painted along the walls and the children, sitting on the floor, had to repeat it sing-song, together with numbers up to ten. They learned basic English by rote (the headmistress didn't speak it fluently), geography, history and science.

'Happy, happy children we, for we know our ABC,' they sang. We applauded and the teacher smiled proudly. Then, in unison, they chanted, 'Butterfly, butterfly, where are you going? Into the garden, dancing, dancing!'

Rural parents were not always interested in their children's education, said the Captain. 'They're not always educated themselves. Some can probably just write their names. That's why there are only sixty-one children here today. When there's work on in the village, there's nobody here. They're all helping out with the harvest in the fields.' He pointed to an eager-looking child. 'See, this girl studies well and has an active mind but what's her future? She'll be here up to the fifth grade, then she'll be married off to somebody.'

Since the school had been built, he said, only four pupils had landed 'useful employment' as teachers or government employees.

At some village schools, he added, children sometimes had to wait until midday for the teachers to arrive. Those same teachers might then offer private tuition, which the parents had to pay for.

He pointed out a small brick building to the side of the school: a toilet he had built. 'But they made such a mess of it! They would use it, but nobody would clean it.'

The head teacher's husband appeared, to report a problem with the drains.

'Problem!' snorted the Captain. 'The most famous word in India. Always remember in India, when all is said and done, more will be said than done.'

As we walked through an orchard, he noticed straggling twigs that needed trimming. One of the gardeners brought his secateurs and pointed out that they were too blunt to cut the twigs. No-one had thought to get them sharpened. We turned round as dozens of boys ran out of the school gates and over to a clump of bushes, where they urinated in unison.

'Look where they're going,' the Captain shouted. 'They're having a wee out there, and yet, if only someone would clean it, here's a urinal!'

The gardener spoke in Hindi again and the Captain barked a reply.

'He says the urinal is just for girls – what nonsense! There's one area for the boys, one for the girls. This should be part of their education – knowing where to wee!' He shook his head in exasperation. 'These sorts of things – nobody bothers about at all. It's an uphill struggle to get anything done. All this could be one big jungle as far as they're concerned. But while I'm around, I'll see that things are done properly.'

It was all, as he would often say, a question of keeping up standards. So was it true to say he was 'master of all he surveyed'?

He laughed, good humour restored. 'Yes, literally! They think there's nobody on earth like me. I am everything to them. I am their father and their mother. That's what they say to my face. But, as I said before, behind my back they may call me other things. They're probably saying, "The sooner you go, the sooner we get your property, your land!"'

After lunch – the staple dahl and rice – we drove out on a bumpy road to the nearby village of Talapar. As we arrived, a woman in a bright floral sari came to greet us and present us with fruit. '*Salaaaaaams!*' boomed the Captain, drawing out the second syllable to several seconds. 'Those are guavas for you – *bihi*. They're ready to eat, actually – you can tell by the nice smell.'

More people emerged from their houses to present the regulation garlands.

'A fellow came here to tell them we'd be here today, so everyone's come to see you. You won't even be visible now; you'll have garlands up to your eyes!'

It was an unfolding education about Indian village life, Abbott-style.

'This man is the chowkidar. He looks after the safety of the village, reports any problems that arise to the police, every Monday. Anyone who's visited the village or has spent the night here – he takes down their name, because they may be running away from the law. And births and deaths – he also keeps that record.'

The Captain himself had a small house and office in the village.

'I stay here in the monsoons, if the road to Behrol is closed. It doesn't happen very often now, but in the old days, before they made the road, the only way to get back to Behrol was to walk. When we first came here there were only horses. We'd take off on white horses, Lillian and I. She was a wonderful rider, very fast. I couldn't keep up with her. We used to race each other but she always managed to get ahead.'

The chowkidar unlocked the padlock on the house door. Inside it was pretty dilapidated.

'The original idea was to build a temple here. The god would have gone in there.' He pointed to a cubbyhole in the wall. 'Then the person who was building it died and no-one continued it. So now the god is downstairs and I'm upstairs. I don't think he likes that much, actually.' And he roared with laughter.

He went over to a group of villagers and the village schoolmaster, an elderly grey-bearded man wearing a Nehru jacket, joined us. Unlike the headmistress in Behrol, he spoke very good English and told the same story as everyone else we'd met since we arrived.

'People are very grateful to Mr Abbott, because he helps them, he does very good social work, he erects this temple, the school building. Many people, they get daily wages. When there are necessities, they come for farm work and get remuneration for it. They call him Rajah. He is a great man.'

The 'Rajah' rejoined us. 'We'll bring someone over to Behrol tonight to dance – a dancing girl, a nautch, from the village across the river. Would you like to have her over for a village concert?

They'd put one on especially for you. It will take about an hour to bring her there, and she'll keep them amused for an hour or so, then we can leave and they'll carry on.'

We imagined the concert would start around 8pm, but it had to wait until after the ritual of the evening bath and changing. Then dinner, with Lakshmi-Bai emerging from the kitchen towards the end of the meal to smile benignly at us. The Captain treated her youngest daughter, Kirti, indulgently, almost like his own granddaughter.

It was getting on for 11pm when we finally left the bungalow swathed in shawls and scarves. A full moon shone down on two dozen villagers – all men – waiting in the square. Eye-stinging smoke from a bonfire was billowing past three red plastic garden chairs placed like small utilitarian thrones for us. The villagers sat on the ground as the musicians gradually emerged from their houses with drums and cymbals.

They were joined by the nautch girl – in her mid-twenties, wearing an ankle-length skirt, or lehenga, and a bright choli (bodice). She had a glittery gold shawl round her shoulders, silver bangles on her arms and, on her bare feet, heavy silver anklets.

'Does the smoke bother you?' asked the Captain. 'Let's move away.' At a word from him, men ran to move our chairs back to a safe distance. The village women stood in their house doorways and watched from a distance, the pallus, or loose ends, of their saris draped across their faces.

The musicians launched the concert with traditional harvest songs sung in the fields – plaintive choruses that erupted into heavy drum rhythms with tinkling finger cymbals. Suddenly, the music started accelerating to a reckless speed as a small man frenetically shook a *khanjari*, or tambourine. The singing abruptly stopped but the percussion carried on, jangling and banging, a flute weaving filigree patterns of melody over it, until it stopped again and another plaintive chorus rose quietly.

The dancer, all expressive fingers and eyes, twirled into a dervish-like frenzy, whirling around the edge of the square, bracelets and anklets jingling. Soon a male villager joined her and a musician with a drum-like tambour strung around his neck broke free from the group and bounded around the square. It was the cue for a third man riding a wooden hobby horse to skip along, rather mincingly. Another walked on his hands. A fifth spun a brass bowl on the tip of his index finger.

In between dances, the nautch girl disappeared into the shadows with one or other of the male villagers. At one point, she approached us for money, pulling at our shawls, and a comic pair of men pranced around us with upturned umbrellas to catch thrown coins. The singing and dancing could carry on until dawn, said the Captain. But, with an early train to catch the following morning at Bina, the nearest mainline station, fifty-odd miles away, we left just after midnight. As we walked back to the bungalow, under a copper-coloured moon, the Captain said he was delighted with the Cracker Barrel.

CHAPTER 5

A CRICKET MATCH AND A DEAD COW

We were back in Bina station a year later after four days in the Hindu holy city of Varanasi. We'd stayed at the Hotel Ganges View, where a form left in the bedroom urged 'Please keep an account of your phone calls and consumations'. Beyond the hotel terrace, the Ganges stretched out into a bluey-grey morning haze. Pilgrims were bathing in the sacred waters, and the smoke from cremation pyres drifted past the loincloth-clad holy men who haunted the city. Human ashes were being emptied into the river, bells rung and prayers chanted. Hippies, time-warped since perhaps 1972, had carefully cultivated a dreadlocks-and-dishevelment style. As we had seen during our travels around India's other sacred sites, they sometimes looked miserable and rarely returned smiles. But then, they had travelled here for enlightenment, not to meet other, older Westerners. This Varanasi was the mystical India of a million backpackers' dreams.

Before India's global economic and technological boom of the 1990s, many people's image of the nation was at least half a century out of date. We'd once shared a train compartment with a young Indian couple who had settled in Chicago five years earlier. The husband, an executive in the oil industry, said he was resigned to spending the rest of his life answering the same three American questions about India. First: does the caste system still exist? (Yes, he said, thriving.) Second: do Indians still ride elephants? (Yes, but not as much as tourists do.) Third: are there many snake charmers? (Only when there's a whiff of tourist.)

Didn't he find some parts of urban India dirty, I asked, when he came back to visit relatives? He looked astonished. No, he said, as the train stuttered past a shanty town built on a rubbish tip where wild pigs snuffled through acres of discarded plastic bags. We passed crumbling buildings, blocks of jerry-built shops and houses half demolished, their façades sliced off, to make way for new flyovers. The 'sleeping dead' lived under them – often villagers who had come to the big cities looking for work and couldn't find even a slum to live in.

'India is getting richer by the day,' the young oil executive insisted.

On the overnight train to Bina, the Varanasi-Lokmanya-Tilak Kamayani Express, fifty or so people surged alarmingly into our four-berth carriage at Allahabad. They were seeing off a family member travelling to Mumbai for treatment for liver disease. Women gathered on the platform and wept through the open window.

On-board dinner was, for once, not lukewarm slop; it was stone-cold slop. We were tempted to open one of the packs of Cracker Barrel we had once again brought for the Captain. Before making up our beds, I asked the carriage attendant to wake us at 5am (we were due to arrive at 5.35). I awoke suddenly at 5.15am and went to find him. He was sleeping soundly.

'Wake up!' I said. 'You were supposed to be waking us up!'

'But sir,' he said, still half asleep. 'You are already awake.'

As we pulled into Bina, we peered through the morning fog and could just about make out half a dozen men on the far platform, slapping themselves to keep warm. With scarves wound round their heads – and one with a rifle slung over his shoulder – they could have been brigands. The smallest of the men ran over. 'For Captain-

Sahib?' he asked. It was, perhaps, an unnecessary question. We were the only Westerners getting off. We drove to the bungalow through a gentle landscape wreathed in smoke from village fires.

Even before the Captain came out to greet us (preceded by his bellowing 'Helloooo!') we were once again engulfed by a stream of garlanders. After breakfast, the petitioners started arriving. They included a man with green eczema and fungal mould on his leg, with flies buzzing around it. He looked seventy but was in fact fifty. A woman described her daughter-in-law's derangement, assaulting people at random; a court case was underway to settle who would take responsibility for her. It would be costly, the woman cried.

A man who had once worked as a gardener here had been sacked because he drank heavily, but the Captain had still paid for his sixteen-year-old son to have an operation for a brain tumour. The boy had been taken out of school three years earlier and now spent every day doing nothing at home. The gardener's wife pulled her sari pallu over her head and wept. Three teachers had not been paid for five months. Would the Captain bail them out? After exhaustive discussion, chits were signed and handed over.

We spent much of the day walking around the farm's orchards and vegetable gardens. The Captain, who was recovering from an attack of malaria, suggested we should start calling him Roy. He told us more about his twenty-five-year-long dispute over land rights but, halfway through a sentence, broke off to tell Shyam to do up the top button of his white jacket. Another servant hurried through the dining room with hot-water bottles for our beds. They were so full, they looked like fat footballs. Monkeys clattered over the roof, and a sweeper crossed the room, pulling in his shoulders as though to make himself invisible.

Roy surprised us by saying that, since we had last seen him, he had revisited England. 'One thing that struck me was that there were very few old run-down cars which, twenty years before that, there had been – what they used to call bangers. And going to London I was quite shocked by the graffiti all over the place, using those aerosol cans.' He had been equally surprised to see a homeless man lying on the pavement near Trafalgar Square.

'But the traffic was very organised, wherever you went, and there wasn't a great deal of waiting in the post offices or the banks. People were always there to attend to you.' He was predictably impressed by British efficiency: 'Seeing all the organisation, where here everything is so disorganised. But the cost of living – *much* more expensive than India. I very much regretted going into Marks and Spencer to buy something and then finding the same thing here, same quality, but much cheaper.'

Was there anything he came across in England that he could not get in India?

'I'm very fond of cheese, a good mild cheese like this...' He pointed to the iconic Cracker Barrel. 'I do miss not being able to get that here, but that's because I live in a small place like Jhansi. In Delhi, there's probably everything you want.'

During his last British visit, when he had stayed with a cousin in East Sussex, he had thought about buying another house there, 'but I was horrified at the price of properties. I wanted to buy one, rent it out, come back here and go back every year after the summer harvest. I'd like to get away for the hot months, or the monsoons, like I did last year. I spent most of August and September there. It's a very nice place to visit, if you have good weather. But you can have very wet summers over there, can't you?'

Surely he would miss his staff and being waited on hand and foot?

'Yes, if I happened to be on my own. But I had some very nice people looking after all my needs, so I didn't miss the servants. Leela was with me, looking after my requirements, washing my clothes and so on.'

'You're spoilt!' laughed Clare.

He nodded. 'Very spoilt! You have people running after you, doing everything for you – even if you're getting a glass of water, you have someone running in: "Sir, why don't you let me do that for you?"'

After dinner, under a sky packed with stars, we joined around 150 villagers in the square to watch a touring theatre group perform part of the *Ramlila*, a dramatisation of the *Ramayana*, the sacred Hindu epic. The square was brightly lit by strings of light bulbs and a bonfire that provided a little warmth on a chilly night.

The two-dozen-strong troupe, which had been touring villages and festivals for twenty-five years, was here for a fortnight. They performed every night from 7pm to midnight, strutting across a specially erected stage with its own proscenium arch and a backcloth painted with homely-looking lions. Over on the right, the musicians played harmonium, *dholak*, *manjeera* and *khanjari* (drums, hand cymbals and tambourines). It would take twenty-two days to perform the whole cycle – something between mystery plays, music hall, soap opera and animated cartoon strips. Moments of high emotion spurred the musicians to manic drumming and stratospheric riffs on the harmonium. The manic quality may have owed something to the dope that some of them were smoking.

Roy, Clare and I sat in splendour on plastic chairs; the rest of the 150-strong audience, shawls pulled tight around them, sat or squatted on scraps of sacking, children at the front. The 'gods', glittering with tinsel and gold, sat impassively on a bench at the back of the stage or circled round a suspended microphone, bellowing their dialogue. The children were particularly taken with Hanuman, the monkey god, whose great curling tail arched up behind him, nicely tasselled.

The show featured slapstick, energetic fights and wrestling matches, the 'competitors' prowling round each other with camply simulated menace. Broad comic cameos included a character wearing a baseball cap staggering drunkenly around. It was like an Indian version of a Christmas pantomime.

Quite a few of the villagers owned televisions, so they were used to more sophisticated entertainment, but that didn't seem to dilute their enjoyment, even during some unintentionally funny moments. The devilish look of a 'frightening' spirit with a red skull mask, for instance, was marginally undermined by the thick, grey, buttoned-up cardigan he wore over his black robes.

The audience shouted wildly as a man dressed as a dancing girl whirled around them. An actor with a huge grey beard splayed out like a bib shouted a commentary, which a teacher sitting next to us kindly translated: 'Ram is ordered to go to the forest area for fourteen years…This is going to show the kidnapping of Sita by

Ravana.' The ten-headed Ravana wore a five-foot-wide cardboard headdress with cut-out painted faces radiating from his own.

Towards the end of the show, the audience made offerings – always adding an extra rupee for good luck (21 rupees, 51, 101) – though some paid the performers with potatoes, peas and cauliflowers. We left before midnight, but the racket continued, with blood-curdling shrieks and loudspeaker-boosted roars echoing across the village. From time to time it was mercifully halted by a power cut.

The night was so cold that we slept under three thick blankets and heavy eiderdowns, with scarves and shawls wrapped round our heads. If we ever stayed again, we decided, we would bring thermals.

Early the following morning, I wrote up a week's notes in the garden, a dustier, far less formal affair than the one in Jhansi with clusters of plant pots and luxuriant bougainvillea. I sat at a small table and, despite the bright sunshine, wore a pullover, jacket, scarf and thick shawl as well as a slightly incongruous straw panama hat. Clare came out on to the veranda.

'The ladies from the fruit gardens have come bearing garlands,' she announced.

We duly presented ourselves to be smothered in marigolds.

After breakfast, Roy took us to a cricket tournament he was officially opening at Khimlasa, a small town near Khurai. Throughout the drive, he kept stopping the car to talk to people, mainly about farming. One man told him that his fields had become infested with aphids. Another complained about a two-dozen-strong herd of blackbuck high-jumping hedges and springing across the fields, damaging crops. Roy told a young man that his yellowing wheat field needed watering and then glanced over the hedges. 'In another fifteen days, the mangoes will come into flower.'

As we reached the main road, we passed a cow lying by the roadside, clearly dying. Roy said his instinct was to shoot it to put it out of its misery.

'But if I do, there'll be protests, because it's such a sacred animal.' Another young man showed him a green pigeon he had just shot and was taking home in a carrier bag.

'You've probably never seen one of these,' Roy said, turning to us. 'Superb eating.'

We also bumped into an elderly water diviner whose technique was to hold a coconut in the palm of his hand. If it tilted itself upright, that signified water below. Roy pointed out a pale mauve bindweed-like flower.

'Ipomoea or *besharam*,' he said. 'Hindi for "shameless" because it will grow anywhere.'

When we eventually reached the Khimlasa tournament, on a scrubby recreation ground alongside a school, the home team was waiting for the visitors, a team from Khurai, to arrive. The tournament chairman, secretary and president hurried over to shake hands with us and make a great fuss of Roy. 'Give us some tips on batting, sir,' said the secretary.

Once again, the three of us sat on plastic chairs and a hundred people stood in front of us, observing us intently. The tournament president chewed paan and spat out red mouthfuls.

Roy presented the team with an impressive 1,800-rupee bat and there was much talk about medium-pace bowlers and the saintliness of Mike Gatting and Ian Botham. I asked if they had heard of David Beckham. Blank faces. Football was less important here than cricket. As one of the team said: 'We say that in UK cricket is a gentleman's game. In Australia it is a passion. But in India it is a religion.'

After half an hour the Khurai team had still not arrived, so the Khimlasa players formed two teams to play each other. Roy bowled the first ball and then gave a short morale-boosting lecture culminating in: 'Remember what John F. Kennedy said: "Ask not what your country can do for you. Ask what you can do for your country".'

Shouts of 'Well hit!' and 'Good shot!' echoed over the ground as we watched a few overs.

'Leg by!'

'Well fielded!'

Roy gave us a running commentary: 'Very well played on the off stump.' He glanced over to the right. 'See that fellow over there? He's scaring away the parrots from the guava trees.'

On the way back for lunch, we passed the cow again. Mercifully, it 'was no more'.

In the afternoon, Roy was a 'VIP guest' (a term much used in India) at a local rally of the Congress Party: three hundred guests, all men. He sat on the platform under framed and garlanded photographs of Indira and Rajiv Gandhi. As friends of a VIP guest, we too were deemed Very Important and sat alongside him. A local 'bard' (they still had them in go-ahead IT-supreme India) sang a Hindi song of welcome to a VVIP (Very Very Important Person) from the Congress Party who was garlanded twenty times and handed gifts including a shawl, a diary, a pen and four coconuts.

'What did the song say?' Clare asked Roy.

'It said they hope the VVIP will solve their drainage problems.'

On the way back to the bungalow, hundreds of farmworkers were being trucked home from the fields. Women were carrying bales of hay on their heads. We passed the dead cow again. It had already been half skinned.

We walked the final half-mile on a path meandering through dazzling green wheat fields. Here and there more piles of 'cow-dung cakes' were drying alongside fragments of discarded clay chai cups. It was sunset, a time of day that Indians poetically call 'cowdust time', when the cows return home from the fields to the villages. That day it was particularly magical, with the sky full of birdsong and a flaming scarlet sun setting in the west as a pale full moon rose in the east. As the sun finally went down over this almost English landscape (give or take the parakeets and the palm trees), we followed boys driving herds of goats back to the village and a man almost bent double with half a haystack on his back. A kingfisher darted past, a flash of blue.

Suddenly a horn blasted across the fields and a railway engine sped along an embankment a few hundred yards away. It must, we decided, have been a mirage. Then silence before the birdsong resumed.

Apart from the Captain's jeep, we generally saw only bicycles and tractors on these rural roads. Sometimes, a procession of bullock carts trundling past village huts suggested we were walking through a medieval landscape. The smoke from village fires wove into the evening mist and there was the occasional whiff of jasmine. Deer bounded across the fields. It was sublimely peaceful.

At breakfast the following day, the green pigeon was brought in twice for Roy's approval. Once with full plumage, then plucked and almost oven-ready. We wrote up our notes in the garden, the quiet disturbed only by children's singing in the village and the relentless call of the coppersmith bird – like a metallic metronome. Women with baskets on their heads sashayed along paths that wound through the fields beyond the hedge. We dozed in the afternoon in our dim bedroom, lulled by the birds, the children's voices and the warmth. The window shutters and the doors on to the back veranda were open. The Captain's voice boomed away in the distance as he joshed with his petitioners. It was like a cosy cave.

In the evening, as we prepared to drive to Bina station for a train to Delhi, Lakshmi-Bai's son-in-law arrived with garlands and wished us 'Merry Christmas and Happy New Year', even though it was 13th January. On the way to the station, jackals scattered in the car headlights. We passed the dead cow for the final time. By now it was smelling horribly of decay.

At the station I said 'Goodbye' to Roy's driver.

'Same to you,' he said and drove off.

It would be two years before we were back.

CHAPTER 6

'HARDLY ANYONE KNOWS WHAT A FOXTROT OR WALTZ IS NOW'

Before returning to Jhansi in January 2004, and our first meeting with Peggy Cantem, we flew to Delhi and spent Christmas there with our American friends, Virgil Miedema and Barbara Spaid. We had first met Virgil, a businessman, in Calcutta (as it then still was) in 1995, together with his elder daughter Stephanie. Clare had been making a radio programme and was recording in the city's Sacred Heart Church when Virgil noticed us. We immediately hit it off and subsequently stayed with the family whenever we were in Delhi, where they lived in the middle-class enclave of Jor Bagh.

Our Christmas with them was an interesting Eastern-Western take on the festival. An Indian Santa with a cotton-wool beard toured Connaught Place, Delhi's central shopping hub, in a horse-drawn carriage as green parakeets swooped overhead. A hotel disco blasted out up-tempo versions of 'Jingle Bells' and 'Rudolph the Red-Nosed Reindeer', with a chorus of stray dogs howling an accompaniment. At the Christmas Day carol service in the austere Cathedral Church of the Redemption – also known as the Viceroy Church – we sang 'In the Bleak Midwinter' as mosquitoes buzzed around our heads.

❖ ❖ ❖ ❖

On New Year's Day, we headed south on the magnificently named Nizamuddin-Ernakulam Mangala Lakshadweep Express, which was only marginally longer than its name. As ever, we were astonished by the bureaucratic triumph of the reservations lists pasted to the carriages' sides – lists sometimes as long as rolls of wallpaper. Alongside each seat number they listed the passenger's name, sex, age (recorded as '99' if not provided), boarding station and disembarking station. At six hours, ours was just a short sample of the train's journey south, scheduled to last forty-nine hours.

It was a foggy morning and most passengers were wearing woolly balaclavas or fur hats that resembled badly made wigs. Many were soon either playing with their mobile phones (one had Strauss's 'Radetzky March' as its ringtone), contributing to a symphony of snoring, or studiously doing nothing. Two very small children wearing balaclavas with knitted ears that made them look like human kittens ran up to us and held out hands for us to shake. 'Good morning, sir. Good morning, madam,' they duetted. 'Welcome to India.'

A young couple joined us in Agra after a honeymoon trip to the Taj Mahal. He was an NRI (Non-Resident Indian) now living in Canada; she was from São Paulo. It was her first visit to India and she was horrified by the dirt, the litter, the ubiquitous discarded plastic, the smells and the sometimes casual attitude to hygiene. She had seen two cockroaches meandering across the floor on a previous train and had been unable to sleep; we didn't mention the small mouse scuttling up and down our carriage. She talked about India's ungraspable extremes of poverty and wealth, ugliness and beauty, and about what she saw as an apparent lack of any sense of collective environmental responsibility.

To lighten the mood, Clare asked what they'd thought of the Taj Mahal.

'I thought: "We're on our honeymoon and it's so romantic",' he said.

'I thought: "This place smells and there's so much hassle",' she said.

He looked at her. 'In India, you choose what you want to see,' he said. 'You have to look through and beyond the problems and the shit to the beauty.'

We had a late lunch at the Jhansi Hotel, although we were staying across town at the Hotel Sita. Yogesh Mehrotra came to say hello. He and his father, he said, were planning to open a new hotel at the nearby, increasingly popular pilgrimage centre of Orchha. Small or large? 'Mediocre,' he said.

He walked us down to Dr Righton's room, little altered from four years before, and then pointed to the dining-room wall. A photocopy of a full-page article I had written for *The Times* about my first visit to Jhansi was framed there, gradually yellowing and slipping from its mount. Headlined 'Last Vestiges of the Raj in Jhansi', it was dominated by the black-and-white picture I had taken of the Captain on his veranda, smiling, erect and dignified.

Rather eerily, a green-lit tank of fish, similar to the one in reception, provided the only light in the almost pitch-black anteroom to the manager's office. The whisky bottles behind the bar, we were later told, were full of coloured water. When people ordered a single or double, staff ran down the road to the liquor store to buy a bottle of the real stuff.

A local politician was about to give a press conference at the hotel and two dozen journalists were due to attend. 'They are being given lunch by the politician,' said a fellow guest. 'They wouldn't come otherwise. Not a word would be reported.'

The journalists spluttered into the hotel grounds on their Lambretta scooters, but within minutes decided not to stay. The politician bustled up and pleaded with them. There was much shouting and waving of arms. Some left, but others lingered in the hope of a little more persuasion. Led by a man in a balaclava, they sat defiantly outside on the lawn under sunshades. The politician hurried into the hotel and, after ten minutes, hurried back with an armful of gift-wrapped books. He distributed them to the journalists, there were smiles all round and the press conference went ahead as planned.

'I understand the politician has promised them not merely lunch, but tea as well,' said our fellow guest. 'He is truly a most astute politician.'

In the four years since I'd first met Captain Abbott, we'd found out more about Jhansi's Anglo-Indian community, and Clare had been commissioned to make a *Woman's Hour* feature for BBC Radio 4 about Anglo-Indian women. So she had arranged to interview Peggy in order to learn more about Anglo-Indian life during 'the good old British days'.

Peggy's paternal grandfather, a British Indian Army man, had lived in the south of India, but: 'We could never trace his roots, though he was utter Anglo-Indian,' she told us over tea and biscuits, as we sat at her crowded kitchen table. 'He died when I was quite young, a very sudden death. The regiment was trekking from Madras, going down Travancore-side, travelling by road. He wanted to relieve himself, so he asked the sergeant major to be excused. He tied his horse to a tree, but he never followed them. When they went back, the horse was still there, but there was no trace of him except his clothes were lying there. And his pay-book was left in his clothes. So it was feared that some animal, a tiger perhaps, took him away.'

Her father, William James Kane, eventually made his way to Jhansi, where he worked on the railway as 'a chargeman in the millwright shop', married and had eight children: six boys and two girls. Only Peggy, born on 21st April 1923, had survived into old age.

Despite being known to everyone as Peggy, her real name was Mabel Ruth. 'My mother was so sick when I was born, she couldn't take me for baptism, so she told my godmother – "Name her Margaret." But from somewhere my godmother picked up the name Mabel Ruth. I don't know where Peggy comes from, but Margarets are called Peggy, so I'm happy with that.'

And her siblings' names? There was Percy, who had died aged eight not long before she was born. And Ernest, who had died when she was a young girl. 'My mother never told me the other children's names,' she said offhandedly. This lack of knowledge or curiosity about family history was something we were to come across regularly among the Anglo-Indian community.

When Peggy was seven, her father's railway workshop had closed and he was transferred to a workshop in Bombay. But then Ernest was killed – 'he was run over by a loco, in 1935' – so the family returned to Jhansi, where her father opened a garage and Peggy was educated at the local convent school.

'My mother wanted to withdraw me from the convent after my father died, but Sister Bernard said: "No, the child is brilliant; don't spoil her future career. We will keep her." I was very grateful to the nuns. I was well educated – for three rupees a month. You can't get an education now such as we got.

'When I finished, my mother wanted me to get married, but I took training in shorthand and typing. I was a very keen story writer, so I wrote to the School of Journalism in England and started a short correspondence course with them. I did do a stint of journalism for a time, but it didn't pay very well for the short articles I did. So it was best to carry on with shorthand and typing.'

At eighteen, she married an 'out-and-out Anglo-Indian, utter Anglo-Indian' – Ivan Eustace Cantem from Bombay, seventeen years older than her.

'He was a good boxer and a good hockey player; very sporty, like me. As a teenager I played a lot of tennis. I was always running, jumping, playing about… Many Anglo-Indians are very good sports people, so my parents liked him. Then my mother was suffering from cancer, and she was very worried that somebody should be there to look after me.'

Ivan Eustace – 'We used to call him "Useless Eustace"!' (a popular cartoon character of the day) – spent thirty years as an engine driver on mail trains – 'senior mail driver A-grade, technically trained' – like his father before him. A framed photograph of him showed a man with dark, piercing eyes and a direct, almost stern, gaze.

In the 1950s, Peggy started work as a stenographer for the local Planning Commission, then for the Collectors (revenue collectors), in the agriculture department, and for the Indian Civil Service – 'in the days when the ICS officers were the cream of society. Their pronunciation was super. I was shifted around like a real shuttlecock!' She had also, she added, taught English to generations of Indians. 'And I still do a lot of typing – though, now computers have come in, the typewriter is becoming an obsolete machine. But people still like a typewriter. Boys who are taking their medicals say: "Aunty, please help us," so I will type their school notes for them. Unfortunately, their spelling isn't always very good and I have to correct it.'

In 1962, she and Ivan Eustace planned to emigrate to Britain, which, like many Anglo-Indians of their generation, they regarded as their mother country. Before they could do so, however, he was diagnosed with cancer of the throat.

'He was gone within fourteen months. I was a widow at forty-two.' Her hopes of emigrating were scuppered. 'But I still have the passport forms signed and kept ready.

'He was a heavy drinker and smoker, that's how cancer got him. In those days Anglo-Indians drank like nobody's business, but nobody bothered because it was so cheap.'

Ironically, Ivan Eustace died three weeks before his railway pension was due to start, so it died with him.

'Financially I was crippled.'

So had she ever visited England?

Her eyes lit up. 'I did go in 1999, through the generosity of my niece – she paid my passage – and I stayed up to the millennium. It was wonderful, I felt happy there. We went into the countryside and saw the style of living and the supermarkets. Everything took me by surprise. It was all very beautiful, clean and efficient.

But people there always gave me Indian food and I was soon tired of it. I said: "I want a roast with Yorkshire pudding and Colman's mustard."'

She paused and fiddled with the cross around her neck.

'It was a lovely place but it wouldn't be good to move to England at my age. I'd only be a burden to the British government. So I'm best off here.

'And you know, when our people went from here to Britain, there was discrimination. They were called all sorts of names, like "the dark-skinned" or "half-baked". And you know those masala grinding stones we have for spices? The English called them tombstones: "Here they come, carrying their tombstones." But they had to stick it out. They were not given an easy time in the beginning, but now they have established themselves, I think they are doing very well in England. They have out-beaten some of the English people in their jobs. Yes, they have put up a good show.'

Peggy wanted us to meet her good friend Cheryl Baines, vice president of the Jhansi Anglo-Indian Association, who lived just across the street. Sheela brought the telephone and Peggy dialled. 'Cheryl?' she shouted, in a voice so loud that Cheryl could probably have heard it without the need of a phone. 'I have my journalist friends Stephen and Clare here. Can I bring them across?'

Ten minutes later we were being served coffee by a pleasant, middle-aged brunette with glossy hair and an appealingly soft voice. Cheryl was, Peggy said admiringly, sometimes mistaken for a Punjabi or a Kashmiri because of her fair skin.

We sat in a living room decorated with family photos and ornaments. There were cream antimacassars on the chairs and divan, peacock-embroidered bolster cushions from Rajasthan, and a cloth cover over the TV depicting Buckingham Palace.

'It's a little of English, a little of Indian,' said Peggy approvingly, with a wiggle of her head. 'Cheryl keeps it very nice.'

The four of us talked about Anglo-Indianness, the first of many discussions we were to have on the topic. Their status, it seemed, had always been ambiguous: betwixt and between, as one subsequently described it; like and unlike. In the days of the Raj, some Anglo-Indians – called Dunstan, perhaps, or Randolph, Myrtle or Blossom – had traditionally thought themselves a cut above their Indian neighbours, while the British had seen them as more than a cut below themselves. Not quite 'pukka'.

At Independence, there was widespread fear in the community that they would be persecuted by the new Indian regime, but that never happened. Instead, they joined the Dalits (formerly known as 'Untouchables') and tribal people under the unflattering label of 'Other Backward Castes'. 'But we objected to that term and it was converted to "Minorities Community",' said Peggy.

Under the British, they had benefited from being allotted a quota of reserved administrative jobs - in the railways, post and telecommunications, customs and police. Then the quota had been abolished, though one seat in the Lok Sabha, the 'lower house' of India's parliament, was reserved specially for them.

In *Plain Tales from the Raj*, Charles Allen offers an uncompromising assessment of the Anglo-Indians, quoting one man who had sailed out to India in 1928, aged just nineteen, to work at the Army and Navy Stores in Calcutta, and stayed on after Independence.

At the bottom of the pyramid, caught between two strongly hierarchical cultures and looked down upon by both, was the Eurasian, who was traditionally said 'to have acquired the worst characteristics of both races'...

So while there was a category of Anglo-Indian that was of high quality, there were a very large number who were pretty wishy-washy... Some of them on the railways did first-class jobs, and some of them as individuals were delightful. But not many companies were prepared to regard them as high management quality.

Nor, as that alternative name of Eurasians showed, were they of exclusively British descent. Cheryl's grandmother, for instance, was German.

'Show them a photograph, Cheryl, my girl,' ordered Peggy.

'Yes, Aunty,' said Cheryl, fetching one from the photo-filled sideboard. It showed a line-up of wedding guests ranging in complexion from 'dark skin tone' to 'wheaten', as adverts for beauty products would describe them.

'That's my family,' said Cheryl proudly. 'My eldest daughter, Sharon, married a Goan boy. His father was Anglo-Indian, his mother Goan, and their children are being brought up as Anglo-Indian Roman Catholics. Sharon is definitely an Anglo-Indian, very keen, and a member of the Nagpur branch. And she likes dancing – ballroom dancing she's very fond of. My second daughter, Charlotte, married an Iranian. She became a Muslim, changed her name, lives Irani-style, reads the Koran and goes to the mosque. Their children are also being brought up as Muslims.

'My third daughter, Judeline, was a senior flying stewardess for Jet Airways for five or six years. She married a Sindhi boy [from northwest India] and also changed her name. But I still call her Judy. She was baptised at St Jude's Shrine and Aunty Peggy is her godmother. So it's a real hotchpotch.'

Cheryl herself was a 'hotchpotch'.

'My mother was Shirley Basket. She married a Jacobs, Pinky Jacobs – named Derek Jacobs, actually. He was Anglo-Indian, Irish from his father's side, if I'm not mistaken. And my husband is Anglo-Indian – Sidney Harry Baines.'

Despite all this confusing cross-fertilisation, the Anglo-Indian community clearly guarded its own integrity. When her two younger daughters had wanted to attend a major Anglo-Indian Association dance event in Pune, they were barred because they had married outside the community.

'They both felt very bad about that. They said: "Mummy, now we are feeling really left out, like outcasts." That time, I really felt it, felt very sad.'

So might Cheryl now represent her family's last Anglo-Indian generation?

'More or less, yes.'

In the astutely observed novels of Rumer Godden, the British chronicler of the dying days of the Raj, the daughters of these mixed-race relationships were always beautiful.

'We have some very, very pretty girls in Jhansi,' agreed Peggy. 'It is the interbreeding that gives them their good looks.' It was a theme we were to return to many times.

Clare recalled how Rumer Godden also portrayed Anglo-Indian girls as a bit 'easy'. In *The Lady and the Unicorn*, published in 1937, she related a conversation between two young Englishmen: one, Stephen, a new arrival in India; the other, William, an old hand, who was inviting Stephen to a party he was shortly hosting.

> *'It's a B party,' he said.*
> *'What's a B party?'*
> *'A and B. B girls.'*
> *'Oh, I see,' said Stephen, and began to wonder about these Eurasian girls of whom he had heard so much, who were so alluring and so dangerous.*
> *'What happens?' he asked.*
> *'Usual thing,' said William. 'They behave very well and we behave very badly, and then they behave worse.'*

Cheryl and Peggy exchanged glances. 'See,' said Cheryl carefully, 'in the old days, an Indian person would like to spend time with an Anglo-Indian family because of the good-looking girls. They were quite free and easy, so the boys wouldn't take them seriously. They would have a good time with them and then leave them. That's why they got quite a bad name. Some of the men wouldn't marry them; they would just go with them for the fun of it. They were taken for granted. No doubt about it.'

'That's true,' nodded Peggy. 'Particularly when the British Army were here, and even the Americans. The girls were taken for a ride and ditched. Some of the Tommies, the soldiers, did marry them and took them to England, and some are happy. But the ones who were left behind suffered; they were often left pregnant, or with children.'

'That's how the Anglo-Indian community increased – with all sorts of tricks,' laughed Cheryl.

Peggy's phone rang and she took the call in another room.

While she was away, Cheryl defined 'Anglo-Indian': 'It means a person whose mother tongue is English and whose father was of European descent. See, we take our descent from fathers or grandfathers, not from our mothers. It always comes through the male line. If the father was Indian and the mother English, then they would be Indian.'

Not all India's young Anglo-Indians now cared very much about their mixed-race heritage. 'Anglo-Indians are fading out, like the Parsis,' said Peggy, rejoining us. 'The few that are left are merging with Indians, taking Indian nationality. And the girls will marry outside.'

'Boys are now going in for Indian girls or Indian Christians,' sighed Cheryl. 'So we don't know what the state of the community will be in years to come. It's very difficult for our girls to find a partner, because Anglo-Indian boys are not always holding good posts, to keep up the style of living girls want. Our girls have empowered themselves so much – they do better at school than the boys, become better qualified, and some do really well in big companies. They're ambitious, but the boys aren't. That's the unfortunate part of it.' Boys who did do well, she added, wanted similarly successful wives. 'They don't want to marry housewives with no education, staying at home cooking and cleaning.'

Because the British had traditionally extended privileges to them, said Peggy, 'some Anglo-Indians felt they were one better than the Indians, and that superiority complex hampered them a lot. The Indians couldn't stand that.'

During the Raj, Anglo-Indians had sometimes been mocked for their chi-chi sing-song accents, genteel manners and aspirations. They had been called 'half-castes' or 'café au lait', neither one thing nor the other. Yet their livelihoods had been secure. Once the British left, however, these loyal servants of the Empire – who had died alongside their rulers in Calcutta's Black Hole and fought beside them in the Mutiny and in subsequent wars – found themselves increasingly marginalised. They were no longer able to take for granted secure government jobs, pensions, protected status, homes in the generally smart middle-class Civil Lines districts of towns and cities. As one once told us: 'In India, the rich despise the poor, the young despise the old and everyone despises the Anglo-Indian.'

'You should read *Britain's Betrayal in India* by Mr Frank Anthony,' said Peggy. 'From that you will see why the Anglo-Indians emigrated immediately. They felt they wouldn't get equal status here after Independence so they got out. A few of us stayed, but we don't have any regrets. I felt I could merge in with the Indians. They're very good people; they look after us in a way. We're happy in India, where we are in our own little sphere. But many of our older members are BPL – below the poverty line. Some of them don't like to admit that they are poor, don't like being called BPL, but from their status, you can see it.'

Others were more fortunate – in demand as teachers or receptionists – 'because of our accent'. Cheryl herself worked at the Little Angels preschool. 'We make sure the children pronounce their words correctly,' she said proudly.

What about their own everyday language?

'At home, English we speak,' said Cheryl. 'We only speak Hindi to our servants or the fruit sellers, or to Hindi friends.'

Peggy nodded. 'Even up to now, I cannot talk the Hindi language very fluently. When I try to talk Hindi, they always say: "*Memsahib, yeh Hindi theek nahin*" – "Your Hindi is not very clear". Because my mother and father spoke English so much, I didn't get the chance to speak the Hindi language well. I only regretted it afterwards. I started learning at a very old age, so it wasn't very easy, getting the correct pronunciation. I have a touch of that British accent still in me.'

Did those Anglo-Indians who had remained in India consider themselves more British or more Indian?

'My first loyalty is Anglo-Indian,' Cheryl said firmly. 'Then natural Indian, then everything else.' She paused. 'I do feel we have lost something from years gone by. Our identity, I suppose. We are neither Indians nor Anglos, you can say; we are just between both.'

After a thoughtful silence, Peggy lightened the tone. 'We have our shows to bring the community together. We're having one in a few weeks' time: a dinner, games and gifts for the children, tombola, housey-housey. I want to give people something to look forward to. We don't want them to think they're a lost community.'

'And Anglo-Indians are very fond of dancing,' added Cheryl. 'Ballroom dancing, foxtrots, waltz, jiving was there and rock 'n' roll. Now they've gone into Indian dancing, our kids.'

'Hardly anyone knows what a foxtrot or waltz is now,' said Peggy sadly. 'They've all gone in for this disco-dancing and DJs. So they just have these rowdy crowds. Hard rock music, as you would call it, and discos – oh, that's their favourite, the modern generation.'

The conversation turned to fashion. The dress codes of both women were a curious hybrid of East and West, Indian and British. Cheryl, who had a nose ring ('I took a liking to it, but we're not supposed to wear them'), was wearing a colourful salwar kameez, the tunic and loose pants outfit increasingly favoured by Indian women. 'From the 1960s, I started wearing salwar tops and saris because if I was wearing a minidress or sleeveless dress, people would say: "You're showing your legs and arms, it doesn't look good." I think we get more respect, wearing a salwar. Very few Anglo-Indians still keep to their dresses, though Aunty Peggy still wears Western clothes. But that's fine because she's seventy-plus.'

'Oh yes, I still wear my dresses,' agreed Peggy. 'But now it's more pants because of my arthritis. They protect my knees.' She was also wearing a blue and white short-sleeved sweater, gold earrings and a scarf tied jauntily at her neck. 'I've not yet worn a sari. I can't manage it. I feel it's going to fall off at any minute.'

'So, apart from clothes and accents,' Clare asked, 'what else makes Anglo-Indians different from Indians?'

'It's our mode of living,' said Peggy. 'See, we keep up our lifestyle, no matter how poor we are. We have to have our little homes kept neat and tidy. We have to have a maid or somebody to help us. We cannot do our own sweeping, etcetera: we're a little lazy in that respect. Whereas the Indians, they can do everything themselves, they don't wait for people to come and help.

'The Indian will always think twice – "I have to save my money. I have to look after my children, keep my family going." If there is one fault with Anglo-Indians, it's that we live for the day, want to live well, and we don't think about what tomorrow will bring. Hospitality is there, love is there and caring is there. No matter who it is, we love to entertain.'

Over the course of our visits to Jhansi we would learn the truth of this as our stomachs tried to cope with a ceaseless round of meals and snacks or 'small eats': 'No, no, you must have one more cake.'

'We are quite a warm-hearted sort of people,' added Cheryl.

'And one more thing,' continued Peggy. 'We have no caste or creed in our status. Everyone is the same, low caste or high caste. Even the menials, we look after them. We treat them equally, no distinction.'

'And they call us memsahib, missy-sahib, baby or *baba*,' added Cheryl. 'Respect is there.'

We were briefly back in Peggy's kitchen the following day for more tea with Cheryl. Almost as soon as we sat down, a dog outside started whining and barking. 'That must be the vegetable-wallah,' said Peggy.

'Or maybe the dog-meat man,' Cheryl suggested.

The trundling of a cart grew gradually louder before stopping outside Peggy's curtain. A man appeared in the doorway. 'It's the dog-meat man,' explained Peggy. 'He's brought the dog's meat, to be cooked up for the evening.'

The cart was stacked with great lumps of raw meat. Cheryl bought one for the slavering *pi*-dog, a stray mongrel, now looking desperately at the cart. 'Not many Indians keep dogs,' said Cheryl. 'They just let them run around, get pregnant and scavenge.'

'Wealthy people – people far beyond our status – keep good-breed dogs here, dogs that are more than we can afford to keep,' said Peggy. 'So the dogs live to a high standard. But everyone in England keeps dogs, don't they?'

Before we could answer, the dog started fighting with another.

'Oh, listen to all that noise!' cried Peggy. 'See, this will be the start of a dog fight. Now there will be more barking than talking!' She giggled. 'Sheela, chase them away!'

Her long-suffering cook moved away from the tiny stove where she was creating one of her enterprising dishes and shouted at the dogs before throwing a piece of wood at them. Then she returned to the stove, her lemon and turquoise sari a thing of beauty among the stained pots and pans and the food-splattered newspapers.

We strolled back to the Hotel Sita through the Sadar Bazaar, a busy microcosm of Market India almost roofed over by a tangled mesh of telephone wires. Tongas – the horse-drawn carts now rarely seen in Indian streets – still survived here, the animals trotting along as though it was 1920. Vegetables and marigolds were piled on trolleys lit by flares in the evening: shopkeepers strung the marigolds together like garlands over their entrances. There were bangle stalls (Clare stocked up), an excellent bookshop, and a small, spotlessly clean and Westernised store selling imported goods. There was Uncle's Shoppe and Life Style Shoppe, Kwality Departmental Stores, Mini Gift Centre and Supervalue Store stacked with brightly coloured plastic buckets and waste bins. Disturbingly realistic Western mannequins stood impassively outside shops selling Havoc Jeans and the ubiquitous Bata Shoes. Women sifted through swatches of cloth in salerooms lined with cabinets of gold jewellery.

A roadside doctor's surgery proclaimed 'Expert in blood, urine, stool, semen & all type of Pathological Investigations'. Mobile phones blasted out snatches of Bollywood music and a barber's salon offered its customers endless shades of hair dye as they sat in solid swivel chairs with split and torn leather seats. An advertisement for one shop located it 'Behind Krishna Talkies'. Cows ambled alongside shoppers. Mindful of the cold nights we could expect at the farms later in the week, we bought a thermal vest for me, a thick shawl for Clare.

For dinner at the hotel, we ordered our standby meal after days of exclusively Indian food: room-service cheese omelette and chips. The first evening, our plates arrived with omelettes on them, but no chips. Where were they, we asked the friendly young waiter whose name, we discovered, was Colin Murphy. 'Chips are inside,' he said. And indeed they were.

He beamed when we mentioned Peggy and told us he was Anglo-Indian himself, with three brothers: Derek, Darrell and Douglas. Anglo-Indianness was not, he added, an important issue to him.

CHAPTER 7

CAPARISONED TUSKERS AND NAKED MEN

We spent the next three days in Orchha, ten miles out of Jhansi. Orchha – its name means 'hidden place' – had grown up among the ruins of a once-important town built in the 16th century but abandoned two hundred years later. Only the palaces and temples remained, scattered across the fields and left to settle into grand decay. Tombs and mausoleums were occupied by farming families who leaned their charpoys, or rope beds, against the ancient walls during the day. Other tombs were grazed by cattle, or had been swallowed up by scrubby jungle, their pineapple-coned domes just surfacing over the treetops. It was the sort of mildly melancholy landscape that would have appealed to the late-18th-century English artists Thomas and William Daniell.

Some of the palaces and temples looked broodingly Transylvanian, with vultures hunched on their battlements and towers. Others were brightly painted – one of them cream and pink, like an ice cream sundae. Outside, holy men with wild matted hair sat cross-legged on the ground and chanted prayers, accompanying themselves on small tabla (hand drums) and finger cymbals.

Backpacking hippies had long been visiting Orchha, enjoying its village atmosphere and stocking up on loon pants and shoulder bags in the market. But now the town, with its nine thousand inhabitants, was increasingly featuring on mainstream tourist itineraries hurtling through India's heritage. Every day the coaches rolled in, telephoto lenses poking through their open windows to capture a bit of ethnic colour from a safe distance. Overseas tourists were lured to the proliferating number of hotels and cafés by enthusiastic guidebook write-ups and by what a hotel manager once described to us as 'mouth-to-mouth publicity'.

The hippies didn't welcome the coach parties, who were trespassing on their secret place and making them feel more like tourists than – as they preferred to see themselves – travellers. As they left their coaches, the passengers were greeted by the local children's litany of demands: 'Bye-bye pen bye-bye chocolate bye-bye photo bye-bye rupee.'

'Why do they say bye-bye rather than hello?' I once asked a shopkeeper.

'Because the tourists stay for very short time,' he said.

Some of the kids were very smart. One persistent boy followed me round demanding, 'One rupee. One rupee.'

I shook my head.

'One rupee. One rupee,' he repeated.

Eventually I said: 'Please go away.'

Quick as a flash he said: 'One rupee to go away.'

Orchha's bazaar gradually expanded over our half-dozen subsequent visits, offering Rajasthani cushion covers, gaudy bags, beaded slippers for trim little feet, and as many papier-mâché elephants as any tourist's heart could desire. It was a good place to get your shoes cleaned or repaired by pavement cobblers, whose livelihoods were increasingly threatened as leather shoes gave way to trainers. A tailor sat outside his stall, whirring away on an ancient Singer sewing machine operated by a treadle. Other tailors sat in box-like kiosks opening straight on to the street. An ironing man wielded a huge and heavy iron as big as a television. A musical instrument shop stocked battered trombones, for baraats, the raucous Indian wedding processions. A sign outside one shop offered 'Digital photos of ancient Orchha'.

In the evening the bazaar twinkled with trinkets, and Indian pilgrims sat cross-legged around the main square singing hymns and chanting. A hundred yards further along, the bazaar gave way to lanes lined with smart, blue-painted houses with bicycles propped against the walls. A twenty-minute walk out of town was the ruinous Lakshmi Narayan Temple, famous for its 19th-century murals of finely moustachioed, musket-carrying British East India Company officers taking tea with rajahs.

At lunchtime we sat on the roof terrace at the Betwa Tawang restaurant in a corner of the main square. It was a good vantage point from which to watch the small-town goings-on below. As we sipped fresh lime sodas, men roared up on motorbikes to the post office or the phone booth which, in pre-mobile phone days, had yellow signs offering PCO (Public Call Office), STD (Subscriber Trunk Dialling) and ISD (International Subscriber Dialling).

We were staying at the Sheesh Mahal, a government-run hotel shoehorned into a corner of one of the old palaces. It was approached through the towering 'Elephant Gate', whose doors were studded with foot-long spikes to discourage belligerent tuskers.

The palace was a warren of corridors, staircases, passages and courtyards, scattered with verandas, balconies and turrets offering views over seemingly limitless forest. In summer, the few buildings we could see from the balconies were almost drowned in a sea of vegetation.

After dinner, we took our beers up the curving staircase past the 'He toilet' and 'She toilet' to sit on the top terrace and listen to the singing and drumming from distant villages, overlaid with the incessant howling of dogs. The sky sparkled with stars, the Milky Way seeming to cascade down like a silver-beaded sari. Thunder rumbled in the distance. We went to sleep lulled by cicadas and awoke to birdsong.

One lunchtime we strolled along the riverbank from the hotel. Spread out on the rocks below us, drying in the sunshine, were the clothes we had handed over as laundry at the hotel that morning. A woman was energetically slapping one of my shirts on rocks to clean it.

We spent many hours wandering beyond the Sheesh Mahal along dusty paths lined by lantana bushes with their yellow, orange, red and pink flowers. The paths wound past overgrown ruins in wheat fields and around mustard and guava plantations almost enclosed in a bend of the Betwa River. Swallows darted over the water, roots of banyan trees reached down to the ground, and the silence was broken only by screeching parakeets and bleating goats nibbling at bushes and herded by elderly women. Cows grazed, monkeys chattered, squirrels scurried, butterflies fluttered around our heads and an owl gazed unblinkingly down at us from the ledge of an ancient stone shrine.

As boys slowly pedalled bicycles along the paths and buffalo trundled along with their ploughs, there was a magical freshness in early morning and a languid stillness in late afternoon, when women carried home baskets of beetroot, cabbage and marrows. An elderly cowherd in a dhoti was making his gradual way along the main path, occasionally squatting on his haunches to let his single cow catch up. Orchha distilled a sense of lost dynasties. When we subsequently told a Delhi hotel waiter that we'd visited it, he looked wistful. 'Too much lovely,' he said.

Over our next few visits, the Sheesh Mahal became ever busier. Parties of young backpackers would settle down after dinner and absorb themselves in their mobile phones. India, after all, may have been fascinating, but it could never be as fascinating as the land of Elsewhere.

On our last day in Orchha, on our way back to Jhansi, we called in at the railway station, which was served by six trains a day, separated by long lulls. Passengers who had turned up hours before their trains were due to arrive dozed in the midday sun. Boys played cricket on the longest platform, goats wandered around. In the stationmaster's office, 'Safety Slogans' were posted around the walls. They ranged from the pithy ('Always alert – accidents avert') to the plodding ('The best safety device is a careful man').

Over the ticketing window was the painted maxim: 'Two magic words: please and thanks'. A picture of Gandhi leading his 1930 Salt March was propped up on top of the 'Key Box'. The stationmaster sat at a desk behind a huge ledger with dozens of columns to fill in. In line with the inventory-obsessed approach of Indian bureaucracy, the desk's dimensions and code number were neatly painted on its side: 'SM/ORC/29/15... 4' 0" x 3' 0" x 2' 6". Before we left Orchha, I asked a trader where the nearest chemist was. He pointed down the road. 'Turn right at the neem tree,' he said.

❖ ❖ ❖ ❖

Back in Jhansi, we took a tuk-tuk to Roy's bungalow, where the *Times* article I had written after my first meeting with him was spread out under a sheet of glass on top of his desk. He drove us down to the farms via Khurai, where for the first time we noticed an office sign proclaiming: 'All-India Ballbearing Merchants' Association'. As an extra comfort for cold nights, we bought two hot-water bottles (*garam pani* bottles, hot-water bags, or 'Duckbacks' as they were variously called).

On the way to the village, we passed a dozen-strong group of villagers squatting by the roadside. They were waiting for a bus, though Roy said they lived only a mile up the road. 'They would rather sit and wait two hours for a bus than walk one mile,' he said. 'People will sit waiting for a politician to arrive for four or five hours. Eventually they'll say: "I don't think he's coming" and only then will they go home.'

Halfway through an afternoon nap at the bungalow, Clare and I were woken by the sound of a crowd outside. Villagers, mostly men wearing dhotis and with scarves tied round their heads, had come – as ever – with their marigold garlands and their salaams and their feet-touching. They updated Roy on village goings-on since he had left for Christmas in Jhansi three weeks before.

One villager's brother had been accused of attempted rape; the villager paid out twenty thousand rupees to support him – eighteen thousand of them for lawyers' fees. To cover this, he had taken out a loan repayable at 30 per cent a year. He said it would be paid 'when the harvest comes', but if the harvest failed he might have to sell some of his land. It was a downward spiral of debt. Another man, we were told, had caught a virus which had swollen his entire body and killed him within three days. A third was about to catch a bus to Indore to arrange his daughter's wedding, at a cost of around fifty thousand rupees.

Then there was the traditional 'distribution of the Christmas cake' – a slice of the cake brought from Jhansi for whoever turned up. Blankets and shoes were also ceremonially handed out as gifts. One old lady complained of poverty and cold, so Clare bought her a blanket which we later saw her wearing around her shoulders as she squatted in front of a neighbour's fire. She couldn't afford firewood of her own.

The next day, a police inspector and his wife were due to come to lunch at Roy's. They arrived ninety minutes late, without apology. When we subsequently called at their flat one afternoon – it was in a monsoon-stained Soviet-style block of police housing – the wife was still in her nightdress. During lunch, the inspector looked up from the huge pile of rice he had just tipped on to his plate.

'You might find it interesting to go to the inauguration ceremony at the Jain temple tomorrow,' he told us. 'There should be caparisoned tuskers there. And a naked man.'

Caparisoned tuskers – elephants with fantastically ornate headdresses – are always a draw. A naked man would be the icing on the cake.

So, the next day, we were driven to the ceremony, which we found in full swing on the far side of a parade ground. As we got out of the car, a man in a smart suit hurried towards us and shook hands. 'Welcome,' he said. 'We are expecting you.' Several other men bowed. We hadn't anticipated a reception committee. The man in the smart suit led us through a crowd of perhaps a thousand people to a stage where rows of dignitaries sat earnestly listening to speeches. The police inspector was already there and ushered us to seats next to him in the front row.

The Master of Ceremonies beamed at us and launched into a stream of Hindi. We understood hardly a word, but the letters BBC and VIP cropped up with alarming frequency, interspersed with the ominous words 'Chief Guests'. There was a burst of applause, a thousand heads turned towards us and half a dozen press photographers snapped away. This could mean only one thing: we had been mistaken for VIPs because Clare was recording more programmes for Radio 4. The BBC link could open all sorts of normally padlocked doors in India, but it could be a mixed blessing. 'I've only come for the tuskers,' I protested weakly to the inspector.

The MC carried on talking. 'He says that Mr Steve and Mrs Clare have come from London especially for this trip,' the police inspector translated. 'And he is inviting you to make a speech and say something about the inauguration of the temple.'

A Richard Hannay moment was about to occur. In Hitchcock's 1930s film of *The 39 Steps*, Robert Donat, playing Hannay, tries to escape the police by dashing into a public meeting. He is mistaken for the chief speaker, makes a speech that moves from inventive nonsense to political passion, and walks off the platform to be greeted by cheers and handcuffs.

I'd already had one of these Hannay moments back in Delhi. We had been visiting the International Museum of Toilets, one of the capital's more specialist tourist attractions, to interview its founder about public sanitation (a pertinent topic in India). The museum was fascinating. Where else could you find an exhibition called 'Great Potties of the World'? Or a replica of the wooden toilet from which Louis XIII of France gave public audiences? Or a sketch of Henry VIII's velvet-padded toilet seat? Or a series of 17th-century 'Poems of the Backside'?

We'd arrived shortly before assembly at the school attached to the museum. 'Good morning, sir,' the children chorused. 'Good morning, madam.'

Painted on the walls was an ABC of Happiness. It began with 'Aspire to reach your potential' and ended with 'Zestfully pursue happiness'. After being garlanded, we'd been ushered on to the platform. As the hymns finished, the museum's founder had strolled to the lectern: 'I would now like to invite our esteemed guests, Mrs Clare from the BBC and her husband, Mr Steve, to address us.'

'Your gig,' Clare had said, gazing straight ahead.

It was no time for nerves. I marched to the lectern and cried 'Namaste!', which had the benefit of getting me off to a good start and the drawback of implying that I was going to speak throughout in Hindi.

Finding something to say was not actually hard. After a working life of listening to British politicians spouting platitudes, I only needed to tell the audience what they wanted to hear. I said what tremendous work they were doing, how important sanitation was, how honoured we were, and what lovely hymns they sang. It went down well, and I hadn't even needed to quote Akbar, the great Mughal emperor and a man of deep fundamental truths. 'A good morning bowel movement,' he had reflected, 'is the happiest moment of one's life.'

The Jain ceremony in Khurai was another matter. I knew little about the religion, except that its followers were so anxious not to kill or injure fellow creatures that they sometimes wore face masks to avoid breathing in insects. So I plumped for more platitudes – the need for unity and peace in a world riven by division, the joy of compassion, how honoured we were to be there… and yes, I'd been to a wonderful Jain temple in the British city of Leicester. The MC translated my speech into Hindi, there was polite applause and as I sat down, someone along the row whispered 'Short and sweet' to his neighbour. The press cameras snapped again and, protocol upheld, it seemed the perfect moment to leave.

Not the case. A man who had been hovering in the background now rushed forward carrying something large and heavy that glinted in the afternoon sun. It was a pickaxe wrapped in silver foil. 'They want you to turn the first sod,' said the police inspector.

I padded in stockinged feet to the sacred site earmarked for the ceremony, brought down the pickaxe, smiled for the cameras and said we had to move on to another engagement. As we left, crowds mobbed us, grasped our hands and asked for autographs. A thousand people waved as we drove away.

'There hasn't been a caparisoned tusker in sight,' sighed Clare. 'Never mind a naked man.'

CHAPTER 8

'GOD-FEARING
WITH SOBER HABITS'

We were back in Jhansi just ten months later, after working trips to
Udhagamandalam – the old British hill station of Ootacamund or
Ooty – in Tamil Nadu, and to Cochin in Kerala. As with so many
car journeys through India, the drive from Ooty to Cochin was
nothing if not entertaining. Along the way we passed signs for a
taxi company called Gridlock Travels, a law firm called Panicker
and Panicker and a garage called Tinkering Works.

Meandering our gradual way up India to Jhansi, we spent two
nights in Chennai. We'd last visited it eight years before, when
it was still known as Madras, and it had seemed sprawling and
amorphous. Now it had transformed into a metropolitan city. It
was hardly recognisable, with an astonishing number of smart new
stores, shopping malls and glitzy hotels. The city centre roads were
lined by huge hoardings which hid many of the tree-filled parks of
a city that was still, for all its size, essentially pleasant, if formless.

Waves pounded the beach, where small boys were splashing
around and a group of middle-class teenage girls was tentatively
paddling. Two of them waded further into the water and were
swept off their feet. Young men gathered round to watch this real-
life enactment of an Indian film's wet-sari scene. In the heat of
early afternoon, people sheltered in the shade of fishing boats or
queued at ice cream wagons.

At the start of a grand tour of British churches and churchyards,
we visited St Andrew's, a spruce, clean, circular kirk with a dome

whose underside was painted sky-blue and studded with golden stars. They formed patterns, we were told, corresponding to constellations seen in Scotland, so the original British congregation would feel at home.

Memorials paid tribute to Physicians General, Surgeons Major, a soldier who died after 'a life of exemplary usefulness' and Handel Manuel, 'organist, choirmaster, composer'. How could he have been anything else with such a name?

The church was decorated for Christmas with sprigs of paper holly tied to its pillars with ribbons. Cupboards were stacked with hymn books and tins of Brasso. Framed photographs in the organ loft showed the church choir gradually becoming more and more Indian from 1930, when Mr Strathie, Miss Timmins and Mr Galbraith smiled in the bright sunshine and Mrs Horwill wore her gay summer bonnet. In the front row, looking very fetching in a cloche hat and a flapper skirt, was 'Miss M. Boys' – Fanny Margaret, aged twenty-one – with a Cairn terrier on her lap. She died just four years later. 'By her gift of song, her vivid personality and her frank nature, she endeared herself to all who knew her', said her memorial. Her father Harry died six months after her. A small, stocky church clerk and 'late Sergeant, Royal Artillery', he stood a few feet away from her in the photo; touchingly, his memorial was a few feet away from hers in the church.

Never ones to miss an opportunity to find echoes of the British in India, we returned to St Andrew's the next day for the Sunday service, with its processions of elders, its breaking of bread and its sipping of thimbles of Cherryade. The hymns (in English) were sweetly sung by the five-hundred-strong congregation, the hallelujahs particularly invested with a rare calm. Hymn No 521 was 'God Save the Queen'. Afterwards, a produce sale included marmalades and mango and sweet lime pickles, with the Indian equivalents of Women's Institute members presiding with well-groomed efficiency. A church elder told us he was a pharmacist and had once spent a year working in London's Notting Hill Gate 'until the cold got to my arthritis'.

In the churchyard, banyan trees entwined tombs like those at Angkor Wat in Cambodia, with creeping tendrils spilling over them and giant centipedes crawling over the stone. There were cobwebs everywhere.

It was much the same in St Mary's churchyard, at Fort St George, the original focus of British colonial power. It was still elegant and charming, despite appalling smells from a canal that was reportedly 98 per cent effluent.

The church, the oldest Anglican church east of Suez, was packed with monuments carved on the grandest scale with sentiments to match. A German pastor, Rev Christopher Gericke, was 'destined to labour in a peculiar vineyard – that of the conversion of the natives of India'. The monument showed one 'native' apparently dozing, propped on his spear, as the pastor expounded the scriptures to him. Josiah Webbe spent his life 'disdaining the little arts of private influence or vulgar popularity'. Here too were Lt Col Hercules Henry Pepper, Catherine Lushington Prendergast and the Rev Walter Posthumus Powell. Other memorials commemorated people who died 'from the effect of a *coup de soleil*' or 'from injuries received in an encounter with a tiger'. There was much weeping and grieving, many hands grasping furrowed brows as mortality caught up with loved ones. Outside was the 1652 gravestone of Elizabeth Parker: the oldest British inscription in India, we later discovered.

Captain Roy Abbott on the veranda of his Jhansi bungalow, January 2000

Peggy Cantem at home in Jhansi's Civil Lines

Anish Khan, Peggy's autorickshaw driver

Sheela Chauhan, her cook

May Coutinho, Peggy's domestic help

Manager Omnath Mehrotra on the veranda of the Jhansi Hotel before its extensive renovation

Captain Abbott's bungalow in Jhansi

Mutiny memorial in the gatehouse of Jhansi's European cemetery

A child's grave in the cemetery

The entrance to the cemetery

An angel gravestone

Religious imagery around the emergency generator at Peggy's home

Roy Abbott in his home office

Lakshmi-Bai Rajput, Roy's cook in Behrol village

Shyam Yadav, his bearer

Lachoo Patel, the deputy bearer

Devera, or Dev, one of Peggy's close Anglo-Indian friends

Cheryl and Sidney Baines with Leela, Roy's housekeeper, having tea and 'small eats' at the Little Angels kindergarten run by Buddie Hars

An alphabet poster at Little Angels

Buddie Hars and her mother
Antoinette Jacobs at their Little
Angels kindergarten

Roy Abbott at his Jhansi bungalow
in 2014

Colleen Barboza

Shop mannequins in Jhansi's Sadar Bazaar

St Jude's shrine, with the Crucifixion in the background

One of Jhansi's main streets

A Jhansi fruit and vegetable stallholder

The village of Orchha, where Peggy and her friends used to have moonlight picnics and dance to gramophone records by Victor Silvester

A Jhansi barber's shop

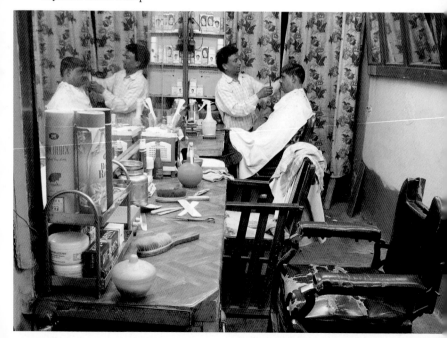

Villagers in Behrol, one of Captain Abbott's four villages in Madhya Pradesh

Portrait of Queen Elizabeth II in Roy Abbott's bungalow in Behrol

A photo of Peggy's late husband Ivan Eustace, with Indian statuette

Roy at dinner in his Behrol bungalow

'The British Empire runs on tea'

An Anglo-Indian family photo

More religious imagery, plus umbrella

Peggy in her forties

Roy as an Indian Military Academy
cadet: 'the Indian Sandhurst'

Peggy and Roy in their eighties

The churchyard was separated from the church by a hectic flyover. Jungles of undergrowth made most of the graves – again, often swamped by banyan tree roots – inaccessible, so we asked the chowkidar to take us round. As we stumbled through the undergrowth, past carved urns draped with stone cloth, large lizards eyed us beadily and then scurried away. Bougainvillea blossomed on many plots but the chowkidar ripped it away so we could see rusting railings, columns, obelisks, pyramids and other once-grand memorials. Here was an 'Army Scripture Reader'; over there Simon Hyman, a sailor who 'died of the bite of a watersnake after three and a half hours illness, aged 21'. A group of youths sat on a tomb playing chequers, with the board chalked on the stone. Dragonflies fluttered like delicately shaken fans.

Along the road, the dark red High Court was a great rambling M. C. Escher-like labyrinth of corridors, stairs, vaults, arches and colonnades. Taking a chance, we wandered in to explore. The rapid clatter of battalions of typewriters echoed along the corridors, their walls lined with full-length portraits of judges. One office was stacked with leather-bound, gold-toothed copies of the 'Madras Law Journal'. Outside, thirty feet of mouldering, tied-up bundles of briefs stretched along the corridor. A clerk blew dust off them as he frantically searched for what was clearly an important document. Sheaves of carbon paper rustled. Lawyers in black gowns strolled purposefully past or huddled in little corner conferences. It felt like something out of the Court of Chancery in Dickens's *Bleak House*.

We edged quietly into a courtroom, elegant with Arts and Crafts décor and stained glass, and sat at the back. A few eyebrows were raised at us, a few wry smiles, as more lawyers petitioned judges, day following day, week following week, and the wheels of justice turning with lumbering slowness. A clerk dropped the remains of his lunch from a high balcony. The food splattered on the ground and crows swooped down after it.

Our last stop was St George's Cathedral, which resembled a chaste white stately home. I made more notes of inscriptions. Henry Valentine Conolly 'fell by the hands of a band of fanatics'; John Mack died in 1832, aged thirty-five, 'Surgeon to the Governer's Body Guard and Physician to the Durbar of his Highness the Nabob of the Carnatic'. Others died of '*jungli* fever' or had their lives 'cut off by the hand of an unknown assassin'. A statue showed Daniel Corrie, the first Bishop of Madras, in his ornate robes clutching a Bible and placing a lordly, patriarchal hand on the head of a small, thin Indian with topknot and loincloth.

A man was kneeling at the altar, praying with fervour, his face contorted, flinging his arms in the air and appealing to the Almighty. Many memorials featured palm trees with broken trunks: one had metal stacking chairs propped ignominiously against it. In the churchyard, another tree's gigantic fronds had totally engulfed one tomb, as though wax from a giant candle had been dripping over it for centuries.

At our hotel, Western classical music was piped out on a loop: Wagner, Shostakovich, Bach, Beethoven. 'We bought ten tapes from an American guest and play them in rotation,' said the manager. 'They add class, don't they?' Classy or not, they added a surreal soundtrack. In the restaurant we ate palak paneer with the 'Dies Irae' from Verdi's *Requiem* thundering around us. Also on the menu was Egg Plant Lady Hamilton.

Our bedroom buzzed with mosquitoes, despite the coils we lit to deter them, which nearly suffocated us during the night. Over breakfast we got talking to a retired British businessman – forty years in the East – with naval tattoos and a Thai wife thirty years his junior. He said he had retired to the coast near Eastbourne for his health.

'Hate it, it's a morgue,' he said. 'When my wife smiled at a woman in the street, she said haughtily: "Do I know you?"'

At dinner, Indian musicians played discreetly in a corner. No-one paid them much attention. As they finished, they shuffled humbly away along a wall.

One red-streaked sunset, we climbed to a rooftop viewpoint. A black-and-white paper kite floated gracefully in the sky before suddenly plummeting on to an adjoining roof. People sat on their verandas, a child pianist in an upstairs room practised Schubert, and a train pulled out of a station with people jammed in the doorways. In the distance, Hindi TV programmes blasted out of the thatched huts in a shanty village.

The following day, I took a letter to be franked at the post office. 'Yes, sir,' said the assistant. 'We will deface it and send it straight to England.'

I also checked train times at the railway station, where a sign announced: 'The following articles will not be booked as luggage: wet skins, hides, explosives, oil, grease, ghee and dry grass'. Another warned: 'Railway Administration is not responsible for damage by rats to packages kept in the cloakroom if eatables are kept in them'. Bats flitted around the platforms at night.

Along the road, a young man was working down a sewer, cleaning out a drain; he was up to his neck in filthy, fetid water and a crowd had gathered to watch. An elderly man rode past on a bicycle, a dozen live chickens hanging upside down from the handlebars, trussed together by their legs. Another elderly man pointed us towards a traveller's cheque bureau where we could change money. As we came out, he was waiting for us. 'Something for my meal tonight?' he asked, hand outstretched.

By way of contrast, in the café of the five-star Taj Coromandel hotel, a pianist was playing 'My Way', and the waitress poured the tea with the concentrated care of a religious rite. The hotel shop had an antique-looking wooden chest on display.

'Is it old?' I asked an assistant.

'Yes sir,' he said. 'At least fifteen years.'

A Hindu wedding party was underway at another hotel down the road. A boy offered me a red turban to wear and said he had just converted to Christianity ('Praise the Lord!'). Outside, a white limousine had red roses stuck all over its bodywork. The bride was led out, eyes downcast, into a posse of video cameras and a shower of rose petals.

We took a taxi to the offices of *Anglos in the Wind*, the whimsically named global magazine for Anglo-Indians, to explore the world that our conversations with Peggy had revealed to us. Before leaving the UK, Clare had arranged to meet Harry MacLure, an elegantly spoken man in his late thirties, with more than a passing resemblance to the Hollywood actor Yul Brynner, who had founded and now edited the magazine. His office was on the first floor of a shopping complex, with the usual air-conditioning unit humming away – to little avail as the sweltering afternoon wore on.

Harry asked a young man at the photocopying machine to bring us chai and settled into the swivel chair behind his cluttered desk to tell us about *Anglos*, with its readership of around twenty thousand. Outside of India, he said, most readers were based in the UK, Canada, Australia and America – wherever the 350,000 Anglo-Indian expats had settled.

He had launched the magazine six years earlier after travelling to different countries every three years for the worldwide annual Anglo-Indian reunion. In 1998, it had been held in Bangalore, and he had realised there was a need 'to connect everyone in the diaspora. And it's not just for older people – it's been very well received by our youngsters because we don't just concentrate on the achievements of older Anglo-Indian people, we feature young achievers as well.'

So what was *his* definition of an Anglo-Indian?

He smiled. 'An Anglo-Indian, in my opinion, is a by-product of the East India Company. After Independence, we were sidelined. We were not given our respect of dues from either the British or the Indians. The British Raj gave us good jobs and facilities, but they left us with almost nothing. When an Anglo-Indian wanted a job in earlier days, even if they didn't have the right qualifications, they usually got one because of their British name. That doesn't work now – we have to compete in the mainstream, alongside all the other communities, so our livelihood is very hard. Lots of Anglo-Indians migrated after 1947, for better living, greener pastures.

'Certain discrimination still does take place, not just to Anglo-Indians but to Indian Christians, too. In government departments and even in the private sector, they don't get promotion on time because they're not Hindus.'

Were Anglos a caste then?

'That word "caste",' he laughed. 'Whenever you fill up an application form in India, it always asks for caste. Even if you are applying for a ration card, you have to mention caste. So we have to put "Anglo-Indian". It's going to take many years for us to become a casteless society.

'It's a funny thing,' he added, 'because we're the only community in India with the word "Indian" in it. Others may be Tamilian, Punjabi, Sikh, but we have "Indian" in ours, and we're proud to have it because we were born and bred here, studied here, go to schools here.

'We're also the only community in India without a state. We adopt the state wherever we were born.'

Like Peggy Cantem, Harry had read *Bhowani Junction* and seen the 1956 film. 'Lots of things are different now,' he said. '*Bhowani Junction* was a railway story. My father was a driver on the railways and I studied in the railway Anglo-Indian school, so lots of memories are there. John Masters must have had a lot of Anglo-Indian friends or he would never have written so feelingly.

'The major change is that we don't have jobs in railways now. Lots of Anglo-Indian girls and boys are taking up jobs mostly in the private sector – the hotel industry, call centres, as medical transcribers, lots of other jobs that in those days, the 1950s, they probably would never have looked at.

'But now we don't have a quota in government jobs. The quota has been recalled, and there is so much competition. Even if they have good qualifications, if they apply for a job on the railways today, there is so much corruption, and we can't bribe people with money we don't have.'

There was a pause as the chai arrived and was handed round, together with glasses of water.

'You like to have some biscuits?' Harry asked. It was a charmingly relaxed scene on a sweltering Indian afternoon. 'Youngsters have changed a lot,' he continued. 'They are now more responsible, getting a good education, good jobs. They're more serious about life in India. And people are not having so many children – they're stopping after three kids. I knew someone in my home town who had twenty-one children – can you believe that? He used to forget their names because so many children he had. He'd say, "Come daughter, come son".

'I come from a family of five, and some of my uncles and aunts had eight, nine, ten children. But now everything is changing. Our youngsters are more knowledgeable about these things. More children means more financial difficulties, and we're not earning that much, unfortunately. If you have two, you can look after them much better.

'Older Anglo-Indians,' he added, 'have good words to say for British people. They have the Queen's picture on their walls. They identify with British people rather than Indian. Still that culture goes on.'

As we already knew from Peggy and Cheryl – and were to hear many more times over the years – 'that culture' included Christmas balls and dinner dances with bands playing.

'Being Christian, being Anglo-Indian, means having a good time and not thinking too much about the future,' laughed Harry.

He himself had never been to Britain, and thought few Anglo-Indians now saw it as their 'mother country'.

'People have gone beyond that stage. In the old days, Anglo-Indians identified themselves with their British past – they always felt England was their home. Even with names like D'Cruz or Pereira or D'Souza, they still identified with English people. So when they left, they wanted to go there as well and it was always called home by people living before Independence.

'But not any more. Now, this is our home. You ask any youngster and they will say that. I'm sure if you ask that young man, he would also say India is our home. We never think about England like people used to before Independence.'

The young man at the photocopier smiled shyly and nodded.

'So wherever you are born, you think of that as your home. And I don't blame those youngsters who were born in London or somewhere – they consider Britain their home. They come here and – as you say, it's very noisy, dusty, dirty – so they see lots of things contrary to what's happening in England. So they wouldn't identify with life here.'

Like Peggy and Cheryl, he reckoned the community might eventually die out.

'Yes, it's a great possibility, especially among people outside India. People I know, they have married Australian men or women, Canadians – so the community is diminishing, integrating into other societies. Their children have nothing to do with the motherland. I reckon it's going to happen very fast. Another forty years, and we will lose our identity, because most who migrated abroad are now in their seventies. In another ten years, they may not be alive to tell the tale.

'So the younger ones now consider themselves Ozzies or whatever. And they cheer for that country's cricket team, not for the Indian team. So yes, we are a dying race, no doubt about it.'

Anglos in the Wind carried matrimonial ads to encourage more marriages within the community. They would say, for instance: 'Anglo-Indian Roman Catholic bachelor, 32 years, 5ft 7ins tall, BSc graduate, working in the Middle East, God-fearing with sober habits, seeks alliance from an Anglo-Indian spinster from India or abroad. Please reply to AITW, box number…'

Or: 'Anglo-Indian Roman Catholic parents invite alliance for their 30-year-old son, 5ft 11ins tall, wheatish complexion, well-built and handsome, working in the Indian Navy. He's God-fearing, sincere, kind and home-loving. Spinster may apply…'

Parents of daughters were just as keen: 'Anglo-Indian RC parents invite alliance for their 30-year-old daughter, BA, spinster, she is 5ft 3in and teaches in a reputed school in Mumbai. Good-natured bachelors with sober habits from India and abroad may write with personal details…'

As we contemplated our own good natures and sober habits, we were joined by a pretty woman in a floral top and knee-length skirt with kind eyes and a big smile. In her early thirties, Sharon Emmett ran her own charity, Smile Cares, which supported Anglo-Indian single mothers, elderly people abandoned by their children, and education and welfare projects for poor children within the community.

'We pay their school fees,' she said, 'school uniform, shoes, tuition fees so they can be educated fully. Because they come from very poor families, and their parents are not educated so much, they earn maximum seventy-five rupees a day – around one pound – which is not sufficient for three meals a day and to pay rent for a house.' Sharon's parents and grandparents were themselves Anglo-Indians: 'So I am a full Anglo-Indian,' she laughed. 'I am British, Irish – my mum's mother has a birth certificate that says she's an Irish person – and half of my dad's family are British. But I've never been to England myself. Even my husband, Justin, is Anglo-Indian. He can trace his family to England and Ireland – he's traced them from the internet. And our son Jonathan is Anglo-Indian.'

She hugged the young boy who had come with her. 'He is eleven years old, studies in seventh grade. For a child like him to come up in life in Chennai is very difficult nowadays,' she added. 'We are given no privileges, so it's difficult to come up in society. There's a lot of discrimination. Other castes have privileges, but we don't, except in Anglo-Indian schools, where we pay a little lesser fee than other castes. But at college, we have no privileges.'

Clare showed her some of the matrimonial ads in the magazine. By Sharon's reckoning, three-quarters of Anglo-Indian marriages were love marriages. Justin, she told us, had been a classmate of her brother's: 'We were good friends, then we fell in love, so finally we just got married. It just happened like that! I wouldn't have married a person outside the Anglo-Indian community because I feel comfortable with my own people. Our ways and habits are different from that of Indians, the style of living is different, their food habits, the way they move, the way they talk – we have the liberty to do so many things. We mix together at parties, meet in church and through friends… That's how we get to know each other.

'Our homes are neatly kept, and we have different rooms – a kitchen, a dining room, a hall. We have a partition where we have a dining table. We don't have Indian things in our home. Although India is our home, we live – what you say? – like English people live.

'As for cooking – generally our cooking is very different. We have coconut rice and ball curry, devil's chutney and biryani and vindaloos. Our taste is much different from theirs – we eat very spicy food!' She laughed.

The following morning, we took a taxi across town to visit two more Anglo-Indians Harry had arranged for us to see: June Beale and her friend Sheila Tully. June's scrupulously neat apartment was in an upmarket part of town, in an exclusive new block, with a central garden atrium.

June, an elegant, gracious woman in black slacks and blue jumper, gave orders to her servant Joseph, a shy middle-aged Indian Christian. 'He's getting us coffee with milk – but Joseph, I don't think they require sugar.'

The living room had Egyptian prints on the walls, Capodimonte figurines on the shelves, and an all-purpose British-American-European feel.

When Clare said it could be in Surrey or Berkshire, there was so little sign of India inside, June replied: 'Thank you for that compliment. We like to have a Westernised home. My son-in-law, Kevin Fernandez, his parents live in London, in Kent, so all my ornaments are from there. I have visited it once, and it also felt like home.

'And Karen, my daughter, works for Singapore Airlines, so every year she goes abroad and from each place she brings something back. So those pictures' – she pointed to Millais's *Ophelia* and other classic prints – 'are from the US. Now they've opened up the markets so much, you can find anything here in India from all over the world.'

Her great-grandfather had been British, and she and her husband Nigel were cousins.

'His father and my mother are brother and sister. My husband looks British – he has to carry an Indian passport to prove he's not!'

Would it bother her if people abroad thought she was Indian?

She shrugged. 'I have my own identity and don't care what people think of me, as long as I get what I want from there and enjoy my holiday. I'm proud to be Anglo-Indian.

'I feel very much at home over here. Although we have problems with noise pollution, car pollution and cleanliness in India, I have a very comfortable life. I have Joseph, and I have housemaids to do the work, so it's the best of both worlds.'

As though on cue, Joseph reappeared carrying a tray set with a coffee jug and neat china cups and saucers. He put them down on the low teak table, then brought another tray of salad and tuna sandwiches, cut into perfect triangles.

'Let's have a munch,' smiled June.

As we munched, June told us more about herself and her family. Until the birth of her first grandchild, she had been a teacher. But she wanted to help care for her granddaughter. She was also involved in the Forum of Anglo-Indian Women, working for, she said, 'the upliftment of the needy in our community, especially Anglo-Indian women... Whatever funds we get, we channel to help the underprivileged.'

Like Sharon, she was dressed Western-style. 'Our generation, we normally keep to Anglo-Indian style – that is, Western.' She laughed. 'I can't wear the sari – even to tie it is a problem – but the sari looks good. When I used to work as a teacher, our school used to take in the cream of society, so then we feel more comfortable when we wear a sari or salwar kameez. But normally we'd be in skirt or blouse.'

Clare touched on the awkward issue of Anglo-Indian women having once been seen as 'women of easy virtue'.

June looked embarrassed. 'In olden days, they were marked that way, because they were pretty. But, um, what should I say? It's not like that now. I mean, it's there in every community but the Anglo-Indian is more open, that's why the Anglo-Indian is also targeted. Even if you look at Indian films, if they have a dancer, or a highty-flighty type, they'll name her Sherelle or Ruby, an Anglo-Indian name, never one of their names. So they still have that prejudice.'

We moved on to the safer topic of entertainment.

'We love our entertainment, our dances and music – everything from slow foxtrot to disco to rap and reggae. In the Anglo-Indian home, there's definitely a sound system – when working in the kitchen, there'll be music playing. I'm very fond of country music, my daughter and son-in-law prefer rap and hip-hop, my husband loves to listen to piano music, saxophones – we love all music. Music is the spice of life.'

It echoed what Sharon had said earlier: 'At school we took part in concerts and that. We were taught to dance – at that time, it was all jives and waltzes. Now, I listen to country, pop, rock, Western, I sing in a choir – we sing all sorts of music, a lot of Handel and Bach, a lot of country and western. I've been doing that from the age of three, in the Emmanuel Methodist choir.'

At this point, Joseph ushered in a sensible-looking woman in her sixties, June's friend and fellow women's forum council member, Sheila Tully. Before retirement, she had been 'confidential secretary' to the chief executive of three companies. 'I'm called Sheila because my grandfather was English,' she said. 'And I've been there ten times because my sister has been there for the last forty-five years, and my daughter lives there, in Croydon.

'I like the cold in England,' she laughed, 'because I'm only there on holidays. Another thing is – compared to India, everything is so disciplined in foreign countries. You stand in queues! And – well, June's home is beautiful, and seventy per cent of Anglo-Indian homes are very well kept, and when you go to England, it's the same there. You have washing machines, and the clothes smell so beautiful because of the detergents.

'All your houses are built to certain standards and specifications, compared to life down here. I love England.'

Although both she and June had married into the Anglo-Indian community, not everyone did – including Sheila's daughter, whose British husband was of Sri Lankan descent. One day, Sheila, who was a widow, hoped to join them and their children in the UK.

'For many years,' said June, 'we would try to find a good alliance for Anglo-Indian girl with Anglo-Indian boy, try to matchmake. It is only now that Anglo-Indians are so scarce that we look at Indian relationships. So many Anglo-Indian women marry Indians now. So Mrs Krishna could be an Anglo-Indian woman, Mrs Brahmasubramanyam could be Anglo-Indian. They have merged well – they marry into Indian culture and give their children names like Sneha or Sabrina or Nisha. British and Indian mix!'

❖ ❖ ❖ ❖

Before travelling up through India to Jhansi, over nine hundred miles away, we took the overnight Charminar Express to Hyderabad and arrived in time for Christmas Eve dinner at the Amrutha Castle. This curious, turreted, pseudo-Bavarian hotel appeared to have been inspired by Neuschwanstein Castle, with crossbows and suits of armour lurking around every corner. We ate Indian food in a Germanic restaurant with a soundtrack of Australian parodies of carols and festive songs:

> *Jingle bells, jingle bells, jingle all the way;*
> *Christmas in Australia on a scorching summer's day.*

Clare was making a *Woman's Hour* feature about women prisoners whose children were in jail with them, so we drove to the Central Jail, not a place high on many tourist itineraries. We were hoping to arrange permission to interview some female prisoners, but it was a slender hope; we had already had plenty of experience of the slowly turning wheels of official, bureaucratic India. The prison director listened impassively to Clare's request, picked up the phone, had a short conversation, put down the phone and turned to us.

'When would you like to see the women?'

'Well, I appreciate that it's Christmas Eve…'

'How about now?'

Everything is possible in India.

CHAPTER 9

'THE PEAFOWLS ARE...
DANCING AND PRANCING'

Our night train to Jhansi, the Hyderabad-Nizamuddin Dakshin Express, took just short of twenty-four hours to cover nearly eight hundred miles. It dawdled through the following day, pausing at village halts where groups of old men squatted on the platform and children tended herds of goats. Occasionally it stopped in the middle of a scrubby nowhere, as though deliberating whether to carry on or not. For most of the morning we shared the carriage with just five other people and a scurrying mouse. We breakfasted on rubbery omelettes and lunched on peppery tomato soup (scattered with croutons which the attendant scooped out of his jacket pocket by the fistful) followed by sloppy curry in tinfoil containers.

Jhansi's station signs loomed out of a murky fog at 10.10pm. A pair of child acrobats, perhaps seven or eight years old, were performing on the platform. One banged a drum while the other, with a painted 'toy soldier' moustache, did cartwheels, handstands and backflips. Thanks to the railway guide I'd been reading on the train, I could have told them that they were performing on the world's seventh-longest railway platform (2,525 feet). But I kept it to myself.

❖ ❖ ❖ ❖

We had breakfast the following day with Roy, Leela and Peggy. In the sunshine, the bungalow's garden looked bright, neat and clean, like a highly coloured painting in a Ladybird book. It was ever more an oasis in a town of dust and ever-increasing pollution. Roy seemed, as he so often did, less relaxed and more preoccupied than in the villages.

Chuman Lal, the elderly 'boy' in white, moved silently backwards and forwards from the kitchen in the same uniform as on that first evening – Nehru cap, gloves, plimsolls – serving the half-grapefruits, porridge, poached eggs on toast and marmalade. The surreality of it wasn't lost on us during this visit – particularly when, three days later, we returned for lunch with the same trio and Devera, or Dev, an Anglo-Indian friend of Peggy's whom we would meet on many subsequent visits.

At one point, Dev turned to me, pointing at Clare. 'And she is your beloved?' she asked.

With Roy's increasing deafness and booming voice, conversations were often loud, with Leela screeching and Dev's voice swooping like a coloratura bird, her hands fluttering like wings. All sorts of confused literary scenarios came to mind – Dev as Dickens's Miss Flite straying into Lewis Carroll's chaotic tea party with a Chekhovian collection of provincial eccentrics far from Delhi/Moscow.

Before we left, Clare said we were going to the Sadar Bazaar. 'Avoid the most costly Johnnies,' Dev warned, knowing the stallholders better than us.

The round of meals began again. Peggy invited us to lunch with an Anglo-Indian friend who brandished a knuckleduster of rings on his fingers. Pastor Rao, the great reciter of Churchill's speeches, turned up again and kissed Clare's hand. We ricocheted between Roy's and Peggy's homes, a breakfast here, a lunch there, a sense of something between amazement and amusement everywhere and generally sharing tables with the same cast of guests. Breakfast at Peggy's would generally be a bowl of 'rumble tumble' eggs, though she invariably also brought out a plastic box of cheese slices.

Several times over our stay she took us to the European cemetery – 'the dead centre of the dead centre of India' as she called it. They were the first of many visits with her, and the first of many hints dropped about donations for its upkeep. We rarely left without letters to send to the Commonwealth War Graves Commission and BACSA, the British Association for Cemeteries in South Asia, once we were back home.

She and Roy had launched a restoration project. 'I want to give the dead the dignity they deserve,' she said, before explaining the reasons behind her campaign. 'I was once at a funeral there and I saw a lady almost slip into a grave because the grass was taller than her, about six feet high. Someone said: "My God, this is the last place I'd want to be buried in!" And then it struck me – "Peggy, *do* something for this place." A lot of history is buried here and history has to be preserved. We should not lose our heritage.

'When I took over in 1984, it was all forest, thick with equatorial forestation. Three decades of neglect: it was worse than jungle! No graves were visible, animals were destroying everything – there were hyenas, there were jackals, there were foxes, reptiles of all sizes… You just could not penetrate it. Huge palm trees and fronds from creepers were making it dark and dismal. It was frightening. There were snakes falling on your head; once there was a huge python. I couldn't believe it. I saw it going into a grave. Come...'

She called Anish and the three of us somehow squeezed into his autorickshaw – 'My BMW – bum-wobbler!' she laughed – and rattled across town to the wider avenues of the cantonment area, dotted with smart army bungalows. Peggy tutted, however, at the occasional pool of muddy water alongside the road: 'They are making it into a cesspit!'

Anish veered suddenly to the left and we bumped over the rough open land in front of the cemetery gates, where we juddered to a halt. Over the fifteen-minute journey, Peggy's mobile phone had constantly pinged. A dog stirred lazily in the sunshine, a tethered goat bleated plaintively and two small children ran excitedly out of the chowkidar's small brick house, whose sign showed it dated back to 1832.

We helped Peggy out of the rickshaw and the children followed us to the sprucely repainted ochre-and-terracotta gatehouse, with its poignant Mutiny memorials. In contrast to its overgrown state when we first visited, the cemetery had been almost completely cleared of vegetation. 'We never knew we had so many people here!' said Peggy.

The restoration was, obviously, helpful for visitors – many from Britain and Australia – trying to find long-dead relatives. But, with its uprooted trees and scrubby earth, it now looked rather bleak and clinical. Its air of overgrown romanticism had been purged; the grieving marble statues looked lonely. But, as Peggy pointed out, the scorpions and cobras once lurking there had now gone and 'the peafowls do not dirty up the graves'.

The clearance project, which Peggy called 'Operation Cemetery', was costing eighty thousand rupees; so far she had raised fifty thousand. The major problem was disposing of the cleared foliage; bonfires could not be lit in the cemetery due to the nearby army ammunition dumps. As 'Honorary Custodian', she employed three men to keep the cemetery clear, paying each of them 250 rupees a month, with a female chowkidar paid a similar amount. At the time the exchange rate was eighty-four rupees to the pound. Her vision, she said, was to create 'a Garden of Remembrance and a tourist attraction… Come, I will show you round.'

A Lambretta throbbed up and a dark-haired woman wearing a black leather jacket over her salwar kameez dismounted.

'Here's Buddie come,' said Peggy. 'Compliments of the season, Buddie!'

'Compliments of the season to you too, Aunty!' said Buddie, who ran the Little Angels kindergarten where Cheryl worked. Her actual name was Claudette Hars, she told us, and she had a twin brother called Claude (nicknamed Buddha) and a sister called Pearline (Buboo).

She joined what was now quite a procession – Clare and me, Anish, Peggy, the chowkidar, his two children and an inquisitive dog.

'The peafowls are a glory in the evening,' Peggy enthused. 'You wait for the sundown and you will see them dancing and prancing all over the place. We have partridges and quails and wild hare: they are famous in this cemetery. They have full liberty.'

Three peacocks and six peahens had gathered in a field beyond the cemetery wall, grazing, occasionally strutting and shrieking.

'Let it get dusk and then all the madams will jump over the wall and do their majestic dance! See, that fellow's a peacock. He's making tracks to jump over the wall here, then he'll give one call and all the madams will fly there. But the jackals are hovering around' – there were two, prowling around quietly and gracefully – 'so they are a little wary. They normally roost on that mango tree.' And then, with the abrupt change of tone that always took us by surprise: 'When there was no restriction on shooting, we used to make peacock roast. We put bacon on the breast so it was not so dry.'

A spectacularly colourful flock of Indian rollers, or blue jays, flew overhead, honking like geese.

'Now the peacock fellow is going back and none of his dames are following him.'

Buddie was talking in Hindi to the chowkidar, so Peggy dropped her voice.

'She is the daughter of Mrs Jacobs,' she explained. 'Now she has a school of her own with her mother – it goes up to five years. She's going to be my successor here, God willing, so I am giving her an idea of how the cemetery has to be run. We have to come here twice a week to see if the work is going on. Otherwise, in India, staff are lax.' She shrewdly returned to the campaigning: 'It costs seventeen thousand rupees a month for the staff alone. Sometimes there is no money and then I have to beg people to give me something towards the cost. God is really helping me and these poor souls. Anish!' she suddenly bellowed. '*Chalo!* Let's go!'

There was an ear-piercing racket as the rickshaw started and spluttered again and we piled back in.

As Anish manoeuvred it slowly around the paths, Peggy continued her guided-tour commentary, shouting over the noise of the engine. Her father and her husband, she said, were buried here. 'And my brother Percy Kane, his grave was there as we entered the gate. Buddie's relations are also buried here.'

'See,' said Buddie, pointing to a nearby grave. 'She was one hundred and two, Gilda Mars.'

Peggy attempted to clarify: 'Gilda Mars was Buddie's brother's wife's father-in-law's...' She trailed off as we all tried to piece together this genealogical jigsaw.

'My aunty's mother-in-law,' explained Buddie. It was easy, we were discovering, to become entangled in the banyan roots of Jhansi's Anglo-Indian family trees.

Anish stopped and laid a garland of marigolds on a small grave. 'See, this is Percy, my little baby brother,' said Peggy, pulling her shawls around her closely. 'I've maintained it and, God willing, I will be buried with him. We never saw each other but we'll be together when we go up to God.'

There was a pause.

'So you see this is one of the best parks in Jhansi. It's become an entertaining place for people, what with the peafowls and the Abbott graves and all.'

To explore the Abbott connection, Roy joined us at the cemetery the following day, and he and Peggy did a circuit of the graves like elderly royals. 'Look at this,' said Peggy. 'Joyce McFarlane. Four years dead already. And poor old Maud has lost her cross.'

Roy gave us a grand tour of his ancestry. 'This black granite one,' he said, stopping at an austere-looking grave. 'That's my grandmother: Linda Kathleen Abbott, died 1942. And here's Uncle George, who died in 1958. Bernadette Enid Cunningham, my father's sister, died 1979. Can it be so long ago? And her husband,

Thomas Glover Cunningham, 1895 to 1982; a good age. And here's their son Thomas Abbott Cunningham, 1927 to 1998. We called him Cookoo Baba.'

We ended at the graves of Lillian and Penny. They were easily the best-kept graves in the cemetery: neat, whitewashed and with borders of pretty flowers. Penny's epitaph was very touching: 'In treasured memory of our precious daughter, Penelope Mary Abbott... You left us broken-hearted, darling. Until we meet again you will always live in the hearts of your mummy and daddy and all those who loved you dearly. Erected by her sorrowing parents Lillian and Roy Abbott.'

Next to it was an empty plot, marked 'Reserved'. 'Reserved for me,' Roy said matter-of-factly.

A few yards away was the grave of Dr Righton, who had posthumously brought us together: 'Dr Major JA Righton, IAMC, 11 Feb 1903 to 14 July 1988. Always remembered with love and affection by brothers Jerry, Walter, Wilfie, and sister Nellie and many friends in Jhansi'. His siblings' names suggested he might also have been Anglo-Indian, but no-one ever confirmed this.

Roy once again said he would spend the rest of his days in India, even though his son and stepson lived in Australia and he had relatives in England. As he had told us before, retiring to England held no allure for him.

Over another lunch at the bungalow – palak paneer and chapatis – Roy told Peggy and Dev that we had gradually brought dinner time at the farms forward from 10.30pm to 9pm. 'You're lucky to have eaten before 11.30,' said Peggy. 'I've told him that Western people must never eat after 9pm.'

Roy's telephone rang and the call lasted half an hour.

'He has verbal diarrhoea,' she giggled as he finally put the phone down. 'And mental constipation.'

At her request, Anish gave us a tour of the town. The Mutiny plaques in the cemetery gatehouse had once been housed in a small temple-like pavilion at the Memorial Well in the market area. 'Constructed by the Britishers in the memory of 66 British', the pavilion had once been at the centre of a beautiful garden in a walled compound. Now the garden had been abandoned to dust and desolation, with debris, including filthy old socks, littered around. The pavilion itself, alongside the well in which many of the victims had perished, was covered with graffiti, with 'Pinky and Raju Ram' scrawling their names for posterity. Behind the compound's containing wall was a shanty settlement of shacks, shops and workshops resounding with the banging and clanging of metal-bashing. It was not a soothing final resting place.

That evening, we caught the Habibganj-New Delhi Shatabdi Express back to Delhi. We sat opposite a female eye specialist and had the sort of unexpected conversation which complete strangers often have in India. We debated the comparative advantages and disadvantages of Western and Eastern ophthalmology before moving on to India's apparent lack of corporate social responsibility beyond the family and family home (neighbours only sweeping the dust from outside their own doors). The eye specialist said she envied Britain's National Health Service and social security system and added that she had visited a few towns in England: 'London, Manchester, Washington.' Another passenger had a factory that made stiffening material for collars and cuffs.

From time to time, I found myself thinking: 'This is where we are. Talking about collar stiffeners on an Indian train. How strange.'

The following April, three months after we arrived back home in Britain, Peggy sent us an aerogramme. True to her secretarial training, it was immaculately typed and tightly spaced to use every available inch of paper. When she handwrote letters, her writing was challenging to read, full of ornate swirls and curls, and she would write in the margins, up the sides, everywhere. Here she reflected on Jhansi's weather:

Our winter is almost drawing to a close. Kashmir and Shimla have had heavy snowfall, and although we are far away from any hill stations, we get the backlash of cold nasty winds, little or no sunshine, intermittent drops of rain, enough to make one miserable. Once the summer starts, by June it is almost impossible to move out of the house after 9am. What with the power cuts and water problems, life becomes a virtual survival of the fittest. In spite of coolers and AC, without electricity it seems pointless and Jhansi, being in the UP, is one of the hottest places. I remain indoors from morning to evening and bear up with the dreadful heat.

CHAPTER 10

MADURAI AND MARRIAGE

Usually, it was fairly easy to reach either Jhansi or Bina by train from wherever we had been. On this brief three-day visit in 2006, however, a little over a year since our last, we had a staggered 1,300-mile journey from Madurai, almost at the southern tip of India, to Chennai. After a time-dawdling eleven-hour wait at the station there, we took another train on to Bina.

Madurai is one of Hindu India's holiest cities and so, naturally, a honeypot for pilgrims. As a result, it was hectic, dusty and suffused with a heady atmosphere of Hinduism. Its vast Meenakshi Temple attracted, we were told, fifteen thousand pilgrims a day. Its gopuras – great, intricately carved towers – loomed over the city, with bug-eyed gods weighing up fish-eyed goddesses. Ash-daubed holy men with painted foreheads, hawkers, touts, beggars with ever-held-out hands, fortune tellers with parakeets imprisoned in tiny cages, dancing elephants, a pandemonium of noise: the visual and aural stimulation was at times overwhelming. Outside the temple, loincloth-wearing men smoked weedy beedis as they lounged on charpoys. Predictably, the city attracted troubled-looking hippies who dangled toddlers on their knees and did their best to ignore us. On the temple wall was a sign: 'All credit cards are accepted for donations'.

We retreated to the Theosophical Society Free Library and Reading Room, which looked little changed inside since about 1900 – dim, dusty and full of antique glass-fronted bookcases with rusty locks. Housed in them were *A Short History of Free Thought*, *Ancient*

India as Described by Ptolemy, books on the French philosopher Diderot, and works by Bertrand Russell and the Indophile theosophist and campaigner Annie Besant. With its garden of tulsi trees, it was a tiny enclave of quiet learning surrounded by streets filling up with new hotels.

One of the city's proudest possessions was the dhoti Gandhi was wearing when he was shot in Delhi in 1948, its bloodstains faded to pale brown. The central exhibit in the Gandhi Memorial Museum, it was displayed in a glass case sealed with masking tape. With it were his slippers, spectacles, pillow, the vegetable bowl he had used during the last year of his life, and a length of yarn he had spun. A copy of a letter addressed to 'Herr Hitler, Berlin, Germany' had been sent just before the outbreak of war. 'You are today the one person in the world who can prevent a war which may reduce humanity to the savage state,' wrote Gandhi.

Displays railed against 'the period of British conquest and rule of India, a period of slavery and humiliation, leading finally to a new birth of the nation through struggle and sacrifice'. English 'high-handedness' had left Indians 'bursting inside with discontent and fury'.

After an overnight journey to Chennai on the Madurai-Chennai-Egmore Pandian Express, we spent most of the day at the Taj Connemara hotel, and had lunch at its new Verandah restaurant. The city's 'smart set' were out in force, piling their plates skyscraper-high from the buffet. We ordered asparagus risotto with sun-dried tomatoes and tomato pasta with olives and basil – and felt utterly effete. Afterwards, we strolled down to one of the great Chennai institutions – a branch of Higginbothams bookshop, one of a cherishable chain operating across India. Many of its station bookstalls offered *Sherlock Holmes*, Agatha Christie, Kipling, *Mein Kampf*, the lighter Dickens, *Femina* and *Savvy* (leading Indian women's magazines), as well as rail timetables and atlases.

It was time to catch the resoundingly named Chennai-Delhi-Sarai-Rohilla Grand Trunk Express. On the station four porters were playing chequers, using stones and a 'board' scratched on the platform with a knife.

We shared the compartment with an Indian businessman who, unexpectedly, was an expert on both Lord Linlithgow, the 1930s viceroy, and the fields of crops we were passing. The journey should have taken around twenty-eight hours but set off two and a half hours late and lost a further two and a half hours on the way.

We had dinner, 'bed tea', breakfast, lunch, another dinner and three large bottles of mineral water. The total cost for both of us was 226 rupees – about fifteen rupees, or fifteen pence, a meal. 'Meals on trains are very costly,' said the businessman. He shook his head and then pointed eagerly at a passing maize field.

Indian rail journeys represent a different concept of time – what Indians call 'unexpected time', to contemplate or interact. Back home, we'd spend train journeys working, reading or taking in the view. In India, journeys became opportunities to talk to complete strangers about anything from the price of white radishes to the finer points of tantric meditation. By the time fellow passengers got off, we'd all be exchanging business cards and pledging eternal friendship.

Earlier on this trip, for instance, we'd sat opposite a man from the Ministry of Human Resources and a young dentist who'd been having an animated conversation about her work. As we sat down, the man from the Ministry leaned across to us and confided: 'In matters of oral hygiene, India leads the world.' Long stretches of Hindi were punctuated by words like 'haemoglobin' and 'diabetes'. As they explored the exciting world of dental cavities, the man from the Ministry reached into his bag and offered us a couple of guavas: 'Very good for indigestion.'

Gradually everyone within earshot was drawn into the discussion, which switched into English for our benefit. A student from Chennai was fascinated by the idea of dental floss and a man across the aisle who slurped his tea made the odd contribution about root-canal work. Mostly, though, he spent his time dissecting family matters with his mother-in-law, a tiny, wizened woman whose voice suggested a small, rusty hinge. They talked straight through the silent, sullen young man sitting between them. A man in a woolly hat further up the compartment looked up from his magazine when the subject turned to fillings. He smiled, revealing an impressive array of them.

We were scheduled to arrive at Bina at 8pm but were delayed until 1am. The 'brigands' Roy had sent to meet us and drive us to the village were slapping themselves to keep warm. We passed the scavenged ribcage of the cow that had died four years earlier, now rearing up like church vaulting. We finally got to bed at 3am. Two hours later, the temple drummers started, parading round the village shouting, 'Ram! Ram!'

Next morning, as before, a table was brought out on to the lawn so that we could write up our journals, surrounded by marigolds, sweet peas and nasturtiums. Four women were painting the brick borders of the flower beds red, using stiff brushes without handles: it was a curiously *Alice in Wonderland*-like scene. A hoopoe strutted around, poking its beak into the soil. Another bird, less flamboyant, flew over to a branch. What was it, we asked one of the servants.

'*Chidiya*,' he said.

We later asked Roy about this unfamiliar *chidiya* bird.

'*Chidiya* just means bird,' he said.

Lakshmi-Bai's three daughters – Kirti, Nilum and Maya – came to show us their photo albums. Studio portraits of them, Roy explained, had been carefully tinted to emphasise the coveted 'wheaten complexion'. Kirti, the youngest, was still living at home; Nilum, married with one child and another imminent, was living with her in-laws; Maya, the eldest, was going through a divorce and had returned to the family home. She seemed very independent-minded. Roy was clearly fond of them, treating them as a benign uncle might treat his nieces.

'Over here, marriages are arranged by the parents, so girls can't say "No, I don't want to get married",' he told us. 'Girls are traditionally controlled entirely by the parents where marriage is concerned. But that's changing fast. They want to see the boy before they arrange the marriage.'

He acted as translator for our conversation. Did Maya know any other single women, asked Clare.

'No-one in the village,' said Roy. 'But she's talking about a lady who stood in the last election. She's a spinster, but then she's a politician. She's more interested in politics than in getting married.'

He talked to her again in Hindi, then turned back to us.

'I asked – if a well-educated girl has been to university and got a degree and is now a doctor or an engineer, why should she have to get married? She says very few girls can be independent through studying, learning a trade or skill and not marrying after that. Girls who aren't educated can't be independent; they have to marry. According to the village culture, they can't say they won't get married. They will be dictated to by their parents and will have to listen to them.'

If a girl wasn't interested in marriage, he added, the assumption would be that she was having an affair.

'And the worst thing that can happen here is for a girl to have a baby outside marriage. That's what they really fear. It would be very difficult then to get her married. There was a case over here. A young girl who'd had a baby out of wedlock threw it in a well and killed it. She was afraid of the repercussions. Her future would be finished. But you can't keep a thing like that quiet in a small village. Everyone found out.'

At seventeen, Kirti was not yet married.

'That wouldn't worry us, but for them it's panic stations. People are saying: "She's mature now, so why isn't she married yet?" And if they get too old, they can't find boys.'

So basically, the family home was simply transitional? Parents brought up their daughters to pass them on to someone else?

'Yes, absolutely, put in a nutshell.'

Kirti, however, was clearly as independent-minded as Maya.

'Lakshmi-Bai says she's not going to marry any Tom, Dick or Harry. Kirti says he has to be a decent boy, someone she approves of. There have been one or two boys come over to see her and she shot them down in flames. "That fellow eats too much tobacco, his mouth is full of paan. I don't like him!"'

In Hindi, Lakshmi-Bai added: 'I was fifteen or sixteen when I got married and I had my first baby seven years later. Now I'm not keeping well, so – I would like to see her married.'

Later, we drove into Khurai to buy beer and toilet paper for the train. 'Nearest toilet paper is in Sagar town,' said one stallholder. 'Thirty-five kilometres.'

Toilet paper-less, we left on a morning train to Delhi. A man on the platform was selling waterproof watches. To show how dependable they were, he displayed them submerged in jars of water.

CHAPTER 11

A VILLAGE WEDDING

A year on, in March 2007, we were back at the farms after five weeks exploring some of the hill stations of north and northeast India. The 'big three' – Simla (called Shimla since 1972), Mussoorie and Darjeeling – were the Raj's boltholes when the summer heat of the plains got too much. To reach them from Calcutta (now Kolkata) or Delhi, the sahibs and memsahibs switchbacked thousands of feet up into the Himalayan foothills in their sola topis and broad-brimmed sun hats. They stayed in bungalows called Walnut Grove and Wisteria, Westward Ho! and Whitby, and possibly dreamed wistfully of 'home'. After Partition, they left behind plenty of this half-timbered Indian Inglenookery. It was as if the Home Counties had been hoisted into the Himalayas but, as time passed, the old colonial outposts were gradually engulfed by modern India.

Returning to Delhi, before once again catching the Nizamuddin-Ernakulam Mangala Lakshadweep Express for an overnight stay at Roy's farms, we drove to an out-of-town bank to change traveller's cheques. It proudly advertised that it was 'fully computerised'. In practice, this meant that the computers duplicated all the bureaucratic form-filling which was such a diverting feature of Indian life. They created what were effectively electronic carbon copies. So each transaction now took twice as long as it had done before.

I mentioned to the counter assistant that this duplication didn't happen in the UK. 'Ah, but comparing India and the UK is like comparing a cow and an elephant,' he said and hurried away.

Mulling this over, we drove back into town, where we passed the barracks of two army regiments: 'The Pulverisers' and 'The Sure-Shooters'.

Tony, a young friend of Roy's, met us off the train in Khurai and showed us his father's grain store. Stockades of sacks filled with red lentils reared up to the roof. Next door was a beedi-packing warehouse where a dozen men sat on the floor parcelling up the slender cigarettes, a dozen at a time, in brown paper, using their feet as well as their hands to crease and fold the paper.

On the way to the farms, we halted at a level crossing as two trains passed. In the West, cars and bicycles generally queue patiently behind the barriers; here they pressed close against them, spreading out beyond the sides of the road, horns honking. As someone once joked to us: 'An Indian queue is one person deep and forty people wide.' Cyclists and pedestrians dodged under the barriers to cross the tracks and one motorcyclist lifted the barrier in order to carry his bike over the track. 'This is the India,' said Tony.

At the bungalow, Roy, his hair ever more hennaed, told us that one of the local Khurai 'scandal sheets', as he called them, had recently run a gossip piece about him. They described him as an Englishman who owned land in India and ruled his villages in the way the British ruled during the Raj. He shrugged it off. 'They can write what they like,' he said.

As we wandered round the village, we involuntarily became a pair of Pied Pipers leading a procession of children around the twisting alleyways and trim courtyards of single-storey houses. Lines of washing were strung across the alleys and calves wandered freely.

On our second evening, Roy took us to Shyam's granddaughter's wedding in a shamiana or ceremonial tent erected in the nearby village of Talapar. As he started the car, he paused and said: 'I wonder if I should take my revolver.' There was a danger of encountering dacoits, or armed robbers, so a guard with a rifle and a cartridge-belt across his shoulder joined us. During the wedding, he stood behind us.

Roy's arrival drew a big crowd. A local bard sang a song of welcome, in a voice so penetrating that it seemed to come from a loudspeaker lodged in his throat. He led us in procession to three thrones-of-honour for the Captain-Sahib and his guests: plastic chairs, unlike the gilded thrones waiting for bride and groom. The crowd stood staring at us, occasionally whispering to each other or giggling. A seventy-five-year-old village elder stalked up to the front on tall, thin legs, like a crane. His skin looked parched, hard and stretched; he wore scuffed old shoes and a weathered Nehru jacket fully buttoned up. He observed us for a few minutes then walked impassively away.

The village barber was there for last-minute trims. How much would a haircut be, I asked Roy. 'Oh, forty annas,' he said (there were one hundred annas to the rupee). 'But you might make it up to a rupee.'

Shyam himself had dyed his grey hair black since we had last seen him. 'You look so young now, you could be the bridegroom,' Clare teased him.

We arrived at 7.45pm, but there was no sign of the baraat, the wedding procession led by a brass band that would bring the groom, wearing maharajah costume and Persian slippers and riding a white horse, to meet his bride-to-be. Indian wedding bands often seemed to have been hand-picked from a register of the world's noisiest musicians. As they blared their trumpets and bludgeoned their drums, they could sound like military-band jam sessions played backwards. Baraats would wind their way slowly along streets, sparklers flashing, fireworks exploding, men carrying chandeliers of light bulbs on their heads. The procession – which bystanders were often invited to join – would stop every few yards so that guests could dance, arms wildly punching the air, as the bridegroom's father waved banknotes over the bandsmen's heads before handing them over. This unfortunately encouraged them to play even louder.

At 9.30pm, however, we still didn't know where our baraat was or how long it would take to arrive. To pass the time, we smiled a great deal.

Eventually, some of the wedding gifts were brought in. A motorcycle, ridden the length of the shamiana; a three-piece suite; a wardrobe; a metal almirah for storing clothes. We wanted to leave but had to stay until we had presented our gifts of money to the bride, who had yet to meet her husband and was being made up in a 'beauty parlour' in a private corner of the shamiana. The female guests had gathered around her and drew veils over their faces as men passed.

A couple of musicians arrived and the men started dancing to the raucous rhythmic music of shawms and tabla. There was much drumming and dancing in the moonlight but, with no visible sign of the baraat, we left at around 10.30pm.

Even at this late hour, we sat down to dinner back at the bungalow, celebrating the wedding at one remove with 'Superstrength' Zingaro beer. 'There's a lot of it being produced in India these days,' said Roy. 'For some people, the main aim of drinking is to get drunk as quickly as possible.'

As we went to bed, he was talking about that year's spectacular mango crops which would push the price down to two rupees a kilo (around ten mangoes) – unimaginably cheap in the UK.

On our last night at the farms, Lakshmi-Bai's daughter Nilum and two-year-old granddaughter Mini joined us in the living room to watch the BBC World News. Without being asked to, Lakshmi-Bai started massaging Clare's legs, rubbing in almond oil, before massaging mine. The news showed smart-suited politicians at European trade talks in sleek modern buildings. It was such a world away.

The following morning, we caught the Punjab Mail from Bina back to Delhi. Behind us on the train a couple of passengers were keeping the present participle alive. 'We were not knowing that one dog is there… Very carefully I was consulting with that person. For two years he is struggling to get recognition.'

CHAPTER 12

MOONLIGHT PICNICS IN THE JUNGLE

It would be more than two years before we were back in Jhansi. In the meantime, we received a couple of letters from Roy. As usual, they were written in a fluent, businesslike hand but were sometimes tricky to decipher. They were sealed with a small adhesive label bearing his address and a drawing of a palm tree, a rather exotic touch for utilitarian Jhansi.

In the first letter, he described problems with his back, hips and knees. 'If you think there's not much hope for me, don't despair, I'm entertaining the same thought myself! No way am I giving up & the battle goes on & I hope that in the end I'll be the winner.' He added: 'Hope you are having a good summer. At least it wasn't too bad when the Wimbledon tennis was on.'

As an 'avid tennis fan', he was disappointed to have missed TV coverage of the men's and ladies' finals and wondered if we could find a recording of them to send him ('all expenses paid to the penny'). 'The staff keep asking about you and very much want you to honour them with your presence. To give them your "*darshan*" (blessing) as it is said over here.'

In his second letter, written in the summer of 2009, he lamented the way his years-long legal case about land rights, being held in Jabalpur, was preoccupying him.

The case drags on endlessly… and by attending in person I think I can bring matters to a head more quickly than the lawyer.… From

Jabalpur, I move on to Bhopal to spend some time with old friends who were once rulers of a small state in MP [Madhya Pradesh]. I feel sorry for them as they have had to come down a lot in life from what they experienced in the past. These are the people who miss the British the most. All you get out of them now is 'Look at the mess self-rule has made of the country'. People talk of progress here since Independence, but it would have been much faster if the British were still here and corruption on a much smaller scale, if at all.

I remember the Raj with great nostalgia and wish I could have seen more of it than I did. I tell people I was born about 50 years too late. If I'd been born right, I'd love to have been a District Commissioner or Forest Officer. What a shame this was not to be!

Leela will soon be back from 'God's Own Country', Kerala. She's been there to spend some time with her parents. Deserves it. Works hard.

We arrived in Jhansi three months later, once again on the Lakshadweep Express from Delhi, where I'd indulged in one of the great rituals of our stays: a haircut at the Verma Unisex Salon in the capital's Jor Bagh enclave. It was an unequivocally upmarket area – even the residents' chauffeurs looked like diplomats.

As ever, we were staying in Jor Bagh with Virgil Miedema and Barbara Spaid and their daughters Stephanie and Allison. Virgil knew more about the history of British India than most Brits ever did. He was fascinated by the old schools, the churches and the hotels, many languishing in far more serious decay than even the Jhansi Hotel, which now displayed a sign proclaiming 'Serving the Nation for Past 110 Years'.

A perfect weekend for Virgil would include a drive around Delhi's imperial sites, admiring the New Delhi that Lutyens had created for George V. One Boxing Day in Darjeeling, he organised a festive walking tour of the town's old British cemeteries. As he once said: 'If you're interested in the British period in India, a lot of it comes alive in the graveyards – so to speak.'

He had introduced us to the Verma Salon in the market a hundred yards from his home and just around the corner from a shop that imported John West tuna and Carr's Table Water biscuits for expats. Roadside flower sellers arranged gladioli, marigolds and roses into exquisite displays and a peanut seller squatted behind a steaming pot of nuts. On the corner, a cobbler sat cross-legged on the pavement surrounded by brushes, hammers, needles and polishes. Small boys brought him parcels of loosely flapping leather that may once have been shoes.

A newspaper stall typically offered acres of baffling headlines – 'Q has taken his money, CBI tells SC...' or 'IA plane wheels jam, jolted TDP bigwigs livid' – and quaintly dated tabloidese. Criminals were 'nabbed' as police 'bust rackets' by 'miscreants'; strikes were 'stirs'; road accidents, however serious, were 'mishaps'.

Across the road, the Verma catered for men and women in separate rooms, both generally humid and scarcely big enough for the barbers and hairdressers to trim a cat's whiskers. Many men had their hair cut by street barbers, who set up chairs at the roadside and propped up their mirrors on a wall or a branch of a handy neem tree. But that wasn't the Verma's style. Its two sturdy chairs and pea-green washbasins attracted a mainly middle-class clientele, which included a fair number of men in late middle age having their greying hair dyed jet-black. The barbers poured what looked like molten tar over their heads and worked it in, as though kneading dough. For all their expertise, however, the result rarely looked convincing and, with their hair slicked back, customers sometimes resembled subcontinental Count Draculas.

Bollywood music played and, from time to time, the radio was tuned to crackly cricket commentaries in Hindi. Waiting customers, however, were generally more preoccupied with their mobile phones. Back in 2007, it seemed the mobile was a gift to India from Nokia, the Hindu god of telecommunications.

The barbers took immense pride in their work and its rituals. These included ostentatiously rinsing combs and scissors in disinfected soap before using them, and ceremonially fixing new blades into cut-throat razors. Customers lounged back in their chairs with greater equanimity than most Western men could have managed while being shaved with such a potentially lethal weapon. The barbers snipped deftly, almost daintily, occasionally standing back to admire their own skill.

There was a complete lack of the chit-chat usual with British barbers – the latest football news, or 'Have you booked your holidays yet?' So customers were lulled into a soothing meditative state, smiling at themselves in the mirror. There was also plenty of time to read the board listing the various treatments on offer: chest hair clean, arms hair clean, fruit facial, head steam, hair spa and, intriguingly, Aroma magic. To have henna applied cost 150 rupees, a 'hair spa' cost 500, and the mysterious-sounding 'rebounding' cost 1,500.

Haircut completed, the barber would, on request, ruffle your perfect coiffure and provide a head massage that began with bright green oil being poured over your hair. He would bang your head with his fists, karate-chop your neck, push you forward and pummel your back with his clenched fists before squeezing your arms as though strangling a snake. The performance would climax with his knuckles rapping on your scalp like castanets. It could have been construed as GBH, but it generally left me feeling exhilarated – and I always slept well afterwards. A haircut here might cost five or six times more than one in Jhansi, but it was a fraction of the cost of one in the UK and offered splendid theatre.

Peggy was waiting for us when our train arrived in Jhansi. She looked older and more bent. Over tea and lurid pink cake at a café near the bazaar, she recalled trips out to Orchha, having 'moonlight picnics' among the deserted ruins of the palaces. 'It was a *jungle*, a real *jungle*, full of insects and creepers and creatures – oh, don't ask! It was full of hairy caterpillars, too. Oooh, they used to climb up the walls. We used to go and burn them…' She laughed at our shocked looks. 'We were youngsters, we used to play hell with them!'

She painted a wonderfully sepia-tinged picture of groups of young people going out to the jungle mid-afternoon, laden with a wind-up gramophone and dance records, and not returning till late.

'We took big hurricane lamps and would pack up our own eats – pilau, some sandwiches, a bottle of squash or lime juice. We'd have moonlight picnics by the riverside, and dancing sessions – we had all the latest hit records. Victor Silvester was our favourite and Benny Goodman – all the jazz musicians we had. Joe Loss – we liked "Chattanooga Choo Choo" – and country and western, Jimmie Rodgers and all those good old-timers.'

Like the Owl and the Pussycat, she and her friends would dance on the riverbank and in the decaying courtyards by the light of the moon.

'We had all the fancy dances – rumba, samba, put your left arm in and all that, shake it all about. But the wild animals! We had to beware of the black-faced fellows, the langurs. One day we stopped by the river and I heard someone shout, "Peggy, get out! There is a black panther coming!"

'Then we would end with "The Last Waltz" and "Who's Taking You Home Tonight?" That was our famous closing item. That's how we would pass our evenings, dancing with Victor Silvester.'

The following day, after breakfast at the Hotel Sita ('The juice is lychee available only,' said the waiter), we inevitably visited the cemetery.

After renovation work costing a lakh – 100,000 rupees – it was spectacularly sprucer than last time, with flowerpots, shrubs and benches, a water pump and lights installed to deter trespassers.

'Look, there is a peacock flying!' said Peggy, still delighted by something she had seen a thousand times before. 'We have one patch that we call their maternity ward because, after the rains, the peahens lay their eggs there. So I won't let the staff touch that plot. And that over there is called the Did-You-Do-It Bird, because that's their call: "Didyoudoit".'

The cemetery walls had been heightened, with barbed wire strung along the top, so the jackals could no longer jump over.

'They were destroying the graves, ruining crosses, ruining plants. You used to hear them crunching the bones of the dead. Now that wildlife is gone, but we still have nilgai, darlings. Huge fellows, like horses, colossal size. They are called blue bulls; they look like deer but they are very aggressive. They can charge at you. They're very good eating but we're not allowed to shoot them. And there used to be cobras here. People say if you kill one, it will haunt you for life.'

Because it was All Souls' Day, we waited around for an open-air Mass, conducted by a Catholic priest with full vestments and incense. The congregation lit candles and scattered marigold petals on relatives' graves. One old lady sat apart from the rest, cross-legged on the grass alongside her husband's grave.

When we later joined Peggy at Roy's bungalow before returning to Delhi, they talked about hunting. 'My father was a great shikari, great hunter,' she said. 'He would sit up on a machan' – a safety platform – 'high up in tree branches with a bird's-eye view.' Then, rather contradicting herself: 'He said you should always fight on equal terms, give them a chance. He shot seventy-seven panthers but not one tiger.'

She paused.

'There are no panthers now,' she added forlornly.

We all thought about that for a moment. Then she rallied.

'And my stepfather, Sidney McFinnegan, was known as "the second Jim Corbett".' Corbett was the hunter-turned-naturalist after whom a major Indian wildlife sanctuary is named. 'And you know, at one time, people would shoot armadillos and stuff them. He was a big fellow, the armadillo.'

Roy glanced across at her and said, almost absently: 'You don't see many armadillos now, either.'

CHAPTER 13

MAY QUEENS AND MONSOON TOAD BALLS

A year later, in the autumn of 2010, with our clothes smelling monsoon-musty, we paid a whistle-stop overnight visit to Jhansi as part of a 2,300-mile rail journey across India. We were travelling from the nation's most westerly station (the port of Okha, in the state of Gujarat, one hundred miles from the Pakistan border) to its most easterly one (Ledo in Assam, near the border with Myanmar). Stopping at, or passing through, six hundred of India's eight thousand or so stations, the journey was conceived as a chapter for *Sunrise on the Southbound Sleeper*, a *Telegraph* anthology of railway journeys.

Before our overnight in Jhansi, we had an even shorter break – nine hours – in Ahmedabad, the Gujarati city celebrated as the home of Mahatma Gandhi's ashram. At the station, a porter took our two heavy cases. We pointed out that they would both wheel along, but it seemed a point of honour for him to carry them on his head.

The ashram, a collection of low buildings beside the Sabarmati river, was an island of calm in a sea of manic traffic noise. Sitting in the bungalow where the Mahatma had lived, a woman was spinning cloth with a biography of Tolstoy open next to her. An exhibition included Gandhi's walking stick, his coconut chopper and a letter addressed simply to 'Gandhiji, New Delhi'. Another correspondent had merely drawn a likeness of the great man on the envelope: no name, no address. Both letters had been safely delivered.

There were aphorisms on almost every wall. 'My feet are tired but my soul is rested', 'Laugh with others not at others', 'Build bridges not barriers', 'Wherever you are confronted with an opponent, conquer him with love', 'Be the change you wish to see in the world'. They were like moral and spiritual versions of the official safety advice signs we regularly saw by the sides of Indian roads.

Jyesh Patel, a young man who had worked to improve conditions in slum communities, was involved in the ashram's education project for young children. 'They have a strong desire to learn about computers, because today computers are necessary,' he said.

What, I wondered would Gandhi have said about that?

'Man is always over machine, not machine over man,' he replied. Many of the ashram's computers had a portrait of Gandhi as their screen saver.

That evening, Ahmedabad station was shrouded in fog and looked evocatively Sherlockian. A hundred-yard-long queue of people was waiting for a local train that stretched several hundred more yards down one platform and disappeared into the mist. When the Sabarmati Express pulled in, passengers boarded in a surprisingly orderly way – not, as sometimes happened, scrambling through the windows. The 'super-slow' train, as Peggy called it, set off at just before 9pm and crawled across India like a gigantic, blue-striped caterpillar.

It was a clammy journey, though after a short shower of rain we picked up the fresh, keen smell of damp vegetation. We often veered off the main line on to a branch line to wait for faster trains to pass. At one station, we waited for half an hour and many passengers – mostly male – got off, bought chai, crisps, pakoras and candyfloss on sticks from vendors and stood talking in small groups. On bigger stations they browsed the book stalls. *Eggs for Delight* and *Mushrooms – A Pocket Companion* were good sellers, said the bookseller. Along the platform a trolley offered a miscellaneous selection of temptations and necessities – belts, plastic jugs, Ludo games, Rubik's cubes and Snakes and Ladders Deluxe.

For all their air of insouciance, passengers on the platform were always on the alert for the engine hoot that meant the train would, in seconds, start pulling slowly away. People would then run to their carriages and hurl themselves through the open doors. The train coursed through the night, hooter blaring. It was answered, hauntingly, by other hooters. Indian trains always look and sound more romantic in the darkness. I lay in my corridor bunk and watched their dark shapes edge out of stations, windows lit, highlighting the passengers within.

We arrived in Jhansi at 5.15 the following afternoon. The train had taken more than twenty hours to cover six hundred miles. A retired colonel along the carriage told us that some services travelled so slowly that passengers sometimes got off to walk alongside their carriage as it dawdled through the countryside. But we were in no hurry.

I had a mission to fulfil at Jhansi station. The previous year I had taken a photograph of one of the porters and used it with a newspaper article on Indian railways. I had brought a copy of the piece to give to him and soon found him. I handed it over, he looked at it, looked at me with some bemusement, said a crisp 'Thank you' and went off to look for new customers.

Peggy met us in a taxi. By this time, we were spending far more time with her than with Roy, who was often away at the farms. As we drove to the Hotel Sita, we passed a retired steam loco smartly painted and given pride of place on a roundabout.

'That's a Puffing Billy,' said Peggy and became suddenly nostalgic for Jhansi's great days as a railway town, when some five thousand men worked as drivers, firemen, guards and ticket collectors and a further five thousand worked in the railway workshop. 'We really liked the British people,' she said. 'There was discipline; there was administration; there was punctuality. The trains kept dead accurate time. But in those days, to work on the steam trains was hell-let-loose, what with shovelling the coal and all.

'In the railway quarter, we very rarely mixed with the people who worked in the government offices and the schools. We were a very strong community. There was a railway school, a railway hospital, the La Scala cinema and over there' – she pointed to the right – 'is the railway HQ. That's where the old Armistice Day service was held.'

Rail workers and their families used to meet every week at the Railway Institute – 'the *most* beautiful place in the world for us railway people' – for bingo, children's games, hockey, football and, crucially, indoor versions of the Orchha dances she'd told us about the previous year. Known as 'Pops', they would last from 8pm to 10pm.

'We used to have fabulous dances – a little waltzing, a little foxtrotting – and a "twilight waltz", with the lights turned off!' Her eyes sparkled with memories. 'Then what-do-you-call-it came in – the twist, disco-dancing. Raymond's Band was the most famous band in Jhansi – all Anglo-Indians – but he lost his players one by one.'

The next morning, we visited her again at her home. Over coffee, she continued painting a romantic picture of the days when Anglo-Indian girls – 'Lovely they were; they won beauty contests' – wore 'flouncy' dresses, with high-heeled stilettos or ballerina pumps.

'Our May Queen Balls were the most outstanding; our girls came full force. We had thirty or forty girls entering – they all wanted to be the Princess of Jhansi. The May Queen used to come out of a beautiful shell when the result was announced – that was her throne. Then the next day she'd be in a cart – her carriage – with a cloud painted at the back. It was beautifully decorated. We used to do it all up in cotton, sprinkled with silver, like snow. And for weddings, they used to have a big heart over the cake filled with confetti. You'd press a button and two angels would pierce the heart and all the confetti would spill out. There was an electrical engineer called Molena, a super engineer – he was European. He used to invent all these things.

'And we had a Monsoon Toad Ball with a competition to find the ugliest man! The ladies were the judges. They would pick the heaviest-looking, the most hideous-looking men they could find.' She laughed her tinkling laugh.

Jhansi's Anglo-Indian community, she said, had been 'in its glory' just before Partition.

'We had a wonderful Anglo-Indian Association, with a very, very strong committee in the railway quarters. There were no intermarriages in those days; people never mixed with Indians to marry them. Jhansi, Sagar, Bina and Delhi – all had big Anglo-Indian communities.

'But after '47, they started to migrate and the community got smaller and smaller. It was almost like an exodus. The people who were left, they had no other alternative but to marry, mixed marriage.'

By the time she took over the Anglo-Indian Association, the community had shrunk to five hundred people plus their offspring.

'We used to buy toys for nine hundred children at Christmas. We had to go out of station to buy them. Our favourite place was either Bombay or Delhi.'

Children had been encouraged to write letters to Santa saying what present they'd like.

'But those little guns for children, we wouldn't give them. They had little pop shots in them, like little corks, and they fired at one another, so we had to be very cautious about buying for them. We had to use our discretion.'

Jhansi's surviving thirty Anglo-Indian families were now 'in old age', she said, because so many younger people had left the town for jobs in Delhi and other cities.

'Some have even migrated to Dubai and the Gulf countries, so it is a dying community, no getting away from it. But people are becoming more conscious of their heritage, the legacy of being an Anglo-Indian. You know, someone once wrote: "The Anglo-Indian has the brains of an Indian and the features of the British".'

Before we could properly dissect this, she veered off to talk about New Year celebrations.

On New Year's Eve, 'no matter where it was, in all the loco sheds in India, all the engines blew their whistles from 11.55 at night right through to 12.05, to bring in the New Year. No matter if they were on the moving trains; they all blew their whistles.'

As if on cue, a train hooter sounded mournfully in the distance. The sound of hooters often punctuated conversations at Peggy's.

'And during the New Year's Eve ball, at 11.55,' she continued, 'an old man – the Old Year – would come in with a big pickaxe.

And a young child in fancy dress, symbolising the New Year, would drop from the top to push him out. The whole stage would be getting brighter and brighter. The decorations were super and we had fabulous prizes for special dances. The person in the best dress would get a hamper from a big shop – whisky, cake, a lovely book, diary, all that. Not in the creation of cats could we have had a better time!'

Before we left, we paid our customary visit to the cemetery. Once again the peafowls were 'dancing and prancing'. We were back at the station just in time to resume our Sabarmati Express journey to Varanasi, almost exactly a day after arriving.

An old man sitting on a bunk across the aisle leaned over and looked me in the eye. 'Because you are from United Kingdom I must treat you as a guest,' he said. Then he leaned back and burped, twice. He spent much of his journey talking in Hindi to the smooth-faced young man sitting next to him. English words and phrases – 'senior citizen', 'a religious point of view' – occasionally popped out, like snatches of copperplate handwriting in pages of Hindi script. He eventually pulled across the curtains of his bunk and burped again from behind them.

We passed pools of white water lilies, egrets perched on cows' backs, people cycling across fields, buffalo basking in rivers and lakes, cotton grass waving in a light breeze, flights of dragonflies darting over the grassland. The scenes encapsulated the lyrical serenity of so much Indian countryside – particularly during and after the monsoon – and just how much of the nation was still rural. It showed why many Britishers stationed in India had loved it so much.

CHAPTER 14

'JHANSI KI RANI' AND 'THE TONY CURTIS OF JHANSI'

We were back on the Sabarmati Express almost exactly a year later, after spending a week in the Gujarati university town of Anand, where Clare had been recording a feature, *Cowdust Time*, for BBC Radio 3. 'Cowdust time' – *godhuli bela* in Hindi – is the magical Indian twilight hour when cattle are herded back to their villages from the fields, kicking up clouds of dust; when farm labourers return home, women light fires for cooking, and villages echo with the bleating of goats and the cries and laughter of children playing. This 'meeting of day and night' had special significance, not just materially but also spiritually. We were to learn a lot more about it over the course of our week in Gujarat.

We had flown from London to Ahmedabad, where Clare had arranged to talk to the artist and art critic Amit Ambalal and his musician sister Sugna Shah. Elegantly dressed in a starched cream and gold silk sari, Sugna played us soulful evening ragas on the sitar in her stylish drawing room, explaining that they 'create a world of their own, a mood of dejection and separation. After day is over, you feel a little tired – "what have I done with my day?" And you go inside yourself. This is the mood of the music, a little bit of sadness because the minor notes give the effect of sadness or surrender to God.

'All our music,' she continued, nodding towards the room's floor-to-ceiling wall painting of Hindu gods and goddesses, 'has connections with Krishna and Radha, which makes it so rich.

The imagination of pure love, of perfect human beings, has been represented by Krishna and Radha, both in music and in paintings.'

To see some of those paintings, we drove across town to the similarly stylish home of her brother. In his garden study, surrounded by his own paintings, he showed us many depictions of Krishna and Radha at twilight. 'When Krishna and his brother and other cowherds bring their cows back from the fields,' he explained, 'their mother performs *aarti* to receive him – the lighting of the lamp. There might be evil spirits in the forest that may harm Krishna, and the lights remove these ill effects. So here we see lot of commotion. Everyone is happy in the palace. The *gopis* – the milkmaids – are telling everyone that Krishna has arrived home safely.

'Krishna himself is in jovial mood, playing his flute. You can see the peacocks and hens are listening, and the *gopis* also listen, like the monkeys and little squirrels – and the gods and their wives in their celestial home in the sky.'

Afterwards, we drove again to Gandhi's ashram, to talk to the Dalit poet Jayant Parmar. He often visited the ashram in the evenings, he told us, to read and write his poetry.

'Evening time is peaceful time,' he said in a soft, kindly voice, 'to relax from physical toil. When you read some poems, that is also prayer. Meditation is running in your body, so it is a good time. Evening gives you message for living more, enjoying life, because the day is short, so enjoy life!'

He read us one of his poems about dusk:

> *In the dust raised by returning cows*
> *Faint stars glow from time to time.*
> *The peepal tree ties bells around its ankles.*

The tinkling sound of bells.
Lit lanterns in the niches
Laughing faces
With peacock feathers,
I'm drawing the moon tikka
On the canvas of the sky
And the dropping leaf of the sun.

From Ahmedabad, we drove on to Anand. It was the tail end of the monsoon, and the sky was overcast, there were puddles everywhere and people wore long plastic macs and used plastic bags as hairnet-like rain hats. With bursts of torrential rain sometimes leaving the streets two feet deep in water, distant peacocks shrieked after every rumble of thunder. We had dinner at the Divine Dining Hall, though the menu at another restaurant tempted us with 'Backed fish', 'Burmish spaghetti' and 'Veg American Chopsey'. As we ate, the waiters grouped themselves around us, watching with great fascination. 'When next you are in Calcutta,' said one, 'you must come to my home.'

We were staying at the VIP Guest House run by Anand University's H M Patel Institute of English in the pleasant, ordered suburb of V. V. Nagar. The emphasis on learning extended to the roadside trees, which were punctiliously labelled 'Sausage tree', 'Rain tree' or 'Margosa tree'.

Parakeets roosted in (unlabelled) neem trees, their screeches mingling with car horns at night, when huge bats flapped around the street lights. A crossroads with a handful of small shops a few hundred yards away could have been used as a film set for an R. K. Narayan novel about everyday Indian life.

In the town centre, shopping was on a less traditional scale. A Big Bazaar had recently opened – a modern mall store with pile-'em-high discount offers. It was a pilgrimage place for the town's new middle-class consumers. Outside, we watched as a mouse scuttled across the pavement and up a man's trouser leg. Giving a shout, he staggered back in classic Norman Wisdom style. We coincided with a Hare Krishna chanting marathon and a festival celebrating Ganesh, the elephant-headed god. All over the city, eight-foot-tall statues of him were erected in brightly lit grotto-shrines.

We had spent many hours acquiring liquor permits (Gujarat is a dry – i.e. non-alcoholic – state) which allowed tourists to buy ten bottles of beer per day. Not refrigerated beer, though. Those were 'the rules', we were told.

To call the Guest House 'VIP' was perhaps stretching things a bit. Our room had the classic features of basic Indian accommodation: mothballs in the washbasin plughole, a plastic green 'turf' doormat, sachets of Odonil room freshener, Dettol handwash, and plastic buckets with plastic jugs hung on them. Two plastic litter bins, labelled 'Use me', were shaped like a penguin and a rabbit.

Clare had an appointment to interview Dr R. P. Jadeja, the institute's unfailingly courteous director, about cowdust time.

'In Gujarat and most of India, evening is sunset time,' he told us. 'Therefore the period is much shorter that in Britain, where people say "Good evening" at 4 or 5pm. That sounds odd in India as that is afternoon. And after 7 or 8pm, "Good evening" is also strange because by then it's night-time.' Although he now lived in a town, he still thought of *godhuli bela* as: 'when the cowdust raised by the returning cows transforms the scene from stark, sharp light to a fantasy world of religious connotations which make it more sacred.

'People, animals, birds, sea creatures – they instinctively know it's time to go and search for food or to return home. Even we in our urban context, following our wristwatch, we still have that biological clock in us. So when the sun is nearing the horizon, going down, internally something tells me "Enough of activity". I must relax, sit down with my family, tell or listen to stories, sing songs or hymns, and eventually fall asleep.'

And it was not just a matter of physical rest, he explained, but also of thanksgiving for the end of a day.

'So meditation, prayer, etcetera, is more effective at this time. Cowdust time is symbolic of the ebb and flow of spiritual energy. A time when the earth does yoga –'

'A lovely image,' said Clare.

Dr Jadeja smiled. 'But, of course, the earth is always doing yoga…'

Even the parakeets chattering in the neem trees, he added, seemed to feel the same energy.

'It's a great pleasure watching them celebrate their existence with a loud twitter, which is their song. Like our human activity, they are celebrating and saying "Thank you God for another day".'

While in Anand, we also visited the nearby village of Ashi, to record the sound of cows returning home from the fields to be milked, of children running home from the village school, of their mothers making fires from cowpats, and of their grandmothers singing devotional songs. We learned that cowdust time is both auspicious – a good time for plucking flowers and leaves for Ayurvedic medicine, and for getting married – and inauspicious. Children were warned not to whistle after dark, and never to say 'Come soon', for fear of conjuring up evil spirits.

Back on the Sabarmati Express to Jhansi (where swallows swooped under the station's platform awning) we had a curry lunch at our seats. Afterwards we gathered together the tinfoil tray and plastic cutlery and tipped them into a plastic bag, along with two empty plastic bottles of Bisleri mineral water. There was a lot of plastic. I took the bag along the carriage to the kitchen area and offered it to the attendant to dispose of. He opened the outside door and invited me to throw it out of the moving train. When I protested, he pointed to the rubbish bin; I put the bag in it.

'Now *you* will throw it out?' I asked. He grinned.

Anand, as we had seen, was embracing urban India's growing shopping mall culture. Not so Jhansi, where we spent the next few days, once more staying at the Hotel Sita. A 1970s atmosphere still lingered over the bazaar, despite an ever-increasing number of shops adapting to new technology and selling or topping up mobile phones. As we climbed into an autorickshaw, we were approached by a small boy carrying a flat, round basket. He lifted the lid; coiled inside was a python.

We had dinner at the Hotel Sita's restaurant. The rituals of an arranged marriage were being played out, with the bride and groom meeting for the first time. The two family groups, huddled in their overcoats, sat stiffly at separate tables, but the atmosphere gradually relaxed and, one by one, the groom's family joined the bride's. It was like a birds' courtship ritual.

We were soon sucked back into Peggy's whirl of lunches here and dinners there with other members of the Anglo-Indian community (Ronnie and Mona; Denzil and Maisie; Joyce and Ivor). Looking a little frailer with each visit, and now suffering from cripplingly stiff legs, Peggy needed help getting down her front steps and into Anish's rickshaw for bumpy rides across town. Her life was, as ever, defined by the cemetery, the church and the railways. With the electricity sockets sometimes sparking alarmingly, she sat much of the day at her dining-room table, her well-thumbed address book open in front of her, her 'mosquito bat' next to it. As before, she was forever telephoning and holding court to whoever turned up.

In the blazing heat of noon, the ceiling fan twirled listlessly in the dark, humid bedroom. Curtained off from the kitchen, it was as cluttered as the rest of her home, its ceiling supported, she later told us, by beams made from recycled railway sleepers. The room was almost completely filled by an enormous double bed with a thin mattress, faded floral bedspread, and a Churchill dog soft toy squatting on the pillow. Somehow a 1940s dark wood dressing table had also been squeezed in. A calendar from the Calvary Bible Church hung on a coat hook and the rest of the room was cluttered with religious symbols: an empty plastic Our Lady holy water bottle, statuettes of Mother Teresa, St Joseph and St Anthony, a poster of Christ, crumpled like a relief map, with the reassuring message, 'I will bless every house in which a picture of my Heart shall be held up and honoured'.

Beyond that, near the back door, were a narrow flagstoned lobby with a sink for washing clothes, and a rudimentary bathroom, with both Western- and Indian-style toilets. A bath on raised concrete blocks had a 'Fragile: handle with care' strip still attached to the rim. A pink plastic soap dish shaped like a swan contained a scrap of strong-smelling soap. A mirror enclosed in a wooden, blue-painted imitation ship's wheel bore the encouraging motto 'Smiling Makes You Beautiful'.

The back door led into a small yard with a gate opening out on to scrubland and a staircase to the upstairs flat, where Peggy's landlord and his family lived. All told, the four high-ceilinged rooms looked as though they had been locked in 1947 and left for half a century.

'Meat men' and 'vegetable-wallahs' continued to trundle their carts to her door. An ever-louder rumbling sound outside would announce the daily arrival of one of them, his trolley piled high with potatoes, onions, white radishes, tomatoes, cauliflowers, cabbages, gourds, beans and brinjal (aubergines). He would hand Peggy vegetables to assess, and weigh the ones she chose on large brass hand scales like the scales of justice. She would waggle her head about the price and beat him down with cunning charm.

There was a constant stream of visitors. One morning, while Sheela was patiently peeling dozens of cloves of garlic, a great jangling and bangling erupted outside. 'Ah,' said Peggy. 'This is the tin- and bottle-wallah.'

A journalist rang to interview her about the cemetery and checked the spelling of her name.

Gazetteer-like, she spelled it out in towns and cities: 'C – Calcutta; A – Allahabad; N – Nagpur; T – Trichy ; E – Erode; M – Madras.'

Thanks to Operation Cemetery, what had once been a jungle was looking ever sprucer, but cutting the grass was an unending job.

'In two months' time, it will be as smooth as a billiard table,' she said.

We again had (a late) lunch at Roy's bungalow. It was a scorchingly hot day (35°C) but the dining room, with its high ceiling and slowly rotating fan, made it refreshingly cool; air conditioning was redundant here. However, with the blinds down and the curtains closed to shut out the dazzling light and heat outside, the whole house felt sallow and ever more like a mausoleum or shrine, not merely to his wife and disabled daughter, but also to the *burra-sahib* way of life.

Roy himself, ever more a throwback to that life, had recently had a less than successful hip replacement and was now sitting in a wheelchair wearing a patient's surgical gown. The house had been adapted to accommodate his infirmity, with the carpets rolled up to ease his progress from room to room.

Ten years on from our first meeting, he might have been stiffer and deafer, but he was still sharp, still a stickler for smartness and routine. And, against the odds, he was in better spirits than we had seen him for several years. His memories were more expansive, reflecting again on his two-year stint living back in Britain in the 1970s.

'I was surprised by what I could do – changing light bulbs!' he laughed. 'But the Britishers we met just weren't friendly. It was just "Hello" and "Goodbye". We didn't like that. I found them very cold, compared to our way of life out here. It was all "darling" and "sweetheart", but they didn't invite you in. The Indian is a more friendly person. Indians will never turn you away. They'll say, "Come in and have lunch. Stay here if you like; we've got a spare bed."

'But, you know, so many people here say they would rather have the British back. There was justice then. Every crossroad had a policeman. He'd pull you up if you were speeding. There was no question of two people sitting together on a bicycle like they do now.'

In the early evening, after the meal, we sat on the bamboo chairs on the veranda where I had first photographed him. The overhead fan was twirling, cicadas hissed, frogs croaked, distant peacocks called, like cats meowing, and lightning occasionally flashed. We looked across the garden, where I'd waited for him to emerge, in his blazer and immaculately pressed trousers, eleven years before.

In ten days' time, he was due to travel to Mumbai for another operation. It was a pity, he said, that we didn't have time to go to the farm. 'You could stay there and sample the ghosts.' It was a wistful, somehow valedictory meal. As we got up to leave, we told him he had given us some of the most memorable and enriching experiences of our lives. He asked us when we would be coming again and, as the rickshaw spluttered its way down the drive, we wondered whether we ever would.

For nostalgia's sake we stopped off at the Jhansi Hotel, which was looking ever more dilapidated. One of the chandeliers housed a bird's nest, though renovations were underway (so far: one bedroom). Early Victorian paintings of British colonials were still caked with grime, almost black after years of decay and cigarette smoke. Dr Righton's room was now let out at 1,500 rupees a day, not the ten annas he had paid right up to the end. Yogesh Mehrotra showed us the dining room again: 'The old tureens are here, the silver tureens to give the lunch. We want to keep the old charm and architecture as it is.'

His father Omnath, the manager, called it 'grand heritage'.

Peggy had naturally organised an itinerary for us, not quite all of it focusing on the cemetery. She took us and her old friend Dev in Anish's tuk-tuk to meet another friend, Colleen. It was a tight squeeze, even though Dev was tiny. As we drew up at what looked like a sizeable mansion, we could see a dark-haired woman sitting in the shadows of the lobby, keeping cool.

'Colleen – I have brought my friends from the BBC to see you,' Peggy called as Anish and I helped her, with some difficulty, out of the tuk-tuk. Colleen, in flip-flops, calf-length blue jeans and a ruched dark pink top, got up to greet us. 'Here, my son, my child,' Peggy said to us. 'This is Colleen Barboza.'

'Come in, come in!' said Colleen, ushering us into another darkened room and shouting Hindi instructions to her servant. She talked very fast. 'Here, you will all have some tea?'

Her father, like Peggy's, had been a train driver and the family had lived in the railway colony.

'We lived just behind Aunty only,' she said, nodding at Peggy. 'My grandparents on my dad's side were in Lucknow and

I had an uncle and some cousins over there, but they were not railway people.'

Clare suggested that Barboza sounded south Indian. 'See!' squeaked Dev. 'I told you! I told you! A lot of Barbozas are there. Most of the people married Indians. Like my mother. So mixed, mixed, mixed!'

Colleen shrugged. 'I don't know about Barboza. Portuguese? My husband's people were from Portugal side.'

Maybe she herself had Portuguese blood in her?

Another shrug. 'Maybe… maybe there is Portuguese in me.'

Given what we already knew about the community's apparent lack of curiosity about personal ancestry, we realised it would be pointless to probe further, but we did so anyway. So where did the British part come in, Clare asked.

'I don't know really,' said Colleen, indifferently. 'I've never followed up the family tree. My mum's parents died when she was very young – her mother when she was hardly three years old. So maybe it's on my dad's side. Do you know, Aunty?'

'Oh yes,' said Peggy, who often knew more about her friends' backgrounds than they did themselves. 'Your father and mummy – all were Anglo-Indians.' Colleen's maiden name, we later learned, was MacFarlane.

Her husband Peter had been a goods driver, then a mail driver, then 'a special driver, on the superfast express trains. So we stayed in the railway colony, but when my father was about to retire, then we came here – in about 1968.'

Her father's older brother had emigrated to England in 1947, her brother when he was eighteen. But, despite all that, her father refused to go.

'My brother tried very much to get my dad to go there for a holiday but he said, "No, it's too cold there".'

She and Peggy started talking about the old days. With Dev a mainly silent presence, they reminisced about the days when Anglo-Indians were called the 'skirt people' because the women wore skirts and blouses. 'And now modern girls wear micro-miniskirts and sequins and all that glittery stuff is all over the place,' said Peggy.

Although Colleen had worn salwar kameez when she was teaching at Jhansi's Modern Public School – the kind of outfit Dev still wore – she now preferred Western clothes.

'In the old days,' she said, 'there was a Muslim tailor – Hussain Bux. He was the best tailor. He would never waste material.' She reached for a family photo album dating back to 1963. The girls looked very sixties Western in their dresses, bouffant hair tied up with bows. 'See those frills? That was all net work, all made by him. He used to get pattern books and all that in the shops and say, "Show me the pattern, I'll make the dress for you".'

'*La Bella* – was it called that, that pattern book?' asked Peggy. 'For evening wear we always wore full-length dresses. Some had halternecks and some had cowl necks, and the *dharjis*, the tailors, were absolutely up to the mark. Women would say: "Mr Bux, don't tell them what clothes you're making, what my dress is".'

'Oh, we used to fight for him – and with him!' laughed Colleen. 'That poor tailor – we used to play hell with his constitution.'

'Every mother wanted their daughter to be the best dressed,' continued Peggy, 'so everyone had their own special tailors. The tailors were paid quite a lot for the dresses in those days, but they were never allowed to disclose what the colour was, what the patterns were, and of course the pattern books came from England.

People had relations in England they would get their pattern books from, but they wouldn't lend them to anyone. They were very competitive, very secretive about their daughters' dresses. And they had the latest up-to-date frocks, mostly the long frocks, flowing gowns. Everything had to be top secret. *Lana Lobell*, that's it – they were the famous pattern books in those days, *Lana Lobell*.'

Their voices had grown louder, shriller, competing with the constant banging of pans from the kitchen next door.

Colleen showed us a photo of her husband. He looked every inch the Teddy boy in his narrow trousers, curly black hair swept back in a quiff. 'They used to call him the Tony Curtis of Jhansi!'

And what did they call her?

She threw back her head and laughed again. 'Oh, I was always called *Jhansi Ki Rani* – like the Rani of Jhansi, Jhansi's Queen! All the girls were called that. We had some very nice-looking Anglo-Indian girls here, didn't we, Aunty?'

Peggy agreed, waggling her head again. 'Jhansi girls' had won many beauty competitions over the years, she said. 'And some have won the prize in England also. My own niece Yvonne won her prize in England, a very pretty girl.'

'The Moray girls were very pretty,' said Colleen.

'You too,' said the usually silent Dev from the sidelines.

'Yes, and Mother also, she was very nice-looking in those days,' said Colleen.

'Still she is,' said Dev, loyally.

Eventually, the tea arrived, with cake, biscuits, Bombay mix and an array of other 'small eats'.

The diversion gave us time to look around the room. The high ceiling had electric fans suspended from it in an attempt to combat

Jhansi's fierce summer heat. Framed family photos hung at jaunty angles on the wall. There were vases of plastic flowers, interlocking wooden shelves for small ornaments – china animals and cottages, a model rabbit sitting alongside a Madonna and Child statuette. A plaque urged: 'In all thy ways acknowledge him and He shall direct thy paths'.

Anglo-Indian homes were always fascinating – similar to British style but different, like but not like. 'Similar but different,' Colleen agreed. 'There's always something on display, no?'

With their ornaments, their souvenirs from abroad and their fridge magnets, they were sometimes reminiscent of British homes in the 1950s and 60s – specifically Roman Catholic ones, complete with religious statues and holy water bowls.

'I have a little altar over there with all my statues and all that,' said Colleen, pointing towards her bedroom. 'I have a statue of Our Lady, I brought her very carefully back all the way from the UK. I normally light a candle there and also by the statue of St Anthony.'

'St Anthony is my patron saint,' said Peggy. 'I have a lot of little statues. I keep them to remind me to pray to them.'

'I tell you,' Colleen added, 'Anglo-Indians – the most important thing is they like to hoard up things, you know. Even if something is not needed in the house, it's hoarded, it's kept on the shelf. It could be as old as the hills, you don't need the damn thing, but it's still kept.' She threw her head back and laughed. 'In the years gone by, we used to get some nice souvenirs and all that in Sadar Bazaar,' she added.

'In those days we used to have quite a lot of foreign shops,' said Peggy. 'Oooh, we had beautiful shops. A Parsi gentleman had the most beautiful departmental store, very well stocked. It was only after 1947 that all that changed. Foreign chocolates we used to get; even Nestlé chocolates we got and Cadbury's. The boxes were lovely for the chocolates. Jacob's cream cracker biscuits…'

'And cheese,' cut in Colleen. 'We used to get that cheese spread in bottles. Lovely Kraft cheese. You can't see a bottle like that again. It's just not there any more.'

'A lot of foreign goods we got,' nodded Peggy. 'Sweets beautifully packed for Christmas with tiny ribbons and all. Huntley and Palmers biscuits, they came from England. You can't see them now, can't smell them now. But it was something we all cherished – those names never die.'

Beyond this nostalgia for British cream crackers and processed cheese there often seemed to be a deeper nostalgia in our Jhansi conversations: for an old way of life when Anglo-Indians had a more central, secure and respected role.

But this was no time for introspection. Peggy was in full flight. 'Meakin's was the famous chinaware in those days – my mother had a very good set. And Johnson Brothers, too, their sets were very famous. If you collected cigarette packets with "Johnson Brothers" on them, for every five packets we'd get a plate. People used to make up their whole dinner set with that. Wives used to tell their husbands: "Smoke that cigarette, we'll make up the dinner set!"'

Now her own crockery – and Colleen's – was plastic, bought at the bazaar.

'Plastic fibre, yah! Plastic crockery is very popular now.' Peggy waggled her head. 'In the old days it was always chinaware. We can't see that now, nothing.' She sighed. 'Those were the good days.'

'And we have dumb waiters and all that,' said Colleen. Then, unexpectedly, she banged on the table, making Dev jump. 'It belonged to my mum and dad, this table,' she said. 'It's – oh, my goodness me! I don't know how old it is. It's teak wood.'

Suddenly, as so often in India, the lights dimmed.

'The wattage has gone low,' Colleen explained. Indian lighting was often muted, sometimes with a blueish tinge, which could make even the prettiest room seem dingy.

'Anglo-Indians, they always kept a good home,' continued Peggy. 'They had their own big room, their toilet, their bedroom, dining room, all inside. But an Indian must have his toilet outside. And their tradition of eating is different. They won't have a meal together. The wife will eat after everybody eats – only after she has finished serving her husband, his friends, or his parents – then she will sit down to eat. That is the tradition. But now they are becoming more Westernised.'

'Now they have become *very* Westernised!' agreed Colleen. 'Before, the husband used to be walking in front, the wife was at the back, miles behind her husband. Now they are hand in hand, or sitting on the cycle, on the handlebar, holding one another round the waist, all these things – oh, they've definitely gone very forward. Before they used to hide their faces, right up to here' – she pointed to her eyes – 'from their husbands and in-laws and all. Now it's, "You can see my face whenever you want!" That's a lot of difference now, yeah.'

More photographs were brought out, bringing back more memories. 'I had two dance halls going at one time,' said Peggy. 'One was with the army band and the other was Mr Raymond's. There were open-air dances also, but they were covered during the winter, and they all had heaters, fires burning. And they were followed by a dinner. The husbands and all would pay, fifty rupees or something – we got sandwiches, hot dogs, coffee, everything.

'We kept on having dances, housey, rummy, bingo till almost 1965 or 1967. We had gramophone music. In those days there were no DJs as they call them now. And we always had a dance on Christmas Eve. We used to have really long ones up to midnight, when people would go to church, come back and carry on dancing.

'You know the palais glide? Whoever you stopped opposite, you had to dance with. And then the valeta waltz – you went round in a circle, then you picked your partners – all those types of medleys. Then we used to have tag waltzes – you know what they are? You're dancing with Mr X, then the next-door neighbour will tag you, or someone who is not dancing will tag you and you'd have to leave your partner...'

She was unstoppably back in the 1940s and 50s. 'Christmas week started from 15th December and ended up at 7th January. Every day there was a function – a hop, dance, bingo – you name it and it was there. Whist drives, card sessions with prizes, fancy dress, children's fancy dress, then hockey matches, cricket matches, all in fancy dress. The ladies might be dressed as men, the gentlemen dressed as ladies. It was no joke, you know, trying to organise these functions!'

She drifted off into reverie and the tone changed.

'As the children grew up they started to go away and the parents were left alone. So the community started to fade out, retiring from the railways, getting smaller and smaller. And now some of them are very poor, not educated, they do menial jobs.

'For people like that, there is a Hindu temple in the Sipri Bazaar. The sadhus, the Hindu priests, distribute food in the morning. They give breakfast, they give lunch, they give dinner, to these people, no matter what caste they are – can be Hindu, Muslim, sweepers, Dalits, OBCs' – Other Backward Castes – 'anything. There is no distinction. Because they say: "God is one, for everybody". It is free food, so if people give a donation, it is accepted very gladly.

'They get a little *subji* – vegetables – some chapati, a banana or whatever fruit is in season. Anyone can go and eat there, poor people who haven't got servants and all, anyone who sits there will get a meal. There are benches, stools. Every day.'

'It's like an ashram over there,' said Colleen.

'It's lovely,' said Peggy.

'Whenever I go on holiday to the UK,' Colleen said pensively, 'I always think of home back here. There used to be a time when my house was so full with the family, and then one by one they all just left. Within three years I lost my mum, my dad, my husband, one by one. And then my children getting married and going away, it just became lonely-like. But my mum used to be very friendly with Aunty, so the only place I had left to go was Aunty's place. And so long as she is here, I'd always like to come back here to Jhansi.

'My children say: "What will happen when Aunty is not there?" I say: "I suppose I'll have to move in with one of you all!"' Peggy and Dev joined her in her laughter.

We all had dinner together that night at the Hotel Sita's restaurant. Peggy said hello to one of the waiters. 'His name is Darrell Murphy,'

she whispered. 'His father was called Spud. And in Bina there was a ticket collector called Ivor Crocker. His dog was called Chippy.'

A woman waved to her from across the restaurant.

'Every second person says hello,' said Peggy.

We mentioned Orchha. 'For a treat, the railway company used to take the railway people from Jhansi out to Orchha on a big train,' said Colleen, whose husband used to play 'Christmas Father', as the Sita's receptionist once put it. 'Oh God, what fun we used to have!' she laughed.

Afterwards we walked outside around the hotel area and talked to an elderly man on a scooter, his wife sitting behind him on an embroidered pillow. He said he had been an engineer in Libya. We mentioned Roy. 'He is an old man and a very decent one,' he said, and rode off.

We had a long train journey back to Anand the following morning – and an early start. We arrived at the station a few minutes before the 5.45am departure of our slow old friend, the Sabarmati Express. As usual, the station was packed with people, sleeping in the foyer and on the platforms, surrounded by stockades of suitcases and sacks of rice. India's trains carry 23 million passengers a day; a quarter of them seemed to be here. They surged to the platform edge when the train pulled in, shoulder to shoulder like kittiwakes on a cliff. It was already testingly hot and we were drenched with sweat, which didn't dry in our air-conditioned carriage. We arrived at Anand at 2.35am the following morning. For once, we were on time. A station sign announced 'Queue for ladies and gents is common'.

Over almost three weeks in India, we saw barely half a dozen Westerners, except in Orchha and a couple on Jhansi station. We saw none at all over our time in Anand, during which we were interviewed on the university's student radio station and introduced as 'beautiful guests from UK'. Before talking to us, the student presenter was advised by her lecturer not to let us keep talking but occasionally to interject. In fact, she punctuated our every answer with 'Yes', 'Really?' or 'That's interesting'. They didn't help the flow of conversation.

CHAPTER 15

'EACH TIME SHE LAUGHED, HER EYEBALLS WOULD COME OUT'

Despite our doubts the previous year, we did see Roy again – a significantly more cheerful Roy. We were back in Jhansi a week before Christmas 2012 – for once, not arriving on the Sabarmati Express. We had spent three idle days in Bekal, a small town in northern Kerala, where accommodation at a plush 'garden village' backwaters resort ranged from 'Superior Charm Room' and 'Premium Temptation Villa' to 'Deluxe Delight' and 'Premium Indulgence'. Butterflies fluttered through muslin-draped bamboo pavilions as bulbuls burbled, egrets stalked and eagles soared.

High-end metro-city families came here to relax, though the businessmen-husbands often paced around the swimming pool, mobile phones clutched to their ears, stress on their faces as news came through from their offices. To help their families relax, there was plenty to occupy children. One mother was pushing a young boy, perhaps seven years old, on a swing. 'You are pushing us with invisible ghost hands,' he told her.

We had never done so little for so long in thirty years of visiting India. Ordering the 'Banana Leaf Experience' for lunch was a major event. 'If Paradise took in paying guests, it would be like this,' said a man at the next table.

At Bekal Fort, our pale skins made us objects of curiosity and amusement. 'One picture only,' people would laugh, clustering around us for selfies.

'Plucking of flowers and littering on the lawn strictly prohibited', ordered a sign. Littering-on-the-Lawn? Surely a Cotswold village? We strolled gently around the market, taking in the bangles, the bindis, the beautifully embroidered saris. One less romantic stall had exquisitely elegant displays of porcelain toilets.

We moved on from Bekal to the southern area of Coorg over the border in Karnataka. Once British India's smallest province, its beauty had so entranced the travel writer Dervla Murphy that, in her 1976 book *On a Shoestring to Coorg*, she wrote that she felt she had been 'miraculously restored to the Garden of Eden'.

We were staying near the town of Madikeri, a sort of smaller, quieter, cleaner and infinitely prettier version of Jhansi. Our base was a sophisticated new hotel complex that sprawled across a hillside, four thousand feet up, with some guests arriving by helicopter. I asked a member of staff what had been here before the hotel was built. 'Nothing,' he said. 'Only rainforest.'

Madikeri's market was a delight. There were pyramids of caraway seeds and cardamom, cinnamon, coconuts and cashew nuts, cloves, chillies and coffee, dates from Iran and figs from Afghanistan. Also, less delightfully, chickens, both alive and half dead. Many of the female stallholders had braided blossom into their hair. In the town's museum, a sculpture of a chubby loinclothed man throwing his arms in the air was helpfully labelled 'Happy Man'.

Sanjeev Kumar, a ponytailed guide from the felicitously named Muddy Boots Co, took us on a 'jungle walk'. It wasn't exactly challenging – no more than a quarter of a mile into semi-jungle. But there was interest at every turn.

'Previously unknown tree frogs have been discovered here,' he said, as we passed a sign to 'Luxury Bliss Villas'. He pointed out a plant that flowered just once every eighteen years. 'It will flower next in three or four years – and the hills will be blue.' There was the web of a funnel spider, which insects unwisely jumped into, and a fishtail tree – 'a favourite of the hornbills and the civet cats… look, there could be wild boar up there, bucking deer, possibly leopards, king cobras…'

He was particularly on the lookout, though, for a Malabar whistling thrush, locally known as 'the whistling schoolboy'.

'I was once playing the flute and as soon as I stopped, it carried on with the same tune. Oh, over there, a barbet singing.'

Large black-and-white butterflies fluttered by, like floating tissue paper.

A motor rickshaw passed in the middle distance. Three men sat in the back, all listening to their mobile phones. 'If you silently walk,' Sanjeev said, 'you can hear a lot of things.'

Two days before Christmas, we drove to Bangalore, or Bengaluru as it had been renamed. On our first visit fifteen years earlier, it had been a quiet, rather staid, city. Known as the Pensioners' Paradise, it had had some of the atmosphere of a retirement village. Now, with its glitzy shopping malls and call centres, its hectic traffic, its new Metro rail system perched on great concrete stilts, and its crowds of young professionals, it had been propelled helter-skelter into the

21st century. I asked a taxi driver what had previously been on the land where the latest mall was being built.

'Nothing,' he said, echoing the hotel employee in Coorg. 'Trees only.'

Before catching our train, we stopped at a luxury hotel for tea; two cups cost five hundred rupees – an eye-watering amount when a roadside cup of chai could cost as little as ten rupees. Still mulling over this inequality, we took the 8.20pm Bengaluru-Nizamuddin Rajdhani Express onwards to Jhansi. Rajdhanis were among the plushest and fastest trains on the Indian network, but the 1,260-mile journey was still scheduled to take the best part of thirty hours.

We shared a compartment with a young couple, both working in IT. They were travelling with their month-old baby and the husband's mother, who seemed to resent our intrusion into their Christmas family journey. The wife and mother-in-law couldn't let the baby rest, singing to it, jigging it up and down, shrieking and clapping. There were more noisy children up the carriage and we were kept awake until midnight by the chatter of two couples in the next compartment. By contrast, the berth across the aisle was occupied by a morosely silent man, who lay in his upper bunk for most of the thirty hours, either asleep or staring at the ceiling. He only roused himself for regular deliveries of tinfoil curries.

We arrived at Jhansi at 1am on Christmas Day, and went straight to the Hotel Sita, where the back alley had gradually evolved into a sort of village compound where women cooked on open fires. With Peggy and her bewildering network of contacts increasingly the reason for our visits, we slept until it was time to have lunch with her.

Christmas was in full swing at her house, with a stream of festive visitors and the phone ringing every few minutes. Sheela was imperturbably chopping a white radish, tomato and onion salad and cooking curries and rice on the two-ring hob. She beamed at us, resplendent in the Queen Elizabeth II Diamond Jubilee apron Clare had brought for her.

The heat and smell of cooked lentils and *subji* made the room welcomingly warm, but Peggy, sitting as usual at the table with its floral oilcloth cover, was still swathed in shawls, scarves and a woolly hat. With her painful legs, hips and feet, where bunions had splayed the toes completely out to the side, she was finding it ever harder to move around.

A car manoeuvred its careful way down the narrow lane and stopped at the front door. Gwendoline Khan got out, elegant and ladylike, with her son, daughter-in-law, granddaughter and baby grandson. There was a flurry of *Merry Christmas*es and instantly the chitter-chatter started. As usual, everyone was talking at once, moving chairs, trying to fit a small crowd into the tiny kitchen. Gwen, as everyone called her, handed Peggy a woollen jumper. 'Oh, I *love* wool!' cried Peggy over the hubbub and introduced us.

'They have met me before,' said Gwen in her gently lilting voice. 'What was that programme you sent me – *The Lollipop Tree*.'

When we had fleetingly met the previous year, Gwen had mentioned this 1970s BBC television documentary about Dr Graham's Homes, the long-established school for Anglo-Indian children in the Himalayan hill station of Kalimpong. A pupil there at the time, she'd appeared in the film, which was narrated by

Cliff Richard, himself of Anglo-Indian descent. 'I was in three or four shots. In one I was opening the window and in another I was playing ball with Mr Minto.'

At eighteen she had married her brother's best friend, a Muslim businessman, and brought up their son and daughter in that faith. Her family background was typical of Jhansi's Anglo-Indians. Born in the railway quarter, she was the daughter of 'a British TTI' (travelling ticket inspector) who had come out to India as an eighteen-year-old soldier, stayed on after Partition and married.

'My dad bought a place near the cemetery – it was called the haunted house. People said we couldn't live there, but we did, very happily, till he decided to go back to England. He sold the house and went back to the UK a few times, but he liked it here, so he came back and stayed on. The house is still there. My mother even one day showed me – "That's the room you were born in"...'

A Bollywood tune exploded from under a pile of papers. 'Oh, where is my phone?' cried Peggy, scrabbling round.

Clare found it underneath a letter from the British High Commission, took it out of its pastel pink-and-green knitted holder and handed it to her.

'Hello, hello, who is here?' Peggy asked. 'Ah, yes baby, I see, hello... How are y'all? How is the weather in Pune? I have a big crowd here. Gwen is here and everyone else is here. I went to Uncle Roy's place and he had a big crowd there.' She put her hand over the phone mouthpiece. 'Will y'all have ginger wine? Anish, fetch the glasses,' she ordered, before continuing with the call. 'I went to the cemetery and laid some flowers on the graves of yours. OK? Merry Christmas and thank everyone for all the cards. Please thank Diana… Daisy's not here today, darling, but I went to see her this morning. OK, darling, OK. God bless.'

The eternally patient Anish disappeared behind the cloth curtain into the small back room. We could hear him searching among the jumble of belongings as the conversation became an unstoppable stream of consciousness. Gwen surfed the mayhem and calmly told us that the emerald and gold salwar kameez her daughter-in-law was wearing had been made by 'the colonel's wife… she also makes the most exquisite cake. Exquisite.'

Anish returned with five rather smeared-looking glasses and an equally smeared bottle of something. 'This was made by that colonel's wife, a very special lady,' said Peggy approvingly. 'It's called wine but it's not actually.'

'Call it ginger ale,' smiled Gwen.

Peggy poured it. 'There's no alcohol in it; just ginger cooked in spices.'

Anish ambled back behind the curtain and emerged carrying a cake tin.

Peggy handed round small plates with large slices of cake on them. 'This cake, I ordered it specially for you. So sweet,' said Peggy. 'Taste the wine, darling.'

We all clinked glasses. If Mr Pickwick had walked in, florid with Christmas cheer, he would have felt quite at home.

'I tell you what,' said Gwen. 'The day after tomorrow, I'll make biryani for y'all and you'll come to the farm. Have you been to Uncle Abbott's farm?' We nodded. 'Well, it's not like that. It's small. I love looking after it, the gardening, the orchards, the field work. We have vegetables and wheat and fruit trees. And we have seven dogs. Do you like dogs?'

'No,' I said.

'Have some more cake,' said Peggy quickly. Once again, she told us her rent was 150 rupees a month: a third of the price of our two cups of tea at the Bangalore hotel.

'My God!' Gwen exclaimed in horror. 'You could feed how many families on that?'

Four mobile phones suddenly rang at once, a carillon of tinny ringtones. 'All the best compliments of the season,' Peggy told one caller. 'I have people here, and the press.'

Events continued to cartwheel along.

Peggy confirmed our first impression of Roy's wife Lillian. 'She was the Ava Gardner of Jhansi – her servants used to feel scared just looking at her.'

She and Sheela had a shouting contest in Hindi.

'You know something?' said Peggy, pointing at Gwen's family. 'These are the best shooters in Jhansi. Husband, wife, son and daughter. They are belonging to the rifle club. They are ace shooters.' Which was unsurprising, given that Gwen's husband ran the town's leading arms store.

'I shoot at targets only,' Gwen explained. 'I could never shoot an animal. I am an animal lover. Now I will go and see Aunty Anto – Aunty Antoinette,' she explained, getting up. 'So nice to see you; come for lunch.' She turned to Peggy and said sternly: 'Aunty, 1pm means 1pm. Not Indian Standard Time, OK?'

'Oh, Greenwich Mean Time?' said Peggy, quick as a flash.

'Yes!' laughed Gwen. 'You have two Britishers with you, so you follow British time!'

'Gwen is a lady of wonders!' said Peggy, as the family left. 'Her biryanis are out of this world!'

A couple of minutes after peace had descended again, a broad-shouldered young man appeared in the doorway.

'Ah, this is my landlord's son, he is from Dubai,' Peggy explained. He was currently living there after five years of medical training.

'Now I am trying to start here in Jhansi,' he told us, 'as a general practitioner or on a surgical ward. I just don't feel like leaving my parents alone now. They are like, "Go back to the Emirates. Go back to Dubai. There is nothing for you here in this town." I'm like, "No, sorry, I can't leave you alone. There is a lot in this town." My parents live upstairs. Aunty is like my grandmother!' he laughed.

'I am trying to persuade his mother to get him married,' Peggy retorted. 'So sweet… I am so happy to have y'all here for Christmas, you're like my family. Otherwise I would have had nobody here for Christmas. I was alone, otherwise. But God sent y'all for me.'

As though God disputed this, the lights went out. Another power cut. The young man left and Sheela muttered something in Hindi.

'Darlings, you'll have cheese – paneer?' asked Peggy. 'Paneer and peas? They are all cooked. Sheela – a soda water for the memsahib.'

As we ate, she told us once again about her home, where she had now lived for nearly fifty years.

'This was once a cottage all on its own, with land around. Then I looked after Mr Abbott's wife for eight years and one time when I was away the landlord built on it. There used to be a little garden at the side there. It had a lime tree, a guava tree, an orange tree and a mango tree. In summer months I liked to sit out under the trees…'

Despite all the hardships she'd endured, Peggy always tried to remain cheerful and positive, always helped others less fortunate than herself.

'It was always my ambition to go out and help the poor,' she said. 'I like to go into the remote villages, to see what their life is like. There is a lot of poverty and it's our duty to help those poor children. We take books, food, clothes, medicines, anything we can get, because they need help, being so far away from the outer world.

'With our own children, we put them into English medium schools. Most of the principals give preference to children who are clever and give all the facilities free, to help them complete their studies. Some are really good in painting and drawing. They want to become commercial artists and we encourage them. It is our duty.'

It was also the Anglo-Indian Association's duty to support poor widows within the community. People like May Coutinho, Peggy's tiny, tired Anglo-Indian maid and cleaner, who drifted in and out of the room like a wraith. She was in her sixties but looked older, with a direct gaze behind large round spectacles that was both beseeching and full of sorrow. She had a tiny government pension of around three hundred rupees a month (the equivalent of £3–4), supplemented by the wage Peggy paid her and money sent by relatives in England.

She had started working for Peggy eight years earlier. 'Aunty helps me, my girl,' May told Clare when Peggy was out of the room. 'She helps me with clothes, with food, with money. Whatever she can help with, she helps me. And I bathe her, change her clothes – whatever she tells me, I do. I won't refuse. Because she loves me and I love her.'

Usually, May could hardly get a word in edgeways, but one day, while Peggy was resting, Clare asked her about her life.

We had picked up information about her over the years, but usually piecemeal. We knew that she had been born in Jhansi to Anglo-Indian parents, that her father had worked as an army clerk and then on the railways, and that her long-dead husband had been Portuguese-Goan. We knew she had two sons and two daughters, and that her only daughter-in-law had walked out a couple of years before, leaving her children behind.

We also knew that she lived with her sons and three grandchildren (a girl aged fifteen, a boy of eleven and a toddler) in one room of a house in the Railway Colony. It was divided into two, she told us, with no bathroom or toilet: 'Like a hut only, it is. Rain comes, everything comes. From 1980 I am staying there, in that outhouse, the servants' quarters of the railway.'

One son worked on a tea stall seven days a week, for a pitifully low income.

'He works thirty days a month, no holidays, nothing. If he doesn't go, he gets no money. From that, he has to buy milk, biscuits, for his child, books for the little fellow. And clothes.'

The other son worked, without wages, for a high-ranking local railway official.

'He washes clothes, looks after the house, waters the garden. Till 9pm at night he works,' she told us. 'He doesn't get time to eat his food.' In return, the official provided the roof over the family's head.

It was a not unfamiliar tale of poverty, deprivation and hardship. May elaborated on it towards the end of our stay when Clare recorded her memories for a radio programme she was hoping to make about our Jhansi experiences.

'My name is May Carroll,' she started formally, in a voice as thin as herself. 'My father was A. W. Carroll. Arthur William. My sister was Ethel Cranston, brother was Irvin Joseph Carroll. The English part was grandparents. I don't know where they came from because they were not alive when I was born. Close to seventy I must be.'

There was that vagueness again.

'When I was nine years old, my daddy died. He had asthma. We had a piece of land – the sowing of wheat an' all – but Daddy sold it because he was sick. Some people defrauded him, too. He looked after me, got me educated, but in the Hindi medium school, St Philomena's Convent.'

She left school when she was fourteen and was married at eighteen.

'Before then, I never worked. But after that, the second month only I had to work because I took up too much of trouble with my husband. He used to drink – he was a pukka drunk, and a gambler. I'd tell him: "Don't drink", but no, he used to drink. I used to work, get money, but he used to snatch the books from the children – "Don't let them study!" And he used to throw things. All the neighbours, they tell you.'

Her husband had been a 'wireman' (electrician) on the railway.

'He left that job in 1980, because of his drinking and gambling. In 2008 he died. Three months I was in the Civil Hospital looking after him. He was not a good husband.'

One of her daughters had married an Indian Christian, the other a Hindu. Both had children, including 'little Kimmy, she's one year old – Kimmy Judeline. Because St Jude Day she was christened, 28th October.'

Although the association helped her financially, and her grandson received a free education and free school uniforms, life was still a seemingly endless struggle.

'Expense is so much, my girl,' she said resignedly. 'Electric bill we have to pay. Two-seater money I have to pay every month. Everything is dear, what you want in the house. Aunty helps me sometimes with the bed sheets. This year she gave me a blanket. So I like to work. I haven't got no-one else, my girl. It is Aunty only.'

In fact, she clarified, she did have relatives 'in England, and in Swansea, Wales. Eight sisters, and four brothers. But I hear nothing.'

One cousin had sent her money every Christmas until he had died four years earlier. Another cousin, who used to help her financially, had recently stopped communicating.

'She too must be having some troubles,' May said resignedly. 'Only I am left in India.'

When she looked back at her life, Clare asked, how did it seem?

'Hard life, my girl. But I got faith and the children are with me. When I was eighteen, I was happy. I used to go to dances, too. My brother he looked after me very nicely. Older than me he was. My mummy used to take me along with her to the dances. My childhood was happy. After getting married, no happiness. All happiness is gone.

'Now I have to see to these grandchildren. I want a roof for them, and a little for studying, to buy them books. If I get a house for these children, even a small one, it is our own. There must be worse than me, too.'

She shrugged her shoulders.

'There might be. My health is all right, but in 2004 I was cancer patient – lung cancer. Aunty got me help from here-there-here-there, so she cure me. Now, no pain nor coughing, nothing. So I pray to God that he keep me in this health.'

Like many of the Anglo-Indians we met, May was Roman Catholic.

'I go to St Jude's. I pray to St Jude and he listens to my prayer. I believe in him and I have faith in him, my girl. Some day he might change my luck…' She tailed off, eyes even sadder than usual. 'So this is my life story. It comes to a life's end. I have one room, and we made it into two. This is only that thing.'

Eventually May's cancer returned and she died in 2019. An abiding memory is of her trailing wearily up the alley on her way home from Peggy's.

Over lunch, Peggy told us that she had been helping out at St Jude's Shrine: 'We used to have a fete there – I like to organise those, and charity shows.' Over the years, she had also been secretary of St Jude's Club and of the Railwaymen's Union. 'I used to ride my own scooter but now I have to rely on someone to take me. It's quite strenuous to run around now at my stage.'

'You're in your late eighties, Peggy!' said Clare. 'Shouldn't you stop pushing yourself so hard?'

'Yes, but as long as there is life there's hope,' she replied. 'And you must try to help people poorer than yourself. You see someone on crutches or on a little trolley scraping his hands on the ground

– dear God, there is always someone worse off. I beg, I borrow, I steal, whatever, so long as I can carry on the work. Never waste your talents, make use of them.'

May's two older grandchildren turned up. 'Merry Christmas, Aunty!' they trilled and then stood in the doorway looking bashfully from Peggy to us and back again.

'Are you coming from church?' asked Peggy. 'Come, have cake.'

Then two young women arrived – one of them the niece of Billy who had been with Peggy when we first met her eight years before. 'You remember Billy?' Peggy asked us.

How could we forget the 'cosmetologist' who had studied the lines on Clare's face? It seemed he had been teaching in Thailand for three years, had married and had a daughter. One of the young women eagerly scrolled through the photographs on her mobile phone and showed us a picture of the child at three months old.

'Will you have a banana?' Peggy asked them, looking around for her fruit bowl, hidden under a copy of the *Times of India*.

'No, we are going now,' said the older niece politely. She leaned down to kiss Clare on the cheek. 'Bye, Aunty, and Merry Christmas, Uncle!'

'The whole colony will come today!' laughed Peggy, sorting through gifts left on the table. 'These are *chikoos*…' She fingered small brown fruits. '…and these are guavas. Taste this one. You like guava cheese? Guava jelly?'

We protested that we were doing all the eating and Sheela was doing all the cooking.

'There is plenty left for Sheela,' said Peggy and handed round some dazzlingly pink slabs of fudge. 'Made by the same lady who made the wine.'

We talked about Roy, whom we now saw less and less of. She told us that his Australian grandchildren, the son and daughter of his son by his first marriage, had recently come over to stay with him.

'They were very nice. Typical Ozzies. Their accent, he could not understand. They have the drawl. The girl was very attractive, because Mr Abbott's first wife was one of the beauty queens of Jhansi. But he has not seen his son at all, doesn't know what he looks like. And I wouldn't call them Anglos now, because their father married an Australian girl... How did you like the *chikoo*?'

The postman arrived and handed over a dozen cards.

'Good afternoon!' she cried. 'This is Mr Postman who loses all my letters!' She opened one of the envelopes. 'Oh, Babs Mollon – she stays next to Buckingham Palace.'

Two months earlier, the Jhansi Hotel had been sold to a local businessman. Mr Mehrotra had left – 'Gone Bangalorey-side,' one of the security guards told us. There were big development plans for it, a radical refurbishment, but for the moment it was a building site littered with piles of earth. Plaster was being stripped back to the basic brickwork, revealing long-invisible Victorian features, including a row of arched alcoves in the old dining room. It was poignant to gaze along the now-ruinous corridor of bedrooms, including Dr Righton's.

We had a Boxing Day trip to Orchha, where more change was underway. Parades of useful small shops were being demolished and roads widened to accommodate ever bigger coaches ferrying in ever more tourists. 'It will lose its village atmosphere,' sighed Peggy.

Certainly, Orchha's charm was dwindling with so many new hotels, restaurants and souvenir stalls. But it was somehow heartening to see that it still attracted plenty of bearded backpackers and their partners. And that they still spooned their lugubrious way through glutinous green mounds of palak paneer in cheap, dim restaurants.

The following day, we autorickshawed our way round to Peggy's before going on to Gwen's house for lunch. Inevitably, within seconds of us arriving to collect her, Peggy's phone rang and, as she answered the call (from Gwen), we talked again to May, who was wearing a strikingly festive gold and crimson sari.

'A Christmas gift from Aunty, my girl,' she said. 'I used to wear dresses, my mummy, too, and my mother-in-law wore dresses, but since starting working, I have to wear these clothes. Before I came to Aunty's place, I worked in St Jude's Hospital. It was ayah's work – looking after children, after old people, patients, changing bed sheets and all. And there I wore a sari and now I have got used to them and I am wearing them only.'

Coming off the phone, Peggy said that, the previous day, Gwen had seen Roy, who nowadays spent long hours indoors. 'She told me he was sitting on the veranda in the sun for once,' said Peggy. 'Not sitting like a purdah woman inside.'

There was a loud clatter outside and a male voice shouted in Hindi.

'Ah, the dhobi boy has come,' said Peggy, and shouted back, '*Kitne*? How much is all that costing?'

Sheela pulled open the curtain and there stood the laundry boy with his wooden trolley piled high with clothes, bed linen and table linen. He handed her a large pile of items and she in turn handed them to Peggy to count.

'How many towels are here?' she asked. 'Is the counterpane here? One tablecloth and seven pillowcases and one towel. *Paise*? *Kitne*? I'll just give him his money. This is really in tatters…' She held up a very ragged-looking towel. 'But it observes all the purposes. Pass me my purse, my son.'

The money was handed over and the boy went back up the lane, shouting as he went, like a costermonger in *My Fair Lady*. Another arrival, this time the shy young woman, the 'sleepy-head', we had met years before at Cheryl's. Smiling awkwardly, she handed Peggy a parcel.

'Thank you, my girl,' said Peggy. Then to us, 'The presents never end till the first of January.'

As the two of them talked, we asked May if she had ever been to Britain. 'Never, my girl. Never been anywhere. All the others, uncles and aunts, they went on P&O liners.'

'Those were the days of P&O,' Peggy explained. 'And it was only costing three hundred and fifty to four hundred rupees for passage. But they didn't have cabins, I suppose. They were deck passengers.'

There were more street calls outside.

'Is this the *subji* man?' Peggy asked. 'May – *subji*-wallah!'

May sidled out to discuss vegetables with the man at his handcart.

'All had to wait their turn for the ships,' Peggy continued. 'They took fifteen days in those days, by the Cape. The families sort of dwindled as the years went on. All our functions stopped. Very sad it was.

'Those that are left are now saying: "We would love to come back to India but there is no scope for our children." It was because of the children that they went. But if the children had had the education, they could easily have made a name for themselves in India. There were a few boys – the Keeler boys, they made a name in the Air Force. And the Peters family – May, bring my bag. I keep a write-up about them, in an envelope…'

She rummaged vainly through the envelopes and newspaper cuttings in her handbag.

'I'll look for it tomorrow, darlings. Here, take this on the Anglos…' And she handed over one of the cuttings.

Anish had fetched his rickshaw, which coughed and spluttered down the alley to take us to Gwen's. Smiling, he stepped into the kitchen. Unlike Sheela, who often had to raise her voice in order to be heard, he always spoke softly. They would often share a joke and he would chuckle quietly in the background, among all the mayhem.

'We can't leave the house unattended,' said Peggy. 'Anish, put a double lock on. Because thieves hide, watch the time you go, especially at Christmas week.'

It took a while to hoist her out of her chair, make sure she was wrapped up well enough, help her down the front steps, and ensure she had her handbag and mobile phone.

'May, where did I put my glasses? I just had them…' She scrabbled anxiously through the bag. 'Something always gets lost. Ah, here they are on my lap! Sorry, darlings, sorry! Come, let's go to Gwen's.'

Anish honked his rickshaw through the streets, its engine going into overdrive. Out of the town centre we passed a dilapidated area of litter-strewn scrubland grazed by pigs.

'This was all the Railway Colony,' sighed Peggy. 'Every house was Anglo-Indian.'

The Khan family lived on an extensive out-of-town farming estate set in fields and orchards. It was alongside three main railway lines, so passing trains hooted every minute or so. 'We don't notice the noise,' Gwen said when I mentioned it.

As with other Anglo-Indians we'd met, her family background was complicated, both her parents having been married before.

'I had one brother from my mother's side, Dempsey; he died recently. And a sister, Penelope, from my father's side, who died in England. She had something wrong with her. Each time she laughed, her eyeballs would come out.'

'Sorry?' said Clare, startled.

'She was operated on,' Gwen continued matter-of-factly, 'but there was a mishap. She rolled off the bed, fell on her head and died. I also have two other sisters, and one brother in England – I don't know if he's alive or not, but his family is there.'

She dug photographs out of a large handbag, including a 1980 picture of her father, brother and other family members.

'This is in Middlesex – London, is it?' The pictures showed a real mix of East and West. 'They would call themselves Anglo-Indian, yes. We're not in touch but I'm hoping to go to England and look them up. I have their address and old phone numbers for them.'

Another photo showed her mother, an attractive woman with long dark hair and a glowing smile.

'She's reading; she didn't know I was taking that photograph. She's enjoying the book – see that big smile on her face?

'Her first husband died. He was a boxer, Edgar Bright. He died at the railway station when going to fight some bout – he just had a heart attack. Dempsey was four at the time. He was named after a famous boxer. He also is no more.

'My parents' marriage was a long and very happy one. And I was always the pet, always pampered. My father would do anything for me – they were both always there for me. My mother was a very soft, gentle person, whereas my father said what he thought of you. He made no bones about it, so people didn't always like his straightforward nature. But Mum was very quiet and very sweet and all that. She was born in Calcutta and, though her father was British, her mother was Spanish – so we are mixed blood. But we always saw ourselves as Anglo-Indian.' She knew little about her mother's English father: 'I never really asked her...'

Gwen had started her schooling at St Francis's Convent in Jhansi but, when her father retired from the railway, the family moved to Pantnagar, in north India, then on to the hill station of Nainital, where she attended another Catholic school. Then the move to Kalimpong, where her mother and father had worked as house parents, with her father also looking after the school's orchards and gardens.

Her ambition had been to become an air hostess, but she gave that up after her marriage. 'I knew him from the age of three. He was my elder sister's boyfriend and it started as an infatuation thing. His parents and my parents would say: "Who are you going to marry?" And I'd say, "Him!" Eventually I went away from here and, when I came back, I was grown-up and he saw me and he was still single and we mingled' – she laughed girlishly – 'and we married. My father was a bit hesitant, but my mother supported me and his parents supported me. We had a civil marriage. There was no problem about religion. I could do what I wanted – I could pray, go to church. I am still Christian. In the house we have pictures of Jesus, Mary, Hindu statues, even his Muslim pictures. We believe in one God, so there is no problem there.'

And what, we wondered, did being an Anglo-Indian mean to her?

'It means a lot. I'm proud to be so. Even though Uncle Abbott and everyone says I am more British!' She laughed. 'I wouldn't want to be anything else.'

After lunch of vegetable curries with raita and chapatis, we drove back into town, passing the St Jude's Senior Citizens' Home – 'The old ladies' home,' as Peggy called it. 'Each lady has her own little room and a toilet room,' she said. 'Edna Bryan lives over there. She's a very short little girl, very sweet.'

Peggy now monopolised our visits to Jhansi and we spent very little time with Roy. Conversations with him had become more like shouting matches due to his deafness. He bellowed hoarsely and now, after two hip operations, spent even more time in his wheelchair.

We did, though, have lunch one day at his bungalow with Peggy, and found him as alert as ever. He was looking forward to the expansion of the town resulting from two proposed new National Highways – north to south and east to west – that would cross near it.

'Jhansi will just develop overnight,' he predicted. 'Even now people are buying up whatever land they can and building on it. A lot of colonies are coming up here now. So it's got a future, definitely. There'll be shopping malls, government offices: the whole state government will be here.'

I asked about the future of the Jhansi Hotel.

'It's being partly demolished,' he said. 'They're opening it up and it's going to make a very big difference. The rooms will be renovated and it will probably be the best hotel here – with Captain Abbott as managing director!' He laughed heartily – a laugh that mutated into a cough.

Clare wondered what might eventually happen to his bungalow.

'It will stay as it is,' he said firmly. 'I like it as it is, manageable. I like smallholdings that you can manage properly, that have a nice garden – fruit trees, a teak garden and so on. My flower garden has thirty varieties in it. But I still prefer the farms, so I take off with even a slight excuse.

'I've been into a lot of homes over here in Jhansi,' he mused, looking around with obvious pleasure. 'But I haven't seen one quite like this. They're all modern homes, recently built – this is an old home. I'm not in favour of modernisation at all. No, I like all the old things as far as possible.' As we had seen, this also extended into his village. 'I try to keep it as it was when I went out in 1950.'

But while he might want to preserve things in aspic, unsurprisingly the villagers wanted their share of modernity – tractors and motorcycles rather than bullock-pulled ploughs.

'Where it's made a big difference is in their health,' he mused. 'It's not as good as it used to be. They used to exercise much more than they do today. Today they hardly walk anywhere. If a fellow is sitting by the roadside, someone will stop and give him a lift. So there's a great increase in heart disease and diabetes. Before, you never heard of a villager just dropping dead from a heart attack.

'And they have television – yes, now in every home! My village is comparatively small, maybe fifty homes, and I think every one of them now has a television. Mobile phones are coming in, and they're able to get loans easily from the banks, so they take advantage of that if they haven't got the money themselves and buy whatever they want. They spend a lot of time sitting around instead of being out in the fields working. What a change I've seen there. What a change!'

His conversation seemed increasingly like an old man's elegy for a semi-feudal past that reform and 'progress' were banishing. But it was also full of contradictions.

'It's been very nice seeing all the changes,' he suddenly said, 'from the time India got its Independence to the present day. That's been a big experience.'

'Good or bad?' asked Clare.

'Mixed, I'd say. If I have to be frank about it, I'd say I don't like it, particularly the discipline side of things. There's no discipline left in this country. Law and order breakdown – very big breakdown. And another thing that's come about since Independence is the destruction of the flora and fauna. Look at the tiger population…'

'But Roy,' Clare protested, 'you've got a tiger's head on the wall in here!'

'Hmmm?' he said absently.

She repeated what she'd said.

'Yes, I've shot a couple of them.' He shrugged. 'I did a lot of shooting – but never indiscriminate. If something wasn't worth shooting, I never shot it just for the sake of bringing it home and making a roast out of the meat. It had to be a trophy. The beaters would drive half a dozen tigers out of the forest, and you picked the one that would make the best trophy.'

This seemed rather skewed logic, but we let it pass and instead asked what else he had shot.

'Oh, all sorts – deer, sambar, spotted deer, four-horned deer, blackbuck, wild boar, panthers, all those sorts of things – but always only if it was worth shooting for a trophy, not otherwise. As soon as the Indians got in power after Independence, it was the indiscriminate issue of gun licences that I objected to. On one occasion, I was out with a government official and they had this tiger beat. Unfortunately, the tiger went in front of where he was sitting, so he shot it. That was his first tiger. He was so excited and exhilarated by this that he told the villagers: "Whoever wants the licence in this village, come tomorrow and you will be issued with one." I didn't like that. I told him: "By doing that, there'll be a lot of shooting done." And he said: "We'll try and control it." But I knew no-one would. These people would just shoot for meat. They'd shoot anything, even female tigers, which we never shot. Calves, little young deer – we never shot them.

'And that's what's affected the animal population. Tigers are down to about two thousand five hundred now. They're really struggling to survive. When Independence came, there were forty to forty-five thousand tigers in this country. So where have they gone? They've all been shot, indiscriminately.' He shrugged again and sighed. 'So there it is.'

The next day, after the inevitable visit to the cemetery (little changed), we turned up at the station in good time for the 5.59pm Habibganj-New Delhi Shatabdi Express to Delhi. It seemed ironic that such a precise time should be scheduled on a railway system whose timekeeping could be so unpredictable. And so it proved. The train arrived at 9.10pm. The familiar mantra of 'Inconvenience caused is deeply regretted' became a mantra, played every few minutes over the station's PA system. The female announcer's grand tone often seemed a little short on sympathy. Our scheduled 10.45pm arrival in Delhi turned into 2.15am. I once asked Peggy if a particular train had been on time in Jhansi. 'Oh, yes,' she said. 'Just two hours late.'

CHAPTER 16

'YOU'VE NEVER SEEN A BETTER JIVER THAN PEG!'

After twenty or so trips to India, we finally visited Khajuraho. Just over 120 miles southeast of Jhansi, it was, after all, a prime tourist attraction, thanks to its 10th- and 11th-century temples. More specifically, thanks to their carvings of globe-breasted women and well-endowed men, all impressively athletic and enterprising in their sexual adventures. We sometimes felt 'templed out' in India, overwhelmed by the intricacies of Hindu architecture and mythology. But Khajuraho's temples were another matter: great sandstone panoramas of abandon. If the Taj Mahal was often described as a monument to love, Khajuraho was a monument to lust.

'I show you very good *Kama Sutra* airo-tek,' whispered one guide touting for custom.

Airo-tek?

'Erotic,' said Clare.

The airo-tek is only part of the Khajuraho story, though.

Away from the busy main temples, where scuttling mongooses reared on their hind legs when approached, we found quieter unrestored ones. We wandered dreamily around on a hot afternoon and timeless India unfolded in front of us. An old man led his cattle down to a stream to bathe them. Small herds of buffalo ambled along dusty roads past abandoned bullock carts. Groups of men sat around talking while the women worked. An old lady unwound her sari discreetly and bathed in the stream, eyes darting watchfully.

Bee-eaters fluttered around scarlet poinsettias. Parakeets flew past, psychedelic flashes of green. It could have been marketed as 'therapy tourism'.

For all its regular influx of tourists, the town that had grown around the temples was unexpectedly charming, like a glimpse of the laid-back rural India we'd found on our first visit to the subcontinent thirty years earlier. It had a pleasant 'village' feel – albeit a village with an unusually large number of men trying to sell you 'airo-tek' playing cards and key rings. The bookshops, too, reflected the temples' preoccupations, with high-rise stacks of the *Kama Sutra*.

Our driver, Asharan Raikwar, invited us to tea at his home, a two-room cottage in a quiet area near the centre of town. He, his wife Mathura and their three children shared a tiny space – a living room (painted bright pink and kingfisher blue) and a kitchen, both of which doubled as bedrooms. Asharan slept on the floor of the living room, with Mathura and their sixteen-year-old daughter Nisha sharing a double bed. The two sons, Sunny and Sahil, shared the charpoy left propped up in the kitchen during the day.

We had come on a newly introduced night train from Delhi, the Nizamuddin-Manikpur-Uttar Pradesh Sampark Kranti Express (the name was a journey in itself). It had finally made Khajuraho easily accessible by rail. The days of travelling to the temples by tonga from Nowgong (forty miles away) or by country cart from Mahoba (sixty miles) – as suggested by *Murray's 1926 Handbook for Travellers in India, Burma and Ceylon* (an invaluable travelling companion) – were long gone. Tastefully, the handbook made no mention of the erotic interest of these 'noble buildings'.

We shared our train compartment with Anupam Verma, a quietly spoken airport official. Based in Khajuraho, he was travelling back there after a weekend with his family in Delhi. 'Life in a small town like Khajuraho is much better than life in Delhi,' he said. 'You have your own time, but in Delhi you spend all your time going to and from your workplace.' He then gave us an impromptu outline of what we still called the Indian Mutiny and he called the First War of Independence, together with an update on recent developments in the government of West Bengal. After two hours, he ventured: 'May I ask your good names?'

At 1am we lurched to a halt at a station platform somewhere that could have been anywhere. We stood at the carriage door and gazed into the foggy darkness. A young man wearing expensive-looking red-framed glasses materialised out of the fog.

'Good evening. How are you?' he asked. 'And from which country?'

We told him.

'Then you are using British Telecom broadband? Are you having any problems?'

No.

He nodded and smiled. 'Have a safe journey,' he said, shook our hands and hurried on. The train arrived in Khajuraho four hours late.

The journey on to Jhansi was less eventful. We were travelling (on the Khajuraho-Udaipur City Express) in a 'First Class AC' compartment, which we had to ourselves. First Class Indian rail travel was all very well but not very sociable. If we'd never travelled 'Second Class AC', how would we have found out so much about the intricacies of Bengali politics? Or about the digestive benefits of guavas? Astonishingly, the train arrived in Jhansi fifteen minutes early. Within two hours, we were back down the rabbit hole.

On an evening swirling with fog, we had dinner with Peggy at the Hotel Sita, surrounded by birthday parties. The latest craze among India's young, it seemed, was to bring birthday cakes and smear each other's faces with cream. Wearing an embroidered Kashmiri jacket and bright blue headscarf, Peggy was, as ever, swathed in thick shawls. Now ninety, she was still dazzlingly active – despite increasingly painful arthritis – and talked about taking toys to the children of tribal people ('a very scary experience'), about 'my good friend the Maharani of Panna' (who lived at Khajuraho), and of course about the cemetery. 'The blue bulls have eaten my hibiscus down to root level,' she sighed.

The following day didn't look promising. 'It's raining,' I said to the Sita's owner, Avnish Talwar.

'No, no,' he said. 'It is the fog lifting. It is the dew.'

Undaunted, Peggy, now wearing a black woollen bonnet that gave her the look of an inquisitive mole, took us to St Jude's Shrine in Anish's BMW autorickshaw – 'my bum-wobbler', as she continued to call it.

'On 28th October, St Jude's feast day, people come to the shrine in truckloads from all corners of the earth,' she said. 'They have good faith in him.'

We found the priest-in-charge, Father Alex Mascarenhas, sitting in the shrine's office, where even more St Judeiana merchandise was on sale, including inch-high statuettes of the saint in lipstick-style capsules for devotees to carry in their purses. Clare bought half a dozen for various Catholic friends. He told us that around eight thousand Catholics often turned up on the feast day, along with fifteen thousand Hindus, hoping for miracles, and that there could be up to sixty thousand pilgrims at Christmas.

'The sick people line up for the procession,' he said. 'When one lady came, she couldn't climb the steps, but she stayed for three days and then she could. And some people who couldn't have children had them after praying to St Jude.'

Rather less sophisticated merchandise was on offer when Peggy joined us on a short trip to Orchha (in, for once, an air-conditioned taxi). She took us to a small, charity-run shop selling bright-stoned jewellery made by local tribal women, along with beguiling, crudely drawn red clay paintings of village life: a woman with a water pot on her head, vegetable sellers holding up weighing scales, two gardeners watering sunflowers, a girl dancing with the sun and the moon – strange, totemic figures.

As we travelled from the dusty town into the dusty countryside, Peggy told us about the charity, Pragathi Ragh, which was connected with St Jude's and in which she was inevitably involved.

'We are doing this for social work in the villages – outlandish villages,' she said. 'We give them education. We have trainers,

Hindi masters, who go with us and can talk their language. The tribal people are out of the sphere of the capital, you know, right in the jungle, and transport is hard to come by, so they have to walk or cycle or go by bullock cart.

'Some go walking miles for even a bucket of water, so we have to educate them in saving their water. In the old days, they had wells; now they have handpumps, but they are very difficult to reach from the most remote villages.

'Some of them are very good at their work. They do matting, make baskets, things out of leather, even shoes, and do rough handwork on saris. So we have to teach them how to go about it in a more refined manner. We work purely on donations and they enable us to reach out to these people.' Educating children was the key to it all. 'Some are very clever and can talk very well in Hindi but they have to walk five miles through jungle to go to a government school. We give them books, pencils, rubbers, slates – well, we used to give them slates.'

The following day, we visited Jhansi's 17th-century fort for the first time in our dozen visits to the town. As it so obviously dominated the surrounding streets, it seemed odd to have left it so long, but there had always been another Anglo-Indian whirl sweeping us up. At the main gate, at the top of a steep slope, a notice instructed: 'Tongas to halt here'. Another warned against 'injuring or imperilling the monument'. An arrow pointed visitors to the 'Jumping Spot', from which Rani Lakshmibai and her horse had leapt so spectacularly in 1858.

The fort offered commanding views. Beyond trees vivid with parakeets, the jumble of Jhansi stretched out far below, with accompanying soundtrack – a racket of noise from the Sadar Bazaar, glitteringly magical by night, but by day a free-for-all of human hubbub, honking horns and blaring Hindi film music. A fort attendant handed us sticks to fend off pestering, possibly thieving, monkeys. Indian families were out in force and, every few minutes, someone would ask to be photographed with us: 'One picture, please?'

Also for the first time we took in the Rani Mahal, Lakshmibai's courtyarded palace, a warren of rooms with decorative panels of canoodling birds. It was littered with dusty architectural fragments including decapitated statues. A veiled old lady sat on a chair in the courtyard, knitting and beady-eyeing visitors in case one of us sloped off with a statue. We called in at the Jhansi tourist office in the Hotel Veerangana, along from the Hotel Sita, and were asked to sign the visitors' book. Ours were the first signatures for five months.

Back at Peggy's house, she was in full flow. People always made a beeline to her house, she said, 'because they know this is the focal point for asking any favours!'

She talked about her work running an unofficial Anglo-Indian marriage bureau.

'They call me Hatches, Matches and Dispatches, because I cover births, marriages and deaths! Anglo-Indian boys in Gulf countries keep in touch with me and ask if I have any girls. They send full bio-data, and a snap is a must. I ask: "Are you interested in getting married?" If yes: "Have you got a photo of yourself? Tell me about your studies and what you expect from each other – if it's sports, outings, everything. Do you like parties, dances, reading books, horseriding, whatever it is?" I tell them to put this data on the computer and I will put them in touch with one another.

'And it works beautifully. Fifteen to twenty marriages I've made and I'm happy they're all doing well. Then they tell me I have to come to their wedding – so many weddings! One person has been married fifty years: Lenny Phillips and his wife, a Blanchette.' Blanchette was an Anglo-Indian surname. 'I arranged that marriage. And her children, I have arranged their marriages. Yes, I am a real matchmaker. And I don't think I have any broken marriages.'

There was a noise beyond the street curtain.

'Just excuse me, darlings. Who is there?'

A tall, dark-haired young woman pushed the curtain aside – Catherina Moss, a PhD student from Kolkata who was staying with Peggy to research and record Anglo-Indians for a doctoral dissertation (she herself was Anglo-Portuguese).

The next fifteen minutes were the usual scrum of confused introductions, laughter, orders to Sheela to make tea and to May to fetch biscuits from the storeroom. Catherina handed Peggy a huge pile of Manila files containing photographs, newspaper cuttings, letters and battered old copies of the magazine *Anglos in the Wind*.

'Who else has been to see you?' she asked, settling herself on a kitchen chair.

'Ellie Fawcett was here ten days ago,' said Peggy. 'She is a student in England, twenty-seven, studying in London. She came here for the first time to Jhansi to trace her grandfather's birth certificate. Then I had another very interesting visit from three boys – Alistair Roberts, Ben Knott and another boy who had come to trace the graves of their ancestors. And would you believe it – I couldn't believe it at all – this Alistair Roberts was the son of my best friend in the convent school, Elma Duffield!' She laughed, still obviously delighted by the coincidence. 'She left after Partition and married in England. I told him: "Ask your mother if she has any autograph books." We all used to have autograph books in those days, so I said: "Ask her, is there any Mabel Kane there?" He rang her and asked her and the first page had my name on it! He told her, "I'm sitting with Mabel Kane, now Mrs Cantem." It was so moving, he nearly started to cry.'

Sheela brought the tea – chai for Catherina, black tea for us – and Peggy continued.

'And Mark Tully is coming to see me, according to what he said on the phone. Gillian' – Tully's long-term partner, Gillian Wright – 'has never been to Jhansi and she wants to see the fort.'

She started shuffling through the papers, which included a cutting about the interview she and Cheryl had done with Clare a decade earlier, for Radio 4's *Woman's Hour*. Papers dropped to the floor.

'So many letters… BACSA, the War Graves Commission…' It was Catherina's turn to be sent into the back room to look for more documents.

Unexpectedly, another visitor turned up: a dandyish young man, wearing a chestnut-brown jacket with cream braided edging and white leather shoes. He looked like a guest at Henley Regatta.

'This boy is a Sindhi,' said Peggy – the province of Sindh, once in northwest India, was now in Pakistan. 'He is one of the lawyers. I call them liars.' She laughed again.

The young man shook hands with us and sat down at the table. We waited for him to say why he had come. But he just sat silent. However, when Catherina emerged from the back room, he was transfixed and went into flirtatious mode, eyes twinkling. When he finally left, he did so reluctantly.

On one of our long train journeys, Clare had bought an Anglo-Indian cookery book from a Wheeler's book stall on a station platform. It wasn't for the squeamish. A typical meal might start with trotter soup – 'Ingredients: 6 to 8 trotters (mutton or pork)' – continue with sheep's head curry, goat's brain curry, sheep's brain faggots or brain pepper fry, and end with plum cake. Perhaps followed by a refreshing glass of Bone Pepper Water, which featured soup bones.

'Oh, our food is famous!' Peggy enthused when we mentioned the book to her. 'Kebabs, mulligatawny soup – that is very great. Yellow rice and ball curry – these are all Anglo-Indian specialities. *Glassy* kebabs and koftas, you put them in the shape of little balls. Mr Abbott is crazy about them. Brown stew, Irish stew, shepherd's pie, toad-in-the-hole – oh, I like toad-in-the-hole very much!'

'And we have *jungli* pilau, where everything is thrown together – vegetables and meat – and cooked in a pot,' added Catherina. 'It's a mismatch of ingredients – *jungli* means someone who is a bit unruly, not civilised, wild – like a wild child, jumping around all the time in a wild and raucous manner.'

'Then there's jalfrezi, *khichri* (kedgeree) and moolis, meals cooked with coconut milk,' said Peggy, very much warming to the theme. 'The kedgeree is not as you know it in England, because no eggs or fish are involved – simple lentils and rice and spices. It's a lot less spicy than the Indian version, a little on the blandish side, basically a chilli fry. We do put a little spice in now, though. So we've learned both styles. I like stews also. I wanted to make one for you today, but I'm sure you have lots of that in England.'

The two of them were well into a food duet. 'It's different to English stew,' explained Catherina. 'It looks bland because it doesn't have turmeric or chilli in it, but it has loads of pepper, ginger and garlic, and that broth that is really nice on a cold winter's day.'

'And our roast is very famous,' Peggy added. 'We train our servants to do this so they can make the dishes we want. But you're vegetarians, aren't you? I was in England when that mad cow disease was going on and my niece was telling me: "We won't have meat, we will have chicken." I said, "I hope we don't get mad chicken disease!"' Her laughter echoed around the room.

What about the goat's brain curry?

'Oh, we eat all sorts of brains!' Catherina exclaimed. 'Even cows' brains – and spare parts…'

Spare parts?

'Heart, inner organs… we eat everything,' she said and again wandered off to find something else for Peggy, who was wondering what time Buddie would be coming. She had originally been expected, then not expected, then expected again.

Suddenly, everyone started talking at once, in English, Hindi and Anglo-Indian. Anish, in Hindi, said he was offended by the thought of cows being eaten. Sheela asked about lunch. May wanted to phone Buddie but Peggy couldn't remember her number, or even her own mobile number. May rang her own grandson by mistake and then called someone called Wally, who was rather bemused. Catherina forgot where she had left her phone and May had to ring her number to locate it. As everyone shrieked with laughter at this unfolding farce, a motor scooter roared up outside and Buddie came in, looking every inch the biker in her leather jacket.

She and Peggy had a shouted discussion about the cemetery, where Peggy inevitably wanted to take us. 'Aunty – you go with Clare and Steve,' Buddie ordered in the end. 'Anish – you take them to the cemetery; Catherina will come with me, yah? We'll meet y'all at the graveyard.'

Thunder was grumbling and torrential rain suddenly started. 'I shall squeeze into Anish's BMW,' said Peggy. We squeezed in with her and Buddie followed on her scooter, Catherina riding pillion. The traffic was even noisier than usual. 'The more they are hooting and tooting, the more they think they will get through,' said Peggy.

Since our last visit, even more barbed wire had been fitted along the cemetery's containing wall to deter the hibiscus-eating blue bulls. Drenched by the rain, the place looked desolate. Even the peacocks looked drab. It was an uncharacteristically short visit.

We went on to Roy's, so Catherina could record him for her project. Now also nearing ninety, he was sitting in his wheelchair, a walking frame and metal crutch alongside. He sometimes dozed off during meals and conversations and had become much deafer, but stubbornly refused to wear a hearing aid. So, between him and Leela, visits to the bungalow were now rarely serene. He was hearteningly jovial, though, and talked frankly about himself in a way he rarely had before.

'Everyone thinks I'm English, you know,' he barked. 'But I'm actually half and half, put it that way. My living habits aren't Indian but I consider myself to be more Indian now than British, having lived here all my life and possibly for the rest of my days. Living in the villages – at Behrol – has also made me more Indian, actually. I don't know what it is about Behrol...' His eyes became misty, his voice softer. 'I really miss that place. I really do. Although I'm there on my own, I can always find something to do. I'm never at a loose end, even if it's giving the staff a pep talk. I'd go back there tomorrow if I could...'

We noticed that he had moved the portrait of his great-grandfather from the office into the hall.

'Oh yes, a very stern gentleman; he was frowning at me, always looking at me, as though to say: "Get on with your work, don't sleep!"'

Astonishingly, despite the Raj-in-aspic atmosphere, he now had email.

'It's not at the farms, though, and I'm glad it's not, to be honest. It means I can just relax there.'

Shyam came in with the tea tray – pretty floral cups and 'small eats' of seed cake and Bombay mix. He was wearing the usual white uniform, white gloves and Nehru cap. He addressed Clare as 'memsahib', which seemed strange after our more relaxed, informal relationship at the farms.

There was a commotion outside. Buddie and Catherina were pulling up on the scooter. 'What a noise!' shrieked Leela, without irony, as they took off their wet jackets.

'This is Catherina from Calcutta,' said Peggy as Catherina shook water off her dupatta.

'Ah, good old Calcutta!' cried Roy as though about to lead a sing-song. 'What a lovely city – is it still lovely?'

Catherina's reply was lost in the laughter and the jostling for seats, but when the noise subsided Roy was recollecting meeting his wife Lillian in Calcutta.

'There she is, there, as a young girl,' he said, pointing to a photo on the wall.

'I want to know all about your family,' said Catherina, switching on her tape recorder.

Roy never needed second bidding to talk about the Abbotts, so we heard again stories we had heard several times before, including that of his great-grandmother, thirteen when she married, seventeen when she survived the Siege of Lucknow. According to a memorial in Jhansi's St Martin's Church, she was 'a heroic figure… when in perils oft, she brought succour to the deceased'.

What was new were the stories about his grandfather, John Harold, establishing Abbott Mount, a colony for Anglo-Indians in the Kumaon hills, bordering the Himalayas.

'That was the one big mistake he made,' said Roy. 'It wasn't too successful – he thought it would flourish but it was too out of the way, and he had trouble with an Anglo woman who lived there. And there was no water there; they had to bring it up manually from the bottom of the mount.

'Twenty or thirty years ago when the harvest was over, I thought I'd go and have a look at it – my grandfather is buried up there. And it's lovely, six thousand five hundred feet up, gets very cold in winter. Leela went when it was snowing and says she won't go again

– she forgot to take her snow boots, so she got stuck.' He roared
with laughter again, shoulders shaking and slapping his thighs. 'The
biggest surprise is that it's still called Abbott Mount and not Gandhi
Nagar! I really must see it again, maybe for the last time.'

A few miles from the Nepal border, Abbott Mount is now
marketed as a 'dwarf hill station' and 'picturesque hamlet' in the
state of Uttarakhand. According to the state tourist board, John
Harold Abbott 'was so mesmerised by the serenity of the place
that he decided to develop it as a European settlement'. Described
as 'obscurely located amidst the Kumaon hills', it offers 'charming
colonial heritage' and 'breathtaking views of sunrises and sunsets'.
As an added inducement, it boasts the world's second-highest
cricket pitch.

Random memories came back to Roy as we all sat around,
drinking our tea. He talked fondly about his older sister, Charmaine,
who had married an RAF officer and settled in Saxmundham, as
had their father. She had died a month before the millennium, aged
seventy-five.

'She was very keen on yoga, every day yoga. She would just get
up from her chair and stand on her head, just perfect! She'd say: "You
want to see my yoga?" I'd say: "I can see it, but don't ask me to do it!"
Then she goes and gets cancer of the bone and dies.' He sighed.

'Anglo-Indian women,' he continued, 'you couldn't get better.
Could. Not. Get. Better. Some real beauties. Lovely. No other
word for it. Good-looking, good company, everything. They had
all the right qualities, put it that way.' He growled with laughter.
'And the Railway Institute – what a place! It was always full –
people drinking there, playing billiards, there was a reading room,
badminton of course, a bandstand with one of the army people

playing every Saturday. Families with young children came. They took them in their prams. There was no age limit – it was a free-for-all. Everyone would be singing and enjoying themselves or having a fight over some girl – "Leave my girl alone!" "Why should I?" "Come outside!"' He threw back his head and laughed even more.

'Every Saturday was a hop,' said Peggy.

'The dances!' roared Roy in full flood. 'You've never seen a better jiver than Peg! I couldn't cope with her; she'd have me on the floor! If she were dancing I'd sit and just watch her.'

'Oh, go on,' giggled Peggy. Then: 'Anish is having to go.' Anish smiled, waggled his head in agreement, and escaped while he could.

Catherina held her microphone towards Roy. 'I've heard your place in the village is haunted,' she said, changing the subject.

'Hmmm… What?' Roy asked.

She repeated the question, but he still couldn't hear it, cupping his hand to his ear. He only understood when the rest of us chorused *'HAUNTED!'* at him.

'Ah yes,' he said, slapping the arms of his wheelchair. 'Haunted. People have seen my uncle. A woman saw him when she came from Bombay and stayed at the farm – Smith was her name, I think. Lillian and I were off in England for a holiday and while we were there she wrote us a frantic letter. "I can't stay here any more, I'm going back to Bombay. There's a man comes here every day and sits at the table."

'She described my uncle to a tee – Charles Abbott, white hair, stockily built. But she'd never met him, so how did she know? And she said, "He sits there, seems to be doing something, then he goes away."

'Now, I've never seen my uncle but I've heard peculiar sounds at the village. I've heard the gate opening and closing at 2am. Who is it at that time of night, going in and out? And there's a child, usually about that time in the morning, I've heard it crying, loudly, from my bedroom that faces what used to be the cremation ground. I even went out one day to see if anyone was there. A nice place to live!' he laughed. 'Some of the dead are still there.'

Shyam appeared again with more tea.

'Ha! You asked about ghosts – there's one here! He appears from nowhere!'

It was Peggy's cue to get a word in. 'I was very ill in 1957,' she told us. 'I was on my deathbed when I was operated on and the doctor told my stepsister I wouldn't survive, that I had forty-eight hours. I was in a coma afterwards and I saw this beautiful palace and gold steps going up with red carpet on. And there was a man standing at the bottom. He told me to take a key, go up the first flight of steps and open the first door on the left. He was in full dress suit, a very handsome man, and when I went up the steps, I saw him again in full white robes and with a glowing face. And he said: "Yes, I am the Lord."

'And then I felt the doctor giving me artificial respiration and I opened my eyes, though I couldn't talk. The matron asked me a week later why I was still in a daze. I told her and she said: "Yes, you were between life and death. But you were too good to go to hell and too bad to go to heaven!"'

The conversation was, as ever, unravelling like a ball of wool, but Catherina was determined to pin Roy down. 'Tell me more about your life,' she insisted.

He returned to his sister Charmaine. 'She was very similar to me as a person. She was also very attached to the village, particularly to the women. They would sit among themselves and at festivals they would carry pots on their heads and she would join them and go to the temple with a pot on her head. She loved it there. Her husband had been posted out here with his RAF squadron. They met in Nainital – my God, how they've ruined that place! It was beautiful, that lake – no rubbish, people didn't throw paper into it. They had a lovely club there; only decent people were allowed to join it. You could have a lovely meal there. You could hire a yacht, go fishing, which I was very fond of.'

Then an old refrain: 'I still look back to British times. Things were more organised, there was discipline in the country. Things were better. It was a great country then because it had a limited population – three hundred million. Now it's gone over into the billions. Bursting at the seams. Look at any two-seater or bus – crowded and packed, people sitting on the roof. Trains are just as bad. They've introduced many more, but still they're not enough.' He shook his head.

A mobile phone started its Bollywood trill, but Roy decided to ignore it.

'It's a good life, though. I wouldn't change it. Anyway, it's too late to move now, but I wouldn't have done it in the early days either. I'm far too attached here. There is only one country for me, this one. If I had to go somewhere else, under compulsion, I'd go to Australia. England? Look at the climate there! And Australians are much more open and free, and you can motor for miles without seeing another vehicle.'

Catherina, defeated, took a piece of paper out of her shoulder bag. 'Could you sign this consent form, Uncle?' she asked, handing him a pen.

'OK, OK, my girl,' he laughed. 'Will I be put away?' He signed. 'How long are you here for? You should stay longer next time. Come back to Jhansi soon – and come and stay at the farms.'

The invitation reminded him of another potential guest. In 1997 he had met Queen Elizabeth during her visit to India. As the British honorary consul in Jhansi, he had travelled up to Delhi for a royal reception.

'I told her that I was possibly the only white farmer left in this country. She said: "I can't believe that." And I said: "Come and see me at the farms, Your Majesty".' As he reminisced, his mind far back in the 'good old days', his tea gradually went cold on the small table next to him.

CHAPTER 17

'THE CRANE FELL DOWN, DEAD AS A DODO!'

We were back at his bungalow, with Peggy, for lunch the following day. More than ever, Leela seemed in charge of the whole household, bustling into the kitchen to bark orders while we helped Roy into the dining room. His wheelchair was waiting at his place.

'Your imperial throne?' Clare asked.

'Ah yes, my mobile throne!' laughed Roy. 'As opposed to my mobile phone!'

'You need to get it motorised, Roy,' I said.

'Ah, you can get those in India now,' he answered. 'But it would be a dangerous exercise out here – avoiding people and running people over and getting into trouble!' He slapped his thigh. 'I wonder if there's any country where you find more jaywalkers than this one? There may be a pedestrian crossing there but they never use it!'

'The traffic never stops for anyone at pedestrian crossings, anyway,' Clare pointed out.

'Ah yes, if you want to get run over, that's the place!' he said. 'I've been told not to drive just now, because of my cataracts, but I'll get back to it as soon as I've had this eye op, and get a lens put in.'

Clare and I went back into the living room to collect Peggy, and half carried her back in, settling her on her chair. 'Thank you, darlings, thank y'all.'

The dining room was chillingly cold so we ate wrapped in shawls and thick woollen Nehru jackets.

'You haven't got a heater?' asked Peggy, hunched inside her jacket and scarf, her woollen hat still on her head.

'Yes, we have a heater,' shouted Leela. 'But this room gets so cold, *nah*? It's not good. When he is not here, I sleep in the bearer's room.'

'He sleeps alone, then?' said Peggy, ever keen to find out whether Roy had secretly married Leela, as rumours had been suggesting over the past few years.

'No,' said Leela. 'I sleep in the *khatiya*. How can I leave him alone? *Khatiya* is like a cot,' she explained, turning to Clare. 'Like a charpoy, an Indian bed, with strings. He has his king-size bed, yah?'

Peggy and Roy started talking at high volume and cross purposes about Catherina and her PhD, as Shyam and Ram Rani, the cook, brought in lunch – palak paneer, with puris arriving, steaming, every few minutes.

'I eat those palak leaves raw,' said Peggy, prodding at her spinach and veering off at a tangent. 'His cabbages were that big!' She spread out her arms. 'When his father was alive, I was in the agriculture department, and they always got the prize! Cauliflowers that big!' Spread-out arms again.

The conversation continued to weave a labyrinthine path through Catherina's travel arrangements, the Calcutta branch of the Anglo-Indian Association and local Anglos, including Randolph Morris. We had met him during a stay at Orchha's Amar Mahal hotel, where he was front desk manager. Naturally, Peggy and Roy between them filled us in on his family connections.

'He was Audrey Thomas's son,' said Peggy.

'From quite a famous local Anglo-Indian family,' added Roy.

'A relative of Colleen's,' said Peggy.

'Sahib? *Ek puri aur?*' asked Ram Rani, offering me another steaming plate of fried breads.

For once, Leela talked about her own family. Her parents, now in their eighties, still lived in Kerala, which she visited once a year. Her youngest brother was a priest – 'a bishop in the denomination of Church of South India. He has a Bible seminary there. He started taking in children who are orphans. He goes around and asks people for money for them.' Another brother was a college lecturer in Mumbai, where her sister also lived, working in the cotton industry. 'They have been here, but in this weather, nobody will come. It is so cold.'

'Not to us, it isn't,' Clare corrected.

Leela laughed. 'You people don't feel it! I feel cold, and he laughs at me in the night when I go to bed because I have my scarf round me. In Kerala there is no winter –'

'I'm an Englishman,' joked Roy, puffing out his chest. 'I come from a cold country.'

As Ram Rani brought round a plate of cake, we said how different the Jhansi Hotel looked since our last visit. Four to six months from reopening, it would be 'Number One in Jhansi', according to Leela.

After lunch, she took some food to Dev, who was now living in the St Jude's Senior Citizens' Home we had passed the previous year. We later learned from Peggy that this quiet, gentle woman who'd once asked me if Clare was my 'beloved' died not long afterwards, of 'loneliness and malnutrition'. It was a haunting image.

❖ ❖ ❖ ❖

The remaining four of us went to sit out on the veranda. Without Leela, the atmosphere was quieter, more relaxed, and Roy and Peggy recalled 'the old days', like the very old friends they were. They looked back nostalgically to the 1950s, an era in which many older Anglos seemed to linger. It was touching, gently Chekhovian.

'Do you remember the skating rink, Peg?' asked Roy. 'And Jhansi Departmental Stores? It was started by my grandmother. It had everything – ladies' tailoring, everything was there.'

'Oooh, everything!' exclaimed Peggy. 'Beautiful coats – she used to go to England once a year and come back before Christmas and put up all her hats, coats, mufflers, everything you could think of! She would bring a whole lot of stuff from England. In those days the Anglo-Indians were in full force, so they used to buy a lot of stuff from there.

'And they had a lovely zoo there. A mini-zoo. All the animals they kept! They had a bear and an aviary. Oh, the bear! I used to be terrified! We paid the bear man four annas to get it to dance and we'd give the bear a banana or something. And we used to have the monkey men coming round, doing all their tricks.'

'My grandmother had everything there,' nodded Roy. 'Even a sarus crane. It met an untimely end. It pecked my grandfather on his head so he grabbed it by the neck and screwed it…' He demonstrated with his hands, roaring with laughter. 'The crane fell down, dead as a dodo!'

Clare and I glanced at each other.

'They can be very dangerous,' said Peggy. 'I had one chasing me but I dodged behind another old lady and it pecked her hat off! I'll never forget that. We were in the railway quarters and I was coming back from school. You'd go up the bridge and down again. And this sarus was at the foot of the bridge, and anyone she saw she chased. So I ran behind this old lady. Her name was Mrs Fernandez. That crane also had an untimely end. Someone else killed it.'

It seemed tactful to change the subject. We moved on to Jhansi's long-gone days as an international airport. We asked Roy to tell us more about the 1938 Air France crash at nearby Datia in which seven people had been killed. We had seen their graves in the cemetery but knew little more.

'Well, in the 1930s – I'm not shooting a line or anything,' said Roy, 'KLM, British Airways and Air France all came here. We were agents for all these airlines at the Jhansi Hotel and, after the crash, my uncle had to take the embalmed bodies down to Bombay to put on a ship back to France. Most people don't believe that Jhansi was so important. It was on the Australian run – Jhansi, Calcutta, Singapore and on to Australia.

'And in the next five years Jhansi will be back on the air map. They've already started work on an airstrip just out of Orchha. It will be worth it – a lot of people are visiting Orchha now, but Jhansi is no longer a stop on the way to Khajuraho. Agra and Orchha are, but not Jhansi. There's nothing to see here, only the fort…'

Then an abrupt right turn into full Raj-nostalgia mode… 'The ICS – Indian Civil Service – what a wonderful service that was, in the old British days,' he sighed. 'That was really something.'

'The cream of society,' Peggy chipped in. 'The heaven-born.'

'They were so totally devoted to this country,' Roy continued. 'But the heat wasn't suitable for them. They spent very little time in their offices, they were always out. They'd go to camp; I went out with one of them, Jim Ferguson, he was a Collector. He was the Rajah of the district; went out on tour, all by horseback, lived in a tent and held court under the peepal tree, a sort of open-air courtroom. Then the camp would move to the next village and everyone would come and air their grievances to him, and he would make immediate decisions. That was why India was so good. It was on-the-spot justice.

'I often think about those days and Ferguson. How I'd have loved to have been in the ICS – a District Forest Officer. There was no better life.' His eyes were very far away – but only momentarily, as the tornado that was Leela returned.

It was the cue for a further five minutes of shrieking, barking, a story about the sex of a fish, a shouted update on Roy's Jarndyce vs Jarndyce court case, a crescendo of noise for all Jhansi to hear. Nostalgia fled.

'I always tell people that God only ever made one person who had so much time on his hands!' said Leela to Roy, laughing. 'I have to go to work – you have plenty of time to spend.' And she bustled off again.

As we looked out across the garden, the quiet reminiscences continued. 'We all used to go out in a tonga to go fishing,' remembered Peggy.

'Those were amazing days, the dacoity days of the fifties and sixties,' mused Roy. 'With shikar, and all our tiger beats and all.'

Peggy touched Roy's arm. 'There are guavas hanging on that tree, Bud.' She was one of the few people who called him Bud – after the American comedian Bud Abbott. We all gazed at the guavas.

❖ ❖ ❖ ❖

Just two hours later, it was time for yet more eating. While Peggy went home to rest, we, together with Roy and Leela, drove to the Little Angels kindergarten run by Buddie. There was a small aviary outside, and a light constantly rotated, flashing on and off. On the veranda were pictures of Gandhi and Christ in front of the cross.

Inside, a picture of Mother Teresa hung on the wall of the parakeet-green-painted schoolroom, together with a declaration: 'Jesus, I trust in you!' Elsewhere were laminated posters of pictorial alphabets, parts of the body, 'Our Flowers', 'Our Birds' and 'Our Animals'. I wasn't altogether sure how many of the kangaroos, zebras and giant pandas they depicted would be lurking in India.

Buddie – no-one ever seemed to call her Claudette – lived here with her twin brother Claude, his family, and her mother Antoinette Jacobs, an authoritative woman in her late seventies whom Buddie addressed as 'Mummy'.

Child-sized red and yellow plastic chairs were stacked on one side of the room and two school tables, pushed together, were covered with sheets of newspaper. Buddie had laid on a huge spread of 'small eats' – sandwiches, cheese balls, pakoras, bhajis, biscuits, fruit cake, crisps, pizza slices, vegetable patties, Bombay mix and slices of cake (Barbie-pink and Kermit-green) – which we struggled to do justice to.

We huddled again in our coats and shawls under unflattering blue lighting that made us all look rather seedy, only a curtain separating us from the wintry outside. We drank ginger tea and listened as Roy, handkerchief as ever in blazer top pocket, held forth. Conversations fractured and broke away, ebbed and flowed over each other, interrupted by the hum of the generator and by phones suddenly trilling into song.

He and Antoinette reminisced about an old Anglo-Indian family they had both known. 'He was only fifty-two or something when he died,' he barked. 'But he drank too much, which they all did, I'm afraid, in those days. They drank some quite palatable liquor – like that fruit drink, but alcoholic…'

'It used to be very harsh, that stuff,' said Antoinette, a blue fleece jacket zipped over her orange and green salwar kameez.

'From the mahua tree,' Roy explained, turning to us. 'It flowers in April and then they dry the flowers…'

'And you made liquor out of it. It ferments. It's very strong. If you ate it raw, you would get a little giddiness,' continued Antoinette.

'People put a little fertiliser in liquor now to give it a bit more kick,' said Roy. 'But they still survive!'

He rocked with laughter and turned to stories Antoinette must have heard a hundred times before about his grandfather, 'the Hay King of Jhansi'.

'When his sons, all four of them, were being extravagant, he would say: "You're like this today, spending money, wasting money, but when I came to Jhansi I had just eight annas in my pocket!"'

'That was a lot!' replied Antoinette absently. 'I used to get one paisa…'

Buddie started handing round the sandwiches and china cups of tea.

'There were four paise in an anna, sixteen annas in a rupee,' Roy explained.

'These are veg patties,' said Buddie. 'And there is chutney and sauce, and sweet things…'

'He had no shoes on his feet,' Roy continued. 'I find it hard to believe, but it's true…'

'These are pizzas,' interrupted Buddie, 'from Nav Bharat bakery here. And we call these Smilies…' She held out a plate of round potato cakes with smiling faces imprinted on them.

As Roy launched into a monologue about mules, Buddie brought out more and more plates of food.

'These are cheese balls.'

Leela bit into one. 'Oh, hot hot hot!' she shrieked.

'Uncle, you want some homemade chutney, green chutney?' said Buddie. 'Try our Christmas cake…' She prepared to dash away again. 'I'll serve the coffee now – or I can make more tea if you prefer? Ginger? Black tea?'

'When's the Mad Hatter arriving?' Clare murmured under her breath.

As she ate, Antoinette talked to Clare about her life. 'We were two sisters, three brothers – Daryl, Era, Andre, Delice and me. My grandfather was – what do you call them? – an officer on the railway in the carriage and wagon department, so he had a lot of people under him. Frank Jacobs – you must be knowing him?' she said, looking at Roy.

He couldn't hear but nodded anyway and murmured, 'Hmm, hmm, hmm…'

Frank's own father had been Anglo-Indian, his mother British. 'I don't know which part of Britain,' Antoinette said vaguely. 'I wasn't even born then…'

She was, in fact, born in 1934, to a goods train driver and his wife.

'My dad never retired,' she said, drawing her fleece closer around her. 'He had to give up his job because in the '47 riots he met with an accident. They reversed the gears when he was on a train and he banged into a dead end and was thrown off. He had compound fractures in his hands and legs – three places his leg was broken, so then he was unfit for duty. He couldn't carry on. Two to three years he was off work. There were not so many medical facilities at that time. He was only on half-pay because he wasn't working for so long. There was no compensation, nothing. So he found it difficult to manage.'

Antoinette was a pupil at St Francis's Convent School at the time. But the accident meant the family could no longer afford the school fees, so she had to leave at twelve. She married her first husband – 'Mr Baines' – when she was 'about twenty'.

What was the Jhansi community like when she was growing up?

'Oh, it was lovely, lovely! You won't get those days again. Very pleasant people they were, always ready to help each other. They were interactive with everything. You've heard of the May Queen Dance? The most beautiful lady from Jhansi was selected. And yes, one year I got!' There was more than a touch of wistfulness in her voice. 'Then things began to change.'

'Those were the days,' sighed Roy as Leela put another slice of pizza on his plate.

'There are hardly any people left now,' Buddie said ruefully, poised to return to the kitchen.

'And that's the end of it,' shrugged Antoinette. 'What can we do about it? Nothing we can do. So let's see what will happen when we all die out.'

Some time after Partition, her father and brother Andre left for England, initially heading for Southall. Her siblings gradually followed one by one.

'But I just couldn't move because of my grandfather. He was so dependent on me. There was nobody else to look after him. My sister, she just disappeared here in India. She was in her late thirties and she left with some fellow. God knows who. After that, we have heard nothing further from her.'

There always seemed to be some mystery attached to Anglo-Indians: a missing sister or brother, a grandfather who disappeared in the jungle, a terrible accident... Antoinette and her five children were one of the few Anglo-Indian families to stay on in Jhansi. Was she glad they had stayed rather than emigrated, as so many others had?

'Well, I couldn't regret it,' she said with another shrug. 'I had no option, actually. Other countries didn't want small children at that time, and my kids were too small to take. By the time they were grown up, they'd stopped the migration.'

Buddie bustled back. 'You want more cakes? See, this is walnut cake and this is ribbon cake. And this is plum – there is more coming...'

'Fairy cakes and butterfly cakes!' exclaimed Antoinette.

'What did I say?' shouted Roy. 'You're going to end up having dinner here!'

Before yet more cakes arrived, Clare and I made our excuses and left. All told, the day had been seven hours of chitter-chatter-chitter-chatter. Not for the first time, we'd seen the bonds that tied India's Anglo-Indians together. It was as though the community had to stick together in their internal exile, clinging tribally to what remained of their heritage.

We had tickets for the following afternoon's train back to Delhi, but, in view of the regular winter fog delays, we decided instead to hire a local taxi to leave at 8am for the three-hundred-mile journey. We drove past mustard fields, sometimes negotiating herds of goats skipping across motorways, sometimes passing through small towns where men sat around drinking chai from clay cups while their womenfolk worked. A detour through Agra took us past the Hotel Alleviate.

As we neared Delhi, the fields gave way to vast estates of multi-storey apartment blocks. The rays of the setting sun hardly penetrated the concrete canyons. Fifteen years earlier, a Delhi-based photographer friend had bought a farmhouse here, in what was then open country; the only people his family saw were occasional shepherds. Now the farmhouse had been swallowed into the ever-growing Gotham City-like suburb of Gurgaon.

At this late point in our journey, we discovered that our young driver had never been to Delhi before and got hopelessly lost when we reached the outskirts. We peered out into the chokingly polluted evening fog on the ring road, passed greengrocers sitting beside their fruit and vegetable stalls, and shouted directions to him whenever we recognised a building: 'Left side!... Right side!... Backside!'

I guided us effortlessly from one traffic jam to another, overtaking whole families balanced on motorbikes like circus stunt acts. We passed a small office with the sign 'Cow World', another for 'The Eccentric Institute for Tuition in Banking'. We occasionally stopped to ask directions from passers-by. Most were studiously polite, telling us what they thought we wanted to hear.

Their relaxed attitude to the subtle difference between 'left' and 'right' added an extra frisson and many extra miles to our journey. We arrived at our hotel twelve hours after setting off from Jhansi. It had taken us two of those hours just to cross Delhi in the rush hour.

On the following day, the last of our trip, we visited Lodhi Gardens, scattered with Mughal tombs and perhaps the capital's most precious green space. Middle-class residents were playing cricket and badminton, practising yoga, picnicking, taking selfies and power-walking in immaculately clean trainers, arms swinging like pendulums. It was a universe away from Jhansi.

CHAPTER 18

'MY MONGOOSE HASN'T COME THIS MORNING'

We were back in Jhansi later that year so Clare could finally make her Radio 4 programme about the Anglo-Indian community. Unsurprisingly, it was to be called *Teatime at Peggy's,* in recognition of the fact that the dwindling cast of characters spent so much time in each other's homes, drinking tea, eating cake and discussing the latest local intrigue.

By now, both Peggy and Roy had turned ninety, so we knew we had limited time to record them. Peggy, in particular, was increasingly incapacitated and suffering from the cold, though still indefatigably cheerful. It turned out to be our longest visit – eleven days – and the most dramatic.

We arrived on the Jabalpur-Nizamuddin Express, after a few days at Kanha National Park in the neighbouring state of Madhya Pradesh. Its tiger reserve was reputedly Kipling's inspiration for *The Jungle Book*, though in fact he never visited it and based his descriptions of central India on what he read in books and heard from friends.

We had reached Kanha after a six-hour drive from Nagpur airport through rapidly encroaching night. The street markets were piled high with the oranges for which the state is famous. Soon we were in densely dark rural areas, speeding past roadside stalls lit by flares and shrines housing garlanded statues of deities. Away from the polluting light of towns and cities, the stars were astonishingly bright, if oddly angled for Europeans. Orion appeared to be poised for a somersault. People huddled in shawls on cottage verandas and jackals skulked at the roadside. 'Tigers cross here,' said our driver, casually.

We stayed at Banjaar Tola, a plush camp offering safari trips, whose main focus was many tourists' obsessive need to see tigers. We saw none, but over two jeep safaris through forests of sal trees and bamboo, we were more than compensated by the extraordinary birdlife – red-wattled lapwings, yellow-footed green pigeons and Indian grey hornbills, white-throated kingfishers, racket-tailed drongos and changeable hawk-eagles. We also spotted grazing deer through a shimmering curtain of dragonflies, with a soundtrack of whistling cicadas.

'Look at the light falling on that spider's web,' said our young but hugely knowledgeable guide Sadhvi Singh. From somewhere in the undergrowth came the tinkling marimba-like call of a tree pie bird. 'And listen – the bugling call of the swamp deer. When we drive along here, always something is watching, watching – tigers, leopards, porcupines, pangolins.'

A small feline face stared out of the long grass.

'A jungle cat. Even rarer than tigers.'

There was a low rumble in the middle distance. What was that?

'Human stomach,' said Sadhvi.

We had dinner with the camp's manager, whose parting shot at the end of the meal was masterly. 'One last quick question,' he said. 'You are well travelled. Tell me: do you think there will be a Third World War?'

The four-hour drive to Jabalpur showed India at its most entrancingly rural, with villages of small houses painted turquoise and lilac, bright green and orange. Blue-uniformed schoolgirls with plaited pigtails and white dupattas cycled to school, satchels on their backs. Skinny old men in dhotis sat out in the sunshine on plastic bucket chairs and herds of bleating goats trotted along the road. Bullock carts, domed haystacks, sunflowers, pots of marigolds, men punting across lily-strewn ponds: all 'too much lovely', as a Delhi waiter had once described Orchha. Only the occasional house walls painted with adverts for Airtel and Vodafone hinted at the 21st century.

Back on the train, I was walking along the corridor when a compartment door opened and a distinguished-looking elderly man peered out at me.

'Which country are you from?' he demanded, eyes narrowed.

I told him and he looked searchingly at me.

'Are you an admirer of Bertrand Russell?'

We had a short conversation about the great philosopher – or, rather, the elderly man talked and I listened – and I mentioned Kipling.

'I have never been attracted to reading him,' he said. 'But I enjoy Conan Doyle.'

Due to arrive at 10.45pm, the train reached Jhansi two hours late, forty-five minutes into Christmas Eve. We later discovered that heavy fog had delayed some Delhi-bound trains by thirty-two hours, with one to Lucknow finally arriving thirty-eight hours late. Inconvenience caused...

Our taxi from the station passed dozens of people sleeping on sacking on the pavements. Jhansi seemed uncharacteristically silent.

❖ ❖ ❖ ❖

For the first time in many visits, we were not staying at the Hotel Sita. The Jhansi Hotel had just reopened after its long-drawn-out renovation and was almost unrecognisable from the place I had first visited nearly fifteen years earlier: sleek, glitzy, stylishly comfortable rooms, smart bathrooms with cascade showers and fragrant bars of guest soap in cellophane-wrapped sachets with an almost heraldic 'JH' crest topped by a crown. Peggy had described it in a letter as having 'seven-star status – one thousand times better than it was'. It seemed not so much a renovation as a resurrection. As one guest wrote in the visitors' book: 'Now my search for a good hostile experience ends with your hotel'.

Our room, with its room-service menu offering 'seismic toast', was a few doors along from Dr Righton's. What would he have made of the hotel's resurrection, I wondered.

We phoned Peggy. 'Roy is away,' she said. 'When he gets back tomorrow, give him a tinkle.' Distant train hooters still sounded reassuringly through the night.

I spent Christmas Day in bed with a stomach upset and watched TV. The adverts had the homespun quality of US TV ads in the 1950s. One featured an enticing 'Dream Bedsheet Combo'.

We were finally round at Peggy's on Boxing Day. The December picture on her Norfolk Coast calendar, sent by a British friend, featured summer photographs of Hunstanton, Sheringham and Wells-next-the-Sea. Another friend had given her a tea towel showing London scenes, including Buckingham Palace.

'I am very patriotic,' she smiled. 'I cherish the Royal Family. The Queen was born on 21st April, the same day as me, and has always been in my mind. At the time of the Coronation, I used to collect all souvenirs of them – plates, little cups, a whole set of the different counties in England: Kent, Derbyshire... And I had little castles, little pigs, all in china.

'We used to buy cigarette packets – Capstans, English 555 State Express brand – and get little photos of the Royal Family or actors and actresses in them. Dorothy Lamour, Bing Crosby... you'd ask your friends for them and if you sent in five pictures, you could exchange them for a big enlargement. And I had a full set of the Royal Family that I collected from Cavendish cigarettes – even our present Queen when she was born... And I have a picture of Diana: the whole family I've got. It's something we should keep in touch with.'

Not for the first time, we were amazed by her powers of recall, maybe connected to her early stenographer training.

'And I had some other weird hobbies,' she laughed. 'Like collecting scarves of different countries – Malta, New Zealand, I have many. About forty countries I have. I don't collect scarves with flowers on, but of famous buildings. They are my legacy.'

Not all her hobbies had stood the test of changing times. 'I was very fond of collecting butterflies – pinning them down, putting them on a big chart. And I was very fond of collecting birds' eggs. I was nearly bitten by a snake once, when I was trying to collect birds' eggs! The bird pecked me, and it was just as well as there was a snake inside the nest! I had eggs as small as that' – her thumb and forefinger registered half an inch – 'they were tomtits. And others as big as ostrich eggs. I think I still have one of those. And

I collected flowers – pressing them into a book. My sister used to tell me I was a robber!' She laughed merrily before subsiding into a bout of coughing.

Nowadays, she stuck to tea towels, including a fine set of British wildlife ones, with pictures of otters and grey squirrels on them. And she was very excited by the mongoose which had started visiting her house, rooting around for snakes and lizards and sometimes sleeping under her bed: 'But he is a destructive fellow. He sometimes nibbles the bedclothes.'

Unexpectedly, the Jhansi correspondent of a national newspaper dropped in. He was pleasant and talkative, and seemed to have an undemanding routine. A church's 150th anniversary celebrations, he said, would make 'a good story'.

Peggy talked again about the Jhansi Anglo-Indians who had emigrated to Britain. 'When they went out to England, they were sleeping on newspapers in hovels. They had to struggle to achieve what they have achieved today. One lady told me: "It has been a struggle for us. We were called the blacks, and whichever county we shifted to, we were treated as though no-one wanted to know who we were. They wouldn't even give us a room." Today those same people are wealthy and writing books about what happened to them in England. They say: "We have all the protection now. What England is giving us, that India would never give" – that is the medical care.'

As ever, there were unending mountains of food to conquer. While Clare was recording Peggy, May made us *bharta*, a curry of chillies, aubergine, onion, coriander and mashed potato – and served it in a hefty naan sandwich for lunch.

Two hours later, leaving Peggy resting in bed, we were tackling tea at Buddie's. As before, we were faced with a vast spread: Indian pizza, battered potato rings, cheese balls in breadcrumbs, pakoras and three sorts of cake – walnut, plum and 'striped' or 'ribbon' cake (coloured sponge) – all laid out on tables in the schoolroom.

'Eat more, you must eat more,' Buddie kept saying.

We returned to the Little Angels school the next day, so Clare could interview Buddie – with Antoinette sitting beady-eyed and sharp-eared nearby.

Buddie talked about Britain, where her sister Pearline lived with her family. 'I go to England for holiday, but not to settle. The weather puts me off. Like at 4pm it's dark, you've just had your lunch and now you're going to bed. Pearline would go out to work and I would be sitting around waiting for them to come back. I'd look out and it's raining or it's dark. At least here, if no-one's in the house, you just take a bike and go out anywhere. Or you go to the neighbours to sit. People in England don't even know their neighbours.' When she'd wished people good morning, she said, they'd never wished her the same.

Antoinette laughed. 'Funny, *nah*?'

I wondered if mother and daughter mixed much with their Indian neighbours.

'Running our school, most of the time we have to interact with them,' said Antoinette. 'We go to their weddings or any functions they invite us to. We enjoy them, then come away.'

'But we are not very good friends, going in and out of their houses, that way,' said Buddie. 'Only with invitation cards we go. We mix with them because at our school we are most of the time in and out only with them, you know? We are more involved with our own people. Whereas with Indian people, Hindus and all, you are more like a guest there.'

'We don't know their traditions and things like that, no?' agreed Antoinette. 'How they celebrate things – we go as guest, then don't know what's coming next. Whereas with Anglo-Indians, you do.'

How, Clare asked, would Buddie feel once Peggy had died?

She looked bereft at the thought. 'I'm going to be lost without Aunty Peggy. Most of the things I have really learned through life, I have learned from her. She's a very, very strong lady, not scared of anything. And she can remember mobile numbers – can you imagine?'

She agreed that Peggy held things together in the Anglo community. 'I doubt there will be anyone else after that; no-one has the time. I will take over the cemetery but not the Anglo-Indian side.'

'Yes, she's the ringleader of the community,' chipped in Antoinette.

Buddie continued: 'In our community, there's hardly anyone left, and by the time our old people die, and our younger generation don't want to stay here…' She tailed off, paused and carried on: 'So the next generation will be like me and Aunty Cheryl – very few left, a handful of people. When Aunty Peggy has gone, I doubt there will be anyone else.'

We strolled back to the hotel through the Sadar Bazaar, past a butcher's called the Honey Pig Shop, to try to find some bubble wrap. Without knowing the Hindi word, I tried to describe what I wanted to a stationer.

'Polythene,' I explained. 'Wrapping paper.'

I snapped my fingers and made popping sounds.

'We call it bubble wrap,' said the stationer.

I mentioned Peggy to him. 'I have met her twice, thrice,' he said.

A woman along the street came out of her house with a newspaper parcel. She opened it, scattered birdseed on the pavement, then screwed up the newspaper and dropped it on the ground.

The next day, we were back at Peggy's, along with Buddie and Gwen. Peggy was still in bed but sitting up and, of course, talking on her phone. There was no sign of Sheela but May moved noiselessly around, providing tea and cake.

'I was going to get an extension cord, to bring the phone closer,' Peggy said in a shaky voice after finishing the call. She winced as she moved. 'I've eaten a biscuit,' she said. 'It's a good biscuit. Company makes a lot of difference…'

With little encouragement, she reminisced about Christmas traditions, and the conversation became ever more surreal.

'In the good old days, we made our own plum puds. And I never forget, as a child, buying a huge leg of ham. I thought it must be fabulous, it was that solid! But I wouldn't eat it. It was supposed to be the leg of a bear – a bear, yah! That put me off as a child. Bear I wouldn't eat; I am terrified of bears. Then it turned out to be English pig.'

The phone rang from the kitchen. 'It's your cousin Jimmy Fernandez,' May shouted.

'Tell him to phone me after half an hour,' Peggy shouted back, and carried straight on with her bear stories. 'My husband knew I was terrified of bears, so once, when we were in the railway quarters, I was reading a book and I must have fallen off to sleep. He was sitting outside and saw the bear man come. All I know, I heard the jingle of those bells. I turned round and there was the bear in the room! You should have seen me – I ran out of the house, out of the bathroom door and called to my husband: "Where did this bear come from?" He said: "I paid the man to bring him in!"'

Laughing and coughing, she lay back against the pillows.

'And my husband's train was delayed once,' she continued when she recovered. 'A bear and a panther were having a fight, and the *pani*-wallah, the water-carrier, was saying: "Don't go, let's see who wins." In the end the bear ran up the tree. My husband had another case of a python and a panther having a fight. Eventually the python coiled around the panther. And the drivers often used to see tigers crossing the line in the night, especially near Bhopal.'

Clare accidentally dropped some cake crumbs on the floor. 'The little ants will bite!' said May, emerging from the bathroom.

'Once, Aunty's bed was full of ants, small red ones!' laughed Buddie. 'I sat on a chair and something was biting me – "What's that?" It was full of ants, all in the legs and pants and everything.'

Peggy nodded placidly. 'I slept on ants one night. I was wondering what was biting me. I got up in the morning and the bed was full of ants. The roof gets damp, full of ants, and they keep dropping – clusters!'

'And another famous thing we used to have at Christmas,' she said, returning to the subject of food, 'was roasted goose. We used to have geese and Mummy would carve the biggest goose, Goosey

Gander. I used to say: "Mummy, don't cut so-and-so." They all had names. We all had our little pets.' She looked round. 'My mongoose hasn't come this morning. She brings her three little *bachchens* – her babies – with her…'

'Just imagine,' murmured Gwen, smiling at us, ever ladylike.

'…and then she goes round the bed and picks up little crumbs. They come regularly – they stay in the drain next door – and I try to feed them. She comes to investigate what's happening in the house here. Under my chair she goes, has what she eats and back again she goes. She's underneath my bed sometimes, too. But I don't get scared. I am quite happy with her. They are very intelligent. They protect us from vipers and any sort of lizard. They put up a solid fight with snakes, a challenging fight.'

'We should have a mongoose round our place,' mused Gwen. 'We have any amount of snakes, a hell of a lot of snakes! In the garden, even in the house. In the kitchen, bathroom, dining room, bedroom…'

'Once when I tried to open the door,' interrupted Buddie, 'the snake wrapped itself round the door handle, around the latch!'

'Everywhere they go!' cried Gwen.

'Gwen was stung by a scorpion,' said Peggy.

'Yeah, last New Year,' said Gwen. 'I had bare feet and I stood on a scorpion. And I'm kicking and it won't leave me, you know. It had stung so badly, it was stuck to my foot. I had to pull it off and then my husband had to take me to the hospital. And after that I got sick, so it became a very great thing.'

'The Indian tradition,' said Peggy, 'is, as soon as you are bitten, if you take an old gramophone record and rub it on the ground, it will automatically stick on the wound. And it draws out all the poison.'

'More cake?' asked May.

Next morning, we drove down to Roy's village, where the orchards were ripe with guavas, sweet limes and mangoes. Over our two days there, the nights were chillingly cold, so the heavy curtains were drawn and the blinds down at midday, even with the brightest sunshine outside. The highlight of the visit was a festival at Singhpur, a village about two miles away. Naked sadhus were promised but, as before, never materialised. We walked back to the bungalow along narrow lanes, stared at by passers-by. The noise of the festival – singing amplified to ear-splitting levels – gradually gave way to birdsong as 'cowdust time' approached again, cows meandered along the lanes and shepherds with long sticks started to marshal their flocks.

We returned to Jhansi on New Year's Eve and found Peggy still in bed and extremely unwell. She complained about feeling weak and clearly needed to visit a doctor. We phoned Buddie, who came straight over on her Lambretta. She said it would be impossible to find an ambulance, and we needed an autorickshaw. Anish was out of town, so I ran up to the main street and flagged one down. The three of us helped Peggy, wearing her nightdress, to get out of bed, struggle down her front step and climb into the rickshaw. She sat wedged between Clare and me, hunched, almost submerged in shawls, glancing anxiously to left and right as we drove across town, occasionally wincing at the jolting. Buddie followed on her scooter weaving in and out of the honking, fume-spewing traffic.

The doctor's surgery was in the busy Sipri Bazaar, which we had never visited before. It was open to the street, with the consultation area curtained off at the rear. We paid the doctor's fee and helped Peggy on to the examination table, in full view of other waiting patients. He decided she needed to go to hospital, so it was back to the rickshaw for another jolting ride to St Jude's Hospital, a dark, gloomy place with characteristically dim blue lighting giving everyone an unhealthy pallor. After paying another fee, we pushed Peggy in a wheelchair along a corridor to a spartan room: a bed, two sheets, a plastic bucket chair and thin curtains on a spindly rail.

While we collected medication from the hospital pharmacy, Buddie got Peggy settled and said she would stay with her overnight, sleeping on the floor. First, she went home to collect an overnight bag, bottled water and food, as none was provided by the hospital itself.

Back at the Jhansi Hotel, another crisis. Before we joined other guests at the New Year's Eve party, Clare scrolled through her tape recorder to check that all her interviews were safely stored. Suddenly the machine started to delete tracks. No matter how many times she pressed the Stop button, 'Track Deleted' messages continued to flash up. In desperation, she wrenched out the batteries. When she replaced them, the message read 'No Audio'.

Panic-stricken, she rang Mike Thornton, her unflappable BBC studio manager back in the UK, and explained what had happened. After a long silence, he calmly asked a few questions and advised her to save the SIM card in the tape recorder, replace it with a new

SIM card and redo the interviews. He would do his best to retrieve the audio when we were back in the UK, he said. Which he did.

Unsurprisingly, we felt decidedly un-festive when we joined the party in the hotel garden. Roy and Leela were there, sheltering from torrential rain and looking rather out of things. They belonged to a world very different from the noisy, glittery dancing going on around them. New Year's Eve hadn't been like this in the great days of the Railway Institute. They left before midnight.

Clare prepared to re-record her interviews. Peggy had stayed a further night at the hospital and, when we arrived at her home, May was helping her hobble back to bed from the bathroom. Wearing a woolly hat, she looked exhausted.

'Hello, my darlings,' she said, obviously in discomfort. Then to May: 'Just rub my back, my girl. I'm not feeling too good today. I've been lying down, and this back…' She winced as May stroked a painful part. 'And this weather is making it worse.'

'This weather is all raining,' agreed May. 'All night it rains. Feel my hand.'

She held out a tiny, cold hand.

The house was somehow colder than the alley outside. 'Anish hasn't come back yet,' sighed Peggy. 'Oh, God!' as another pain hit her. 'He's gone to the bank.'

After returning to Jhansi, the ever-faithful Anish was staying with her at night, sleeping on the narrow sofa at the bottom of her bed. We propped her up against her pillows.

'Just pull this thing over me,' she said, indicating the well-worn quilt.

'Don't you have a heater, Peggy?' I asked. We had bought her one the previous year.

'Oh, it went short circuit, the sparks went flying,' she said. 'Thank God we were awake, otherwise it could have caused fire. The electricity is very bad here; the fluctuation is so bad, I cannot tell you. One time it will be low, then sparks are flying, even in the TV.'

Clare remarked on how cosy she looked, snuggled down in the bedclothes with a hot-water bottle.

She laughed and waggled her head. 'I'm very cosy now. Father came in the morning, yes. He gave me Communion and all. And I had my breakfast – porridge and oats, tea with a full lot of medicines. But they're not making me feel any better.'

May went next door to make us tea.

'And seed cake,' called Peggy in a frail voice. 'It's made without any almonds or dried fruit in it. It's very nice. And I've got a plum cake here. May, bring the plum cake!' Always there was plum cake.

Clare explained about the recordings and asked if she felt well enough to be re-interviewed. Indomitable as ever, she valiantly agreed. But first she wanted to explain about the cake.

'The fruit is soaked in rum, whisky or brandy,' she said. 'We take all our ingredients to the baker and he mixes it and bakes it. We provide everything – even the butter, we have to give – and we take our own containers. You know, the Anglo-Indian speciality during Christmas is *kulkuls*, like little shells of pastry. And cheese straws. But all that tradition is dying out because people don't have the time for it and the cost is too much, so we just make the bare necessities for Christmas. Put on the bright light, May.'

'It's not working,' said May, jamming the light switch up and down. Clare switched on her tape recorder and, inevitably, someone outside started drilling loudly.

'May, bring that cream cake in the fridge,' ordered Peggy. 'It's made all with fresh cream,' she explained. 'It was presented to me by Mr Pankaj – he's the engineer who helped me to start the cemetery.'

May brought in a startlingly white, creamy sponge cake, covered in fluorescent pink icing. On top were a plastic rose, cherries, pineapple slices and assorted foliage.

'My goodness, this *is* a special cake!' said Clare. It was tooth-achingly sweet.

'Why do you think I called y'all here?' laughed Peggy. 'May, open the cake and give Aunty some. Cut-cut-cut. It's from Nav Bharat bakery in Sadar Bazaar. Layered cake they call them, with three layers. Cheers, darling.'

May handed Peggy an envelope. Inside were a Christmas card and a photocopied photograph.

'A photo from England. "I hope to visit you this year",' she read. '"I hope you got the money I sent you for the cemetery".'

She handed us the photograph. It showed a row of Anglo-Indian women from the 1950s or 1960s, all wearing Austrian dress, as though from a production of *The Sound of Music*.

'Elma Duffield, see here, was in school with me. Middle row, third from left – this is Elma.' This was the same Elma we'd heard about a couple of visits earlier.

She summoned up energy from somewhere for the repeat interview but looked very tired afterwards, so we left her to rest while Clare rerecorded May in the kitchen. After half an hour, the lights started flickering again and Peggy tut-tutted from the bedroom.

'It is very erratic electricity,' she said when we rejoined her. 'It may go off at midnight, come back at 3am, go off at 8, come back at 10, go off at 12pm. You cannot do anything if you have a microwave or anything, so it's better to live without the electric. But there are people who use too much consumption, so you can't blame the government. Air conditioning and all these gadgets have come out.'

May draped her shawl around her shoulders and head. 'I am leaving,' she said, 'because my son wants to go to work; he is looking after the baby. More tea you want?' She scurried off to catch her bus. 'Think of me, my girl,' she said to Clare as she left.

Buddie was due to arrive later that afternoon, so we stayed reminiscing with Peggy about 'the good old days'. Much of what she said we'd heard before, but we knew we might never hear the tales again, so the tape recorder was once again switched on.

'Our girls were very good-looking,' said Peggy, returning to a very familiar theme. 'A mixture of Indian culture and British. They had that beauty in them and that expression, a way of talking. And their education and background was so different to other people. Some have made very good names for themselves.'

We told her about the Jhansi Hotel's party, sparking off more memories of previous New Years.

'We used to have a bonfire outside the open compound after New Year was heralded in. Couples danced around the bonfire and we'd start singing "For he's a Jolly Good Fellow" and "Daisy Daisy", and all the old numbers we used to sing. That Scottish song – "My Bonnie Lies Over the Ocean". I cannot forget all those days. There were a hundred and fifty couples marching around the bonfire and all the crackers going off. A lot of people would cry at New Year, thinking about what they'd been through, but it was also a good experience. I lie in bed here and think of what days we have seen.'

She broke off to eat the rather unappetising-looking food May had left for her.

'It is egg – you don't eat egg, darling? It's boiled with salt. All mashed up.'

Clare suggested that the cemetery must also remind her of the old days, with so many people she had known lying there.

'Yes, it does. And I have one feeling as I enter there. I say: "My dear souls, I have managed to give you back some dignity and love. Now your dear ones can come and see your graves and I want God to bless y'all. But there is only one request I ask God. If God would give me one fraction of a minute to see how happy you are, I'd be so happy. Let me see y'all. Not for thanking me, but so I can pray for you. You were lying in dense jungle, but now you can see from one end to the other".' She sighed. 'Life has its own span, my darlings. We have to do something for the dead as well as for the living.'

Disconcertingly, she started to cry.

'I don't know why I'm crying,' she apologised, wiping her eyes. 'But so many of my friends and dear ones are buried there and their lives were very precious.'

We told her the cemetery would be one of her major legacies, along with all the help she had given to the living over her own long life. She wiped her eyes again and smiled bravely at us.

❖ ❖ ❖ ❖

Although Clare had interviewed Gwen earlier in the trip, that recording was also one of the casualties of the tape-wiping. So the next day, Gwen came over to the Jhansi Hotel to talk to us again. She was dressed Muslim-style in velvety salwar kameez, headscarf and embroidered slippers.

'I'm wearing these because it is winter,' she explained, smiling gently. 'As you know, our farm is a little way out of Jhansi, village-side. When I was first there, I used to wear dresses and jeans and all that stuff, but village people look at you in a different way if you are dressed like that. So I started dressing this way so as not to be like a sore thumb. We don't usually cover our heads, *nah* – I just roam in the salwar and kameez at home, or the leggies as we call them and a top; that's it.'

She said she had known Peggy since childhood.

'She was Mum's best friend; she was always on the scene. My mother loved her and I love her. Peggy tells me that when she had her operation and was semi-conscious, my mother went to see her. She kept rubbing her hand and saying, "Come on, Peggy, you've got to get through it, come on, you're going to be all right, don't worry." Peggy could hear her voice and says it made her feel better.

'They were always at dances and parties. My mother was a very good dancer, my father, too. At every party, every dance, they were asked to do solos. Any occasion when there was some excuse to have a party, all the Anglo-Indians would be there, at the club. Those were really good days. I don't know if they still have any dance parties.'

Like Peggy, Buddie and Roy, she reflected on the exodus of Anglo-Indians from the town, leaving 'only old people. The young ones marry out of the community, like me. There are not so many

Anglo-Indian boys. And, if there are any, they may be going the wrong way in life, so girls find it hard to get boys. So there may be a time when there will be no-one left. That makes me very sad. Aunty Peggy is my anchor and Uncle Roy Abbott is always there for me. I just love both of them.'

She wiped her eyes with a handkerchief and gave a little half-embarrassed smile. Outside the room, workmen started banging and drilling. It was as though a gang of them were following us around in order to disrupt any recordings they knew were going on.

She composed herself again and talked about Peggy's social and charity work and her fundraising abilities. 'She is highly respected. I take my hat off to her. In her old age she goes to the cemetery every second day in her tuk-tuk and checks it all out. She's so happy to do it. Many a time I go along with her. I love it there. It's so calm and peaceful. I like to go and just sit. My mother is buried there, my brother is there – and I will be buried at the foot of my mother's grave. I've already got a plot.

'Aunty Peggy has a lot of stamina,' she continued. 'She's very hard-working, has a lot of patience, is ever ready for anything.' And she recalled impromptu trips she'd taken with Peggy and other Anglo-Indians over the years. 'We never had any plans, wouldn't book into a luxurious hotel, we'd rough it out, cook our own meals, take our things with us and a stove, go from one place to another. We'd stop when we saw a river and cook a meal. I had a lovely time with her. But now, sadly, since her legs are giving way, she hasn't been on any trips.

'She was always joking. When she was young, she joked with everybody. She is still fun, real fun, even though she is so old. I enjoy every moment with her. Everyone loves her. And if you show her love, you get it back tenfold. She always says I am like her daughter, and I regard her as a mother also. And she always has a solution for everything, is always there to help. Her home is open day and night to me.

'And she never lets you come away without a meal. Even if you've had breakfast, you have to have breakfast again! She is a wonderful person, a lovely person, there is no-one like her. She's my anchor. She and Uncle Roy, they are my favourites. I just love them both.'

That evening, Clare and I were quiet over dinner, sad in the realisation that something was coming to an end.

On our last day in Jhansi, we had a final tea with Peggy. She was much revived and in good spirits, talking again about her role as a matchmaker, and persuading us to leave a further donation to the cemetery.

It was the last time we saw her. She died fifteen months later, on 26th April 2016, five days after her ninety-third birthday, in the hospital opposite St Jude's Shrine. An obituary in India's national *Telegraph* newspaper described her as 'the glue that held Jhansi's tight-knit community together'. It quoted Sir Mark Tully, who recalled a tour she had given him of the cemetery. 'She was a great doer,' he said, 'a very persistent lady.' Another obituary called her 'The New Rani of Jhansi'.

Back home a month later, we received a letter from Roy, posted in Jhansi.

I was at the farms when I got the tragic news of the passing of our dearest Peggy. I rushed back here & made it in time for her funeral at 4pm, which was very befitting for a much respected & loved person of this town. About 300 people were there to bid her farewell and it was clearly visible that most of them were grief-stricken. There's no doubt she was a legend in her time…Way back in the late 40s and 50s we were probably the best dancing pair in the Railway Institute. I used to call her my dancing queen…With much love & regards,

Roy-Sahib of India.

He enclosed an obituary which quoted Irene St Anne, Peggy's eighty-year-old niece, who had come to the funeral from her home in Lonavala, a hill station between Mumbai and Pune. 'Defying all her ailments, Peggy aunt was very active till her last breath, keeping the graveyard "alive". She would bring small plants from my garden, which have now become big trees in the cemetery. She will live along with these.'

Fortunately, Peggy lived long enough to hear Clare's radio programme about her, *Teatime at Peggy's*. Clare had sent her a tape of it and she had telephoned us in Britain to say how much she'd enjoyed it. She subsequently wrote to us to thank her 'very dear and special friends… for the boost given to me in the declining years of my life'.

She said that despite her difficulty in 'moving about', she was still visiting the cemetery two or three times a week to check how renovation was going. Work was hampered by the late monsoon.

I am at my wits' end how to fight the elements and keep the vegetation under control…The main objective is to raise the status of the cemetery to a 'heritage site', an added attraction for tourists who visit the Jhansi Fort en route to Khajuraho.

Roy left for his village two days ago with Leela. Their stay can be nothing short of 2–3 weeks. We will be having an Anglo-Indian Show Dinner with games on August 15, Independence Day. Let's hope it goes off well... PS: Please excuse my bad writing. My typewriter needs servicing. No mechanic around.

It was the last letter she sent us.

At the end of *Teatime at Peggy's*, Clare asked her if she had reserved a plot for herself in the cemetery. Yes, she said, next to her brother's.

'I'm going to make benches so that, after I die, I can see who goes and comes! Because then I can still go round in the night and see the work that is going on. That will be my job – to protect everybody there. I'll make all the dead come along with me and have a walk.' And she laughed that lovely, life-affirming laugh. 'We'll have a ball!'

CHAPTER 19

END OF AN ERA

We spent most of New Year's Eve 2016 driving backwards and forwards along the broad leafy avenues of South Delhi, trim-hedged home of high court judges, lieutenant generals and air vice-marshals. We strolled in Lodhi Gardens and had coffee and lemon cake at Café Turtle in nearby Khan Market, the upmarket haunt of Western expats. We browsed the Full Circle bookshop and the branches of Anokhi and Fabindia, the modish fashion chains popular with Westerners and 'frat pack' young Delhi-ites alike. Jhansi's Sadar Bazaar it was not.

The next day, we caught the late-morning New Delhi-Thiruvananthapuram-Kerala Express, a pronunciation challenge that was embarking on a fifty-one-hour journey to India's southern tip. Our six-hour journey to Jhansi was an eye-blink by comparison.

Ten minutes after the train pulled out, a middle-aged man in a baseball cap made his way along the carriage. He had a large, heavy rucksack on his back but, more unusually, was carrying a three-foot-high stack of paperbacks. As well as Harry Potter, *To Kill a Mockingbird*, *A Brief History of Time* and books by the bestselling contemporary novelist Chetan Bhagat, there was a good showing of the motivational titles that had flooded the Indian book market over the last few years: *The 7 Habits of Highly Effective People… The Magic of Thinking Big… Ignited Minds… Super Fast English (Part I & II).*

This mobile bookseller was Shushell Mishra, who lived in Mathura, two hours south of Delhi, and had been commuting backwards and forwards to the capital, selling his books, on an almost daily basis for twenty years.

'There is no guarantee that I will sell anything,' he said, with a look that clearly meant: *But I am sure you will buy.*

After some good-natured bargaining, he gave the woman sitting across from us a 15 per cent discount on a Chetan Bhagat book. When Clare showed interest in *I Am Malala,* by the Nobel Prize-winning Pakistani schoolgirl Malala Yousafzai, he jumped straight in.

'Thirty per cent discount on this – four hundred rupees for two hundred and eighty rupees.'

An attendant brought round the lunchtime biryanis passengers had ordered, served in smart plastic containers stacked in a grubby washing-up bowl. Another attendant walked through the carriage repeating the mantra: '*Pani* water, cold drinks, buttermilk.' The train was due to arrive in Jhansi at around 6pm but was delayed by four hours. At 7.30pm another attendant came round to take orders for the following day. 'Morning tiffin?' he enquired. Clare politely said she hoped we'd be in Jhansi by then.

At the Jhansi Hotel, another New Year Party was well underway. Roy and Leela were once again there, smartly dressed but, as before, looking detached, almost withdrawn, and sitting in uncharacteristic silence. It was a particularly busy evening, with an unexpected party of Scandinavian tourists to cater for. They'd been heading back to Delhi from Agra but train delays meant they were billeted here for dinner.

Halfway through their meal, a wedding baraat could be heard approaching along the street outside, led by the usual raucous brass band. There was much whirling and shouting. The tourists flocked outside to watch and one of the dancers urged an attractive blonde woman in her late thirties to join them. She stepped into the baraat and whirled with the best of them, looking utterly happy.

On New Year's Day, we joined Buddie and Anish at the cemetery to see Peggy's grave. As yet, its black marble slab had no inscription, but 'Forever remembered – forever missed' was the plan. They had brought marigold garlands for us all to drape over it. Anish looked heartbroken. As she had wanted, the grave was next to that of her brother Percy, who had died aged eight in 1923, the year she was born. The lettering on Dr Righton's gravestone was rapidly becoming illegible.

We strolled through the Sadar Bazaar, a little disorientated by not having our Jhansi visit choreographed by Peggy. It was a Sunday and the bazaar would normally be closed, but it was thought auspicious to open on New Year's Day. Genial shopkeepers and stallholders wished us Happy New Year as we dodged bicycles with high-rise piles of cardboard boxes strapped over the back wheel. We nodded to Bollywood-esque representations of the Hindu gods and browsed a stall that encompassed coconuts, brushes, twine, Uncle Chipps crisps and bags of cement.

I handed one of my visiting cards to the manager of a bookshop. 'You got these cards printed in India?' he asked.

I nodded.

'It looks like it,' he said dismissively.

Anish came with me to buy cans of beer at a 'wine shop'. Wine was, in fact, rarely stocked in such places. Most of the trade was in whisky and beer (including super-strong beer that could power a space capsule). How many cans, the assistant asked.

'*Teen*,' I said.

The assistant looked blank.

'Three,' Anish translated.

We spent just one night in Orchha. The small town's ever-expanding commercialisation and touristification was edging it inexorably towards becoming Trinket Town.

We stayed, as ever, at the Sheesh Mahal. 'You must come to my home when you are here next,' said Mr Omri, the longest-serving of the waiters. From far below, we gazed up at the array of windows on the hotel's towering walls, realising for the first time that there was a sheer two-hundred-foot drop below our bedroom. It was next to the Maharani's suite which boasted a toilet in a turret. We had lunch at the Betwa Tarang rooftop restaurant, reflecting on the changes we'd seen in the town.

'Tell me we're not turning into Peggy and Roy,' said Clare. 'Or Tusker and Lucy,' she added, referring to the central characters of Paul Scott's celebrated novel, *Staying On*.

Mr Omri organised a 'special dinner' for us, including a superb smoky-tasting aubergine curry. Three folk musicians played at the far end of the restaurant: drum, tambourine and harmonium. Towards the end of their performance, they were joined by an elaborately made-up dancer with a screechingly high-pitched voice.

'Where is she from?' I asked Mr Omri.

'*He*,' he corrected. 'Not she.'

And where did the songs originate? Rajasthan?

'Bollywood.'

Next day before breakfast we walked through the fields. The only sound was birdsong, including trilling bulbuls, one of the most endearing of Indian birds. Kingfishers darted along the water of the Betwa, parakeets flapped, crickets chirped and cormorants perched on the riverbanks drying their oil-black wings. It had all the shimmering freshness of a perfect Indian morning. When we returned to the Sheesh Mahal, a dozen-strong group of Italians were sitting round a table, heads bowed as though in prayer. In fact, they were all absorbed in their mobiles and tablets.

We took a taxi back to Jhansi and had lunch at Roy's. He had a St Jude's calendar on the wall and a mug proclaiming 'The British Empire Runs on Tea' on his desk. The mournful bust in the corridor had been surreally garlanded with Christmas tinsel, and the ringletted bust in the sitting room now sat behind a nativity crib decorated with cotton-wool snow.

We had tea at Buddie's with him, Leela, Gwen, Cheryl and her husband Sidney Baines, a quiet man whom we hadn't previously met. Tea stretched into early evening. It was a curious get-together, like a shadow of earlier times, although Roy was in good jovial form. Naturally, there was much talk of Peggy.

We had just one more day in India before flying home. Anxious to avoid another massive rail delay, we booked a taxi to take us back to Delhi, at a princely cost of nine thousand rupees – around £90. The taxi owner told us: 'There are two routes to Delhi – the fast one on the Expressway, or the slow one, where you will be held up in traffic jams. Which would you prefer?'

The (fast) journey still gave us plenty of time to reflect, as we generally did at the end of trips, on what we would miss about India when we returned to Britain. There was so much. At random: the courtesy, curiosity and overwhelming hospitality of most Indians ('To us, guest is God,' a hotel receptionist once told us). The colour and excitement and ceaseless stimulation. The squawking parakeets, the scurrying squirrels and the occasional sinuous mongoose. The warm winter days, the cheap books, south Indian masala dosas, the glorious sunsets at 'cowdust time'. The unpredictability, the lulling contentment of sleeping on overnight trains, the sheer fun that put the frustrations in perspective. As one travel company used to advise its clients, among the most essential things to pack for a trip to India was 'a sense of humour'.

And very high on the list of things we would miss when back home were our friends in Jhansi.

Before we left for Delhi, I photographed Roy again on the veranda of his bungalow. He fixed the camera with the same benevolent smile as on that January morning seventeen years earlier when I'd first photographed him. It was the last time we saw him; he died ten months later, on 23rd November 2017.

After saying our goodbyes, we spent our last night at the Jhansi Hotel and wandered along the corridor to Dr Righton's old room, where our Anglo-Indian adventures had started. Fourteen journeys to Jhansi had come full circle. And, to echo Peggy, we'd had a ball.

AFTERWORD

Our involvement with India's Anglo-Indian community began with Stephen making a serendipitous discovery during a two-day press trip to Jhansi in January 2000. It subsequently became very much a joint adventure.

Clare's own family has an Anglo-Indian connection. Her Irish maternal great-grandfather served as an army schoolteacher in India, where four of his eight children were born. Family legend has it that one of these, Vincent, died after falling from a window while sleepwalking, possibly at the family home in West Bengal. Another, Harry, died in Bangalore after being bitten by his pet monkey and developing what we were always told was hydrocephalus, but which may have been rabies.

Then there was Great-Uncle William, who became a tea estate manager in the northeastern state of Assam. At some point, this 'devout Roman Catholic' (according to Clare's mother, his niece) married an Indian woman, quite possibly a worker on his tea estate. They had two children together: a daughter called Theresa and a son, Vincent, who eventually worked for the Indian Civil Service or 'heaven-born', as they were nicknamed.

Shipped back to England in 1916 on medical grounds, William never returned to India, and the family have yet to discover any record of his wife.

Theresa, who was educated at a Catholic convent school in Calcutta, came to the UK some years after her father. She married and had three sons, but never talked to them about her mother, never even telling them her name. According to research conducted by a friend of one of those sons: 'I have found no evidence whatsoever that [William's] wife ever came to England. One theory could be that in fact she had died, either in childbirth or shortly thereafter. It seems unlikely that she would have "abandoned" her children. This could explain why Theresa, and possibly Vincent, too, were put into a "boarding school", both for a Catholic upbringing and because William could not cope with two little children even if he had the help of an ayah (nanny).'

And that remains all that we know, despite various visits to West Bengal and Assam, where the trails frustratingly peter out. This is not an uncommon experience among Anglo-Indians, which helps explain why some are so vague about their ancestry. However, while the hunt for 'she who has no name' continues, our knowledge of the Anglo-Indian community has been widened enormously through our years of visiting 'Peggy Aunty' and Captain Roy Abbott.

Stephen McClarence & Clare Jenkins, April 2024

GLOSSARY

aana aur jaana	coming and going
aarti	Hindu prayer ceremony with lights
achaar	pickles
almirah	a large iron locker
aloo gobi	potato and cauliflower curry
anna	unit of currency, worth a sixteenth of a rupee
ayah	nanny or lady's maid
baba	baby
bachchen	children
baraat	wedding procession with band
beedi	Indian cigarette
besharam	Ipomoea or Morning Glory (flower)
bhaji	fritter
bharta	an aubergine-based side dish
bihi	a type of guava
bindi	coloured dot in the centre of the forehead
biryani	a mixed rice dish
brinjal	aubergine
burra-sahib	an important man
chai	tea boiled up with milk and sugar
'Chalo'	'Let's go!'
chapati	unleavened flatbread
charpoy	rope bed
chidiya	bird
chikoo	a fruit
chini	sugar
choli	bodice, usually worn with a sari

Chota Rajah	little king
chowkidar	caretaker or gatekeeper
dacoit	armed robber
dahl	a lentil dish
Dalit	the lowest of the Indian castes, formerly called 'Untouchables'
darshan	blessing
dharji	tailor
dhobi	laundry
dhobi-wallah	laundryman
dholak	drum
dhoti	loincloth
dupatta	shawl-like scarf
'Ek puri aur?'	'One more puri?'
garam pani	hot water
glassy kebab	a rich Anglo-Indian curry
godhuli bela	twilight, or 'cowdust time'
gopi	milkmaid or female cowherd
gopura	intricately carved gateway tower of a Hindu temple
gulab jamun	a sweet confectionery, a dumpling in syrup
hijra	transgender or third gender person or community
jaggery	cane sugar
jalfrezi	a stir-fried curry dish
-ji	honorific term attached to the end of a name
jungli	wild or uncultivated
jungli pilau	Anglo-Indian rice and meat dish
khanjari	tambourine

khatiya	cot
khichri	kedgeree
'Kitne?'	'How much?'
kofta	meatball
kulkuls	deep-fried pastry shells
lakh	100,000 rupees
lathis	solid wooden sticks carried by police officers
lehenga	full, embroidered skirt
Lok Sabha	the lower house of the Indian Parliament
machan	a safety platform
maharajah	ruler or king of a former Indian state
maharani	wife of a *maharajah*
mali	gardener
manjeera	hand cymbals
masala	spice
masala dosa	south Indian dish, a filled pancake or crêpe
memsahib	madam
missy-sahib	young mistress
mooli	radish
naan	leavened flatbread
Namaste	a greeting or blessing
nautch	dance or dancing
paan	betel leaf with areca nut
paisa	unit of currency; 100 paise = 1 rupee
pakora	fritter
palak	spinach
palak paneer	spinach and Indian cheese
pallu	loose end of a sari
paneer	Indian cheese

pani-wallah	water-carrier
peepal tree	sacred fig tree
pi-dog	stray dog
pilau	a rice dish
pukka	genuine
purdah	isolation (for women)
puri	Indian fried bread
raita	yoghurt with vegetables or spices
rajah	king
rupee	unit of currency
sadhu	Hindu holy man
sahib	sir or master
Salaams	greetings
salwar kameez	a woman's outfit of loose tunic and pants
samosa	fried pastry with savoury filling
sati	the banned ritual of a wife being burned to death on her husband's funeral pyre
shamiana	marquee or tent
shawm	musical wind instrument, like an oboe
shikar	hunt/shoot
shikari	huntsman
sola topi	sun hat or pith helmet
subji	vegetables
subji-wallah	vegetable-seller
tabla	drums
tiffin	lunch, often carried in a steel tiffin-carrier
tikka	a mark painted on the forehead
tonga	horse-drawn, two-wheeled carriage
wallah	a person with a particular duty

GLOSSARY

vindaloo	a very spicy curry
yeh Hindi theek nahin	your Hindi's not very good
zamindar	landowner